CHARACTERISTICS

Bottlenose dolphins have teeth, but they do not chew their food.

CHARACTERISTICS Bottlenose dolphins often work together to catch fish.

SOCIAL LIFE
Bottlenose dolphins communicate with one another by making sounds and using body language.
CHARACTERISTICS
Bottlenose dolphins breathe through blow holes on the top of their heads.

California Science

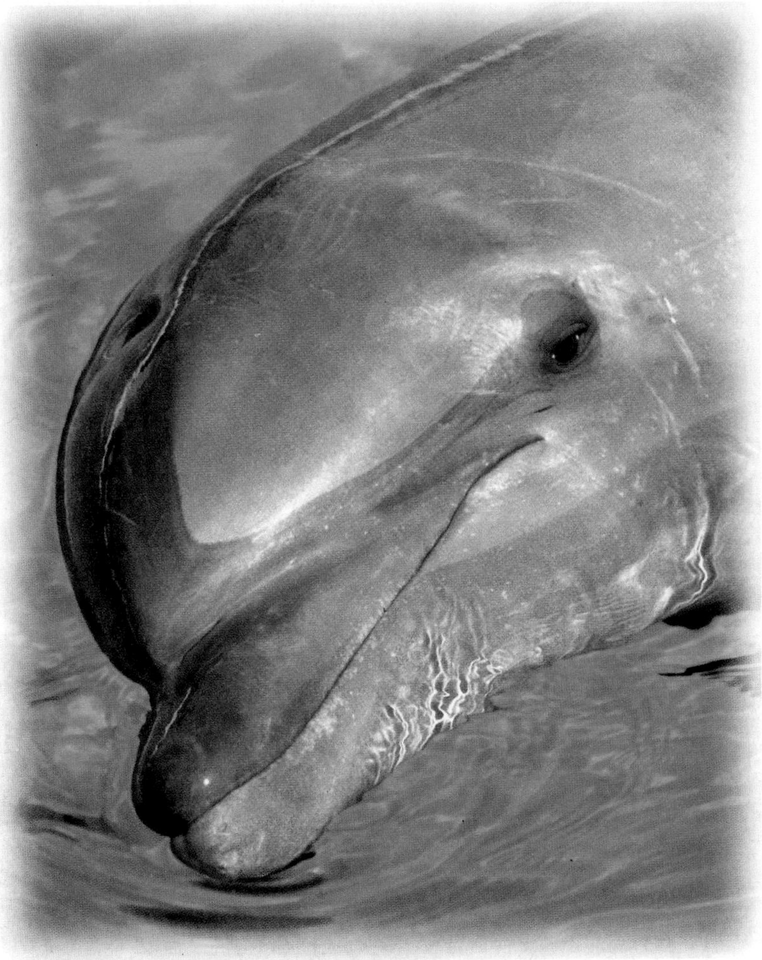

Harcourt
SCHOOL PUBLISHERS

Visit *The Learning Site!*
www.harcourtschool.com

California Science

Pacific bottlenose dolphins

Series Consulting Authors

Michael J. Bell, Ph.D.
Assistant Professor of Early Childhood Education
College of Education
West Chester University of Pennsylvania
West Chester, Pennsylvania

Michael A. DiSpezio
Curriculum Architect
JASON Academy
Cape Cod, Massachusetts

Marjorie Frank
Former Adjunct, Science Education
Hunter College
New York, New York

Gerald H. Krockover, Ph.D.
Professor of Earth and Atmospheric Science Education
Purdue University
West Lafayette, Indiana

Joyce C. McLeod
Adjunct Professor
Rollins College
Winter Park, Florida

Barbara ten Brink, Ph.D.
Science Specialist
Austin Independent School District
Austin, Texas

Carol J. Valenta
Senior Vice President
St. Louis Science Center
St. Louis, Missouri
Former teacher, principal, and Coordinator of Science Center Instructional Programs
Los Angeles Unified School District
Los Angeles, California

Barry A. Van Deman
President and CEO
Museum of Life and Science
Durham, North Carolina

Series Consultants

Catherine Banker
Curriculum Consultant
Alta Loma, California

Robin C. Scarcella, Ph.D.
Professor and Director, Program of Academic English and ESL
University of California, Irvine
Irvine, California

Series Content Reviewers

Paul Asimow, Ph.D.
Associate Professor, Geology and Geochemistry
California Institute of Technology
Pasadena, California

Larry Baresi, Ph.D.
Associate Professor
California State University, Northridge
Northridge, California

John Brockhaus, Ph.D.
Department of Geography and Environmental Engineering
United States Military Academy
West Point, New York

Mapi Cuevas, Ph.D.
Professor of Chemistry
Santa Fe Community College
Gainesville, Florida

William Guggino, Ph.D.
Professor of Physiology and Pediatrics
Johns Hopkins University, School of Medicine
Baltimore, Maryland

V. Arthur Hammon
Pre-College Education Specialist
Jet Propulsion Laboratory
Pasadena, California

Steven A. Jennings, Ph.D.
Associate Professor in Geography
University of Colorado at Colorado Springs
Colorado Springs, Colorado

James E. Marshall, Ph.D.
Professor and Chair, Department of Curriculum and Instruction
California State University, Fresno
Fresno, California

Joseph McClure, Ph.D.
Associate Professor Emeritus
Department of Physics
Georgetown University
Washington, D.C.

Dork Sahagian, Ph.D.
Professor of Earth and Environmental Science
Lehigh University
Bethlehem, Pennsylvania

Curriculum and Classroom Reviewers

David Appling
Curriculum Specialist
Anaheim City School District
Anaheim, California

Christina Duran
Teacher
Primrose Elementary School
Fontana, California

Darryl Gibson
Teacher
Salinas Elementary School
San Bernardino, California

Michael Lebda
Science Specialist
Fresno Unified School District
Fresno, California

Ana G. Lopez
Science Specialist
Fresno Unified School District
Fresno, California

Harcourt
SCHOOL PUBLISHERS

Science and Technology features provided by
SCIENCE Spin from WEEKLY READER

Printed in the United States of America

ISBN 13: 978-0-15-347118-6
ISBN 10: 0-15-347118-2

3 4 5 6 7 8 9 10 048 13 12 11 10 09 08 07

Introductory Unit

Ready, Set, Science! viii

Big Idea **People learn about science by asking good questions and doing careful investigations.**

Essential Questions

PHYSICAL SCIENCE

UNIT 1 Motion 50

Big Idea **The motion of objects can be observed and measured.**

Essential Questions

roller coaster at Knott's Berry Farm

LIFE SCIENCE

UNIT 2 Life Cycles 146

Big Idea **Plants and animals change as they grow. The stages, or times, of their lives make up their life cycles.**

Essential Questions

EARTH SCIENCE

UNIT 3 Earth Materials 222

Big Idea **Earth is made of materials that are different from one another. People use these materials.**

Essential Questions

References

Ready, Set, Science!

California Standards in This Unit

4 **Scientific progress is made by asking meaningful questions and conducting careful investigations. As a basis for understanding this concept and addressing the content in the other three strands, students should develop their own questions and perform investigations. Students will:**

- **4.a** Make predictions based on observed patterns and not random guessing.
- **4.b** Measure length, weight, temperature, and liquid volume with appropriate tools and express those measurements in standard metric system units.
- **4.c** Compare and sort common objects according to two or more physical attributes (e.g., color, shape, texture, size, weight).
- **4.d** Write or draw descriptions of a sequence of steps, events, and observations.
- **4.e** Construct bar graphs to record data, using appropriately labeled axes.
- **4.f** Use magnifiers or microscopes to observe and draw descriptions of small objects or small features of objects.
- **4.g** Follow oral instructions for a scientific investigation.

What's the Big Idea?

People learn about science by asking good questions and doing careful investigations.

Essential Questions

Science in California

Hi Jin,

My aunt took me to a coin show in Sacramento. I saw coins with pictures of people and animals and other things on them. The coins were made of different kinds of metal. They were different shapes and sizes, too. I learned a lot!

Your friend,

Rosa

What did Rosa learn about ways coins can be different? How do you think that helps explain the **Big Idea?**

California Standards in This Lesson

LESSON 1

Investigation and Experimentation

4.a Make predictions based on observed patterns and not random guessing.

4.b Measure length, weight, temperature, and liquid volume with appropriate tools and express those measurements in standard metric system units.

4.c Compare and sort common objects according to two or more physical attributes (e.g., color, shape, texture, size, weight).

Essential Question

What Investigation Skills Will We Use?

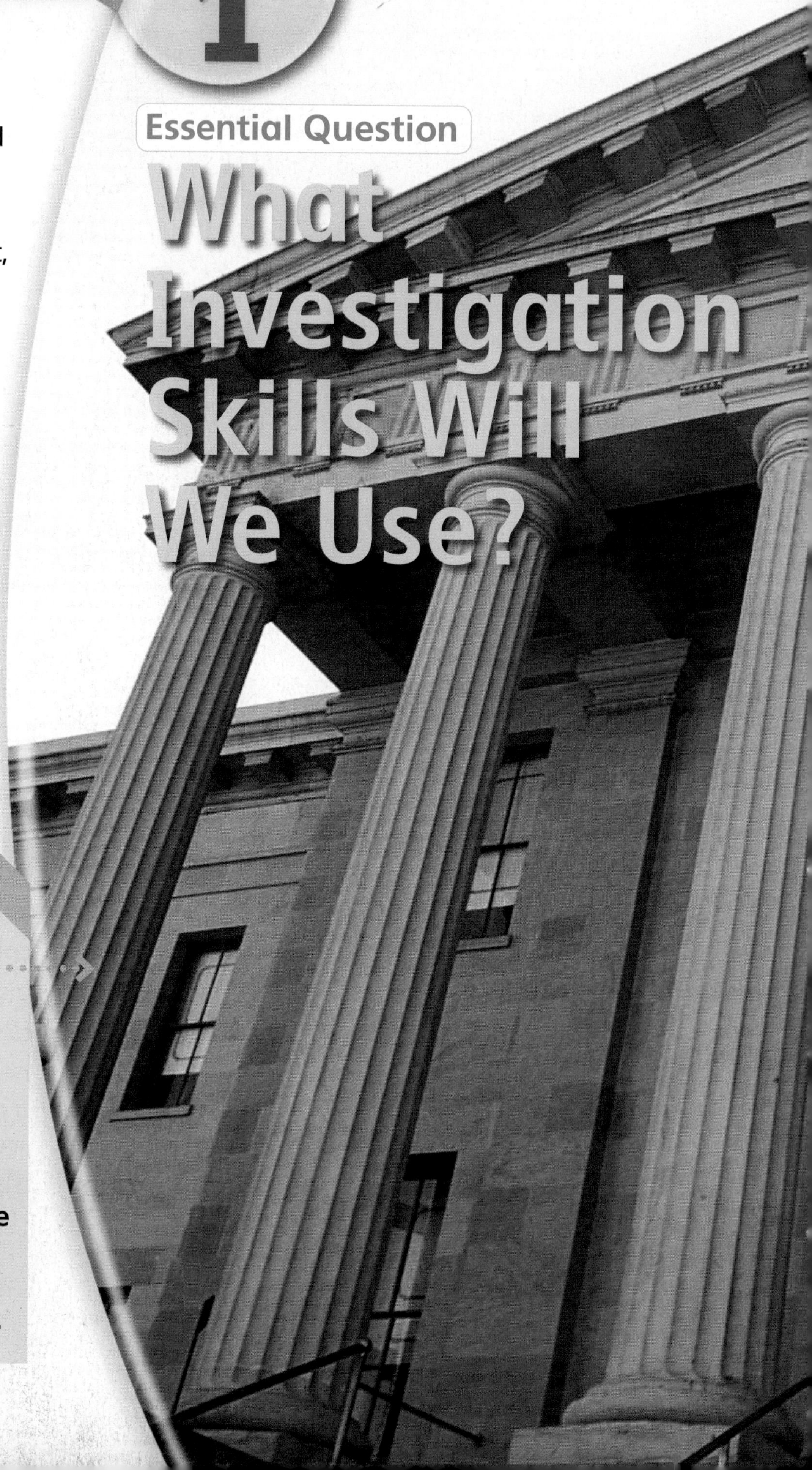

California Fast Fact

United States Mint, San Francisco

The San Francisco mint makes coins and medals that honor people and events. The letter *S* on the coins shows that they were made in San Francisco.

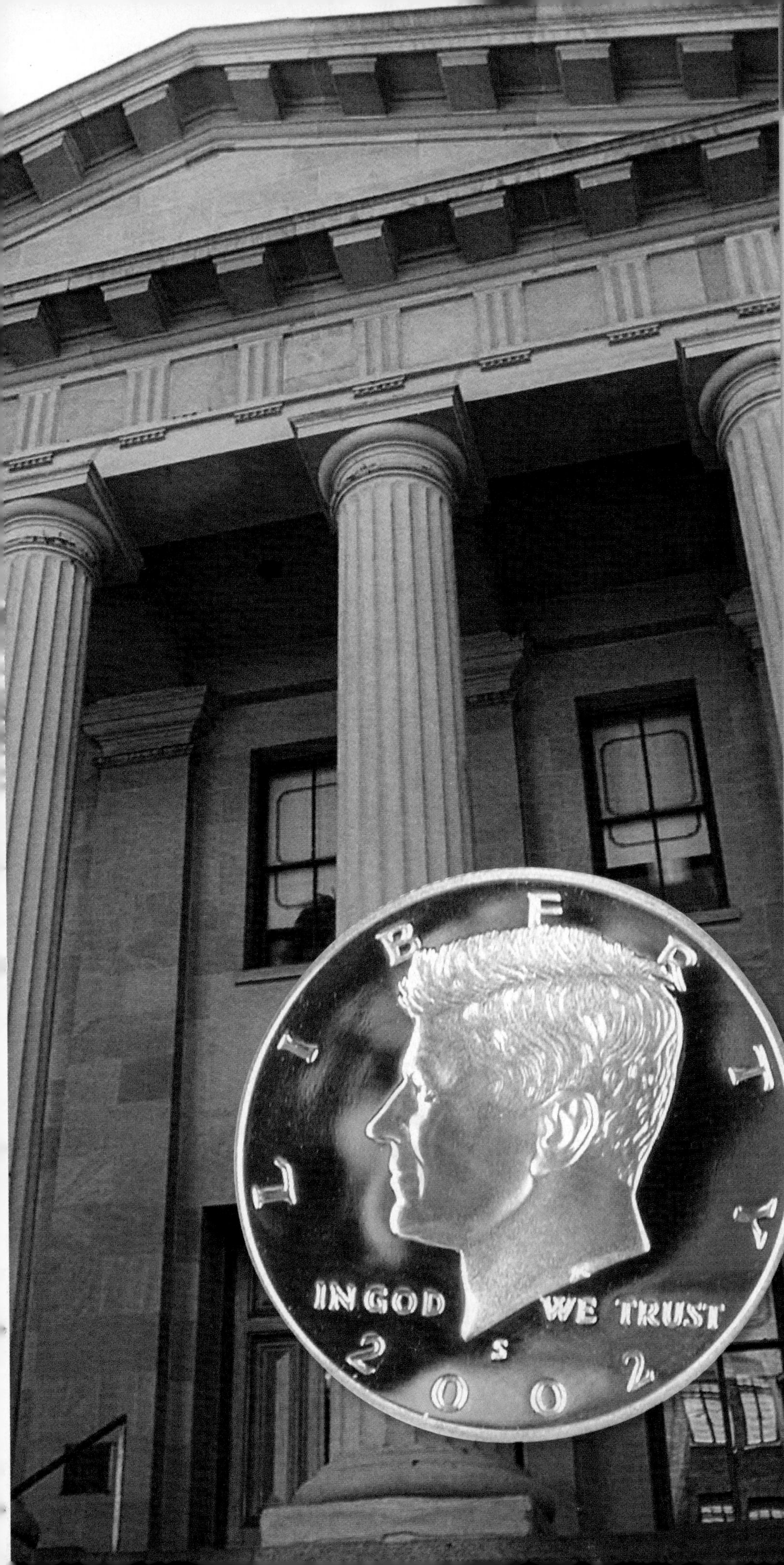

Vocabulary Preview

Investigation skills are a set of skills people use to find out about things. p. 6

When you **observe,** you use your senses to find out about things around you. p. 6

How Many Pennies?

Directed Inquiry

Ask a Question

What can the children do to observe the coins in this collection?

Get Ready

Investigation Skill Tip
When you observe, you can use your senses of sight and touch.

You Need

pennies

small plastic jar

What to Do

Step 1

Observe some pennies and a jar. Predict how many pennies will fill the jar. Write the number.

Step 2

Fill the jar with pennies. Count them as you put them in. Write the number of pennies that fit.

Step 3

Compare the number of pennies in the jar with the number you predicted.

Draw Conclusions

How did the size of the jar affect your prediction? **4.a**

Independent Inquiry

Observe some dimes and the same jar you used for the Investigate. Predict how many dimes will fill the jar. Then fill the jar. Was your prediction correct? **4.a**

4.a, 4.b, 4.c

VOCABULARY
investigation skills
observe

MAIN IDEA AND DETAILS

Look for details about the investigation skills that scientists use.

Investigation Skills

Scientists use investigation skills when they do tests. **Investigation skills** help people find out about things.

Observe

Use your five senses to **observe**. Learn about things around you.

Compare

Observe ways things are alike. Observe ways they are different.

Classify

Classify things by comparing them and sorting them into groups to show ways they are alike.

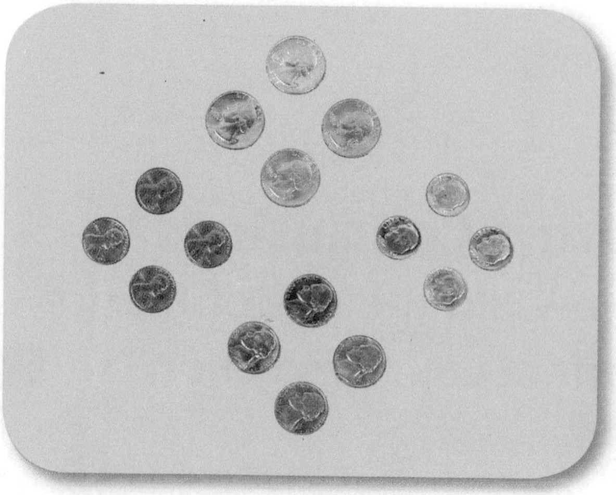

Sequence

Put things in order to show changes.

sequence of size

sequence of value

Measure

Use tools to find out how much or how many. You can measure how long, wide, or tall something is. You can measure how much something weighs. You can measure how much space something takes up.

Make a Model

Make a model to show what something is like or how it works.

Focus Skill **MAIN IDEA AND DETAILS**

What are some investigation skills?

A magnet attracts things made of iron.

Hypothesize

Think of a scientific statement that you can test.

The ball goes faster when I throw it hard. My hypothesis was confirmed!

Draw Conclusions

Use the information you have gathered to decide whether your hypothesis is confirmed.

Plants need water to grow well.

Infer

Use what you know to make a good guess about what is happening.

Predict

Use what you know to make a good guess about what will happen.

Record

Record information by drawing or writing about it.

Tell

When you tell, or communicate, you share with others what you learned.

Focus Skill **MAIN IDEA AND DETAILS** **Why are drawing conclusions and predicting investigation skills?**

Insta-Lab

Stacking Pennies

Set a tray on a table. Predict what will happen if you try to stack 50 pennies. Stack the pennies on the tray. What happens? Was your prediction correct?

Standards Wrap-Up and Lesson Review

Essential Question

What investigation skills will we use?

In this lesson, you learned about the investigation skills that scientists use.

Standards in This Lesson

4.a Make predictions based on observed patterns and not random guessing.

4.b Measure length, weight, temperature, and liquid volume with appropriate tools and express those measurements in standard metric system units.

4.c Compare and sort common objects according to two or more physical attributes (e.g., color, shape, texture, size, weight).

1. Focus Skill **MAIN IDEA AND DETAILS** Make a chart like this one. Fill in details about the main idea **We use investigation skills.** **4.a, 4.c**

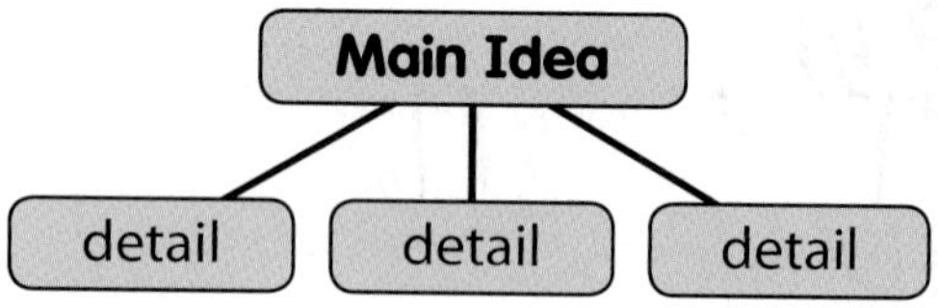

2. **SUMMARIZE** Write two sentences that tell what the lesson is about. **4.a**

3. **VOCABULARY** Use the term **investigation skills** in a sentence. **4.b**

4. **Critical Thinking** Predicting is an investigation skill. Tell how predicting the weather can help people. **4.a**

5. What are you doing when you are finding out how tall something is? **4.b**

A drawing conclusions
B measuring
C predicting
D sequencing

The Big Idea

6. Why is it important to know how to use investigation skills? **4.a**

Writing — ELA-W 1.1

Write to Inform

1. Observe a penny and a nickel.
2. Write a few sentences about them.
3. Tell ways the penny and the nickel are alike.
4. Tell ways the penny and the nickel are different.

Math — NS 1.1

Counting Coins

1. Look at a pile of coins.
2. Sort them into groups of pennies, nickels, and dimes.
3. Count the coins in each group.
4. Write the number of coins in each group. Tell which group has the most coins. Tell which group has the fewest coins.

For more links and activities, go to **www.hspscience.com**

California Standards in This Lesson

Investigation and Experimentation

4.a Make predictions based on observed patterns and not random guessing.

4.b Measure length, weight, temperature, and liquid volume with appropriate tools and express those measurements in standard metric system units.

4.f Use magnifiers or microscopes to observe and draw descriptions of small objects or small features of objects.

LESSON 2

Essential Question

What Science Tools Will We Use?

California Fast Fact

California State Quarter

The California quarter was first made in 2005. The fifty state quarters are being made in the order in which the states joined the United States. California was the thirty-first state.

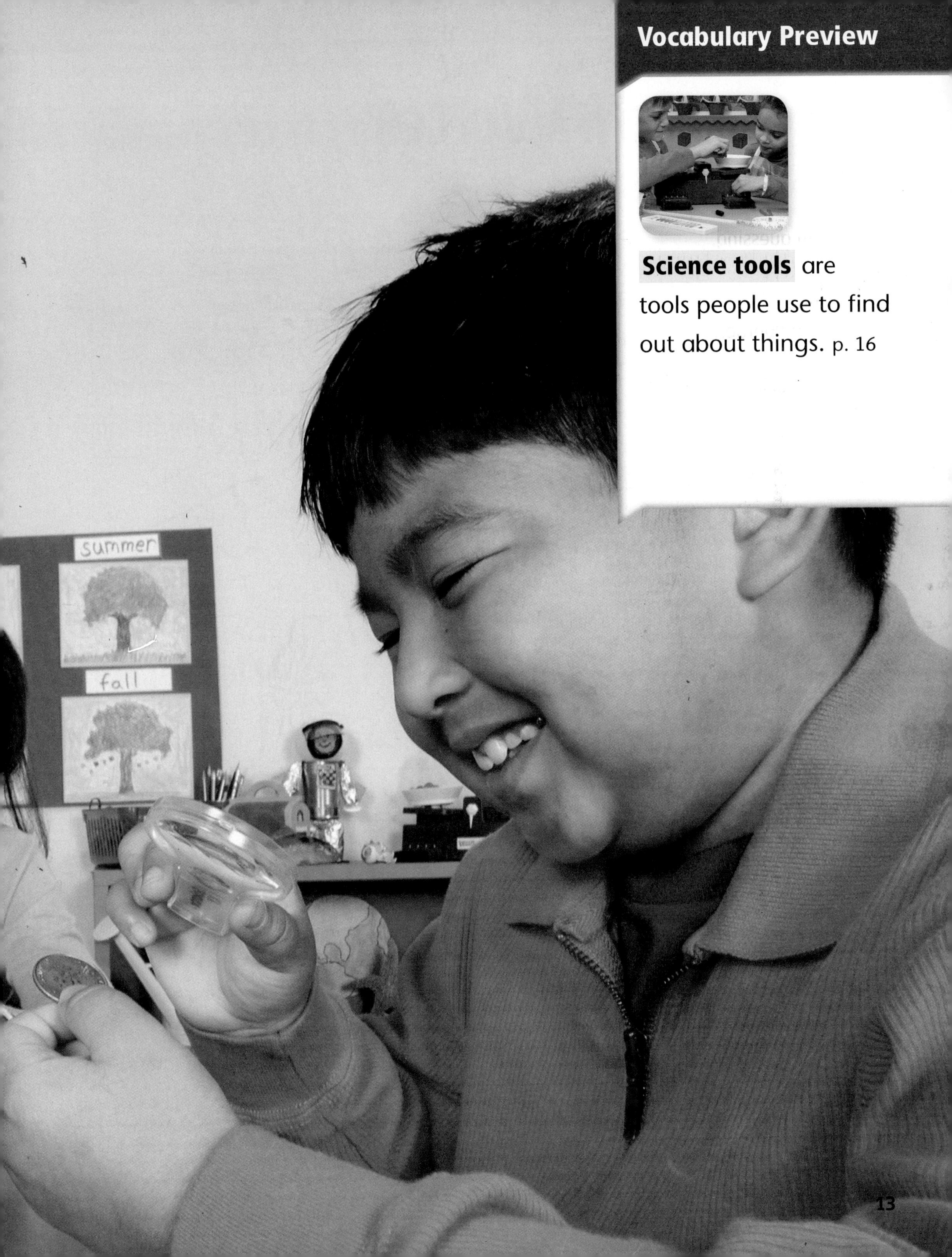

Vocabulary Preview

Science tools are tools people use to find out about things. p. 16

Investigate

Drops of Water on a Penny

Directed Inquiry

Ask a Question

What are the children predicting?

Get Ready

Investigation Skill Tip

When you predict, you tell what you think will happen.

You Need

dropper

cup of water

coin

What to Do

Step 1

Predict how many drops of water you can put on a coin before the water runs off. Write your prediction.

Step 2

Use the dropper to drop water on the coin. Count the drops. Stop when the water starts to run off the coin.

Step 3

Compare the number of drops you were able to put on the coin with the number you predicted.

Draw Conclusions

Did you predict more or fewer drops than you were able to place? Why do you think this happened? 4.a

Independent Inquiry

Predict the number of drops of apple juice you can put on the same coin. Then try it. Was your prediction correct? 4.a

VOCABULARY
science tools

MAIN IDEA AND DETAILS

Look for details about science tools.

Science Tools

Scientists use special tools to find out about things. These **science tools** help people observe and measure things.

Hand Lens

Use a hand lens to magnify objects, or make them look larger. Hold the hand lens near your face. Move the object until you see it clearly.

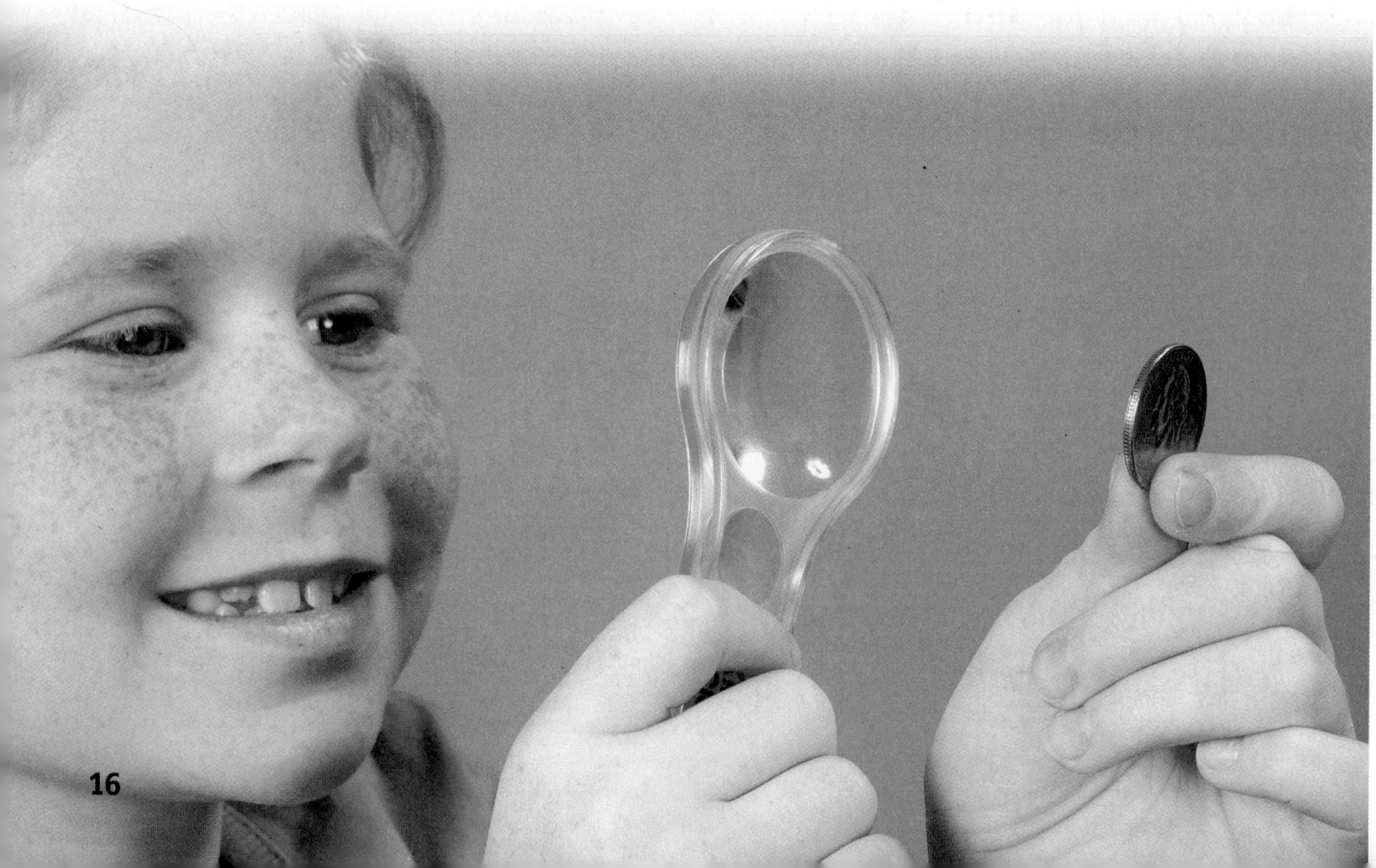

Magnifying Box

Use a magnifying box to make objects look larger. Place the object in the box. Then look through the top of the box.

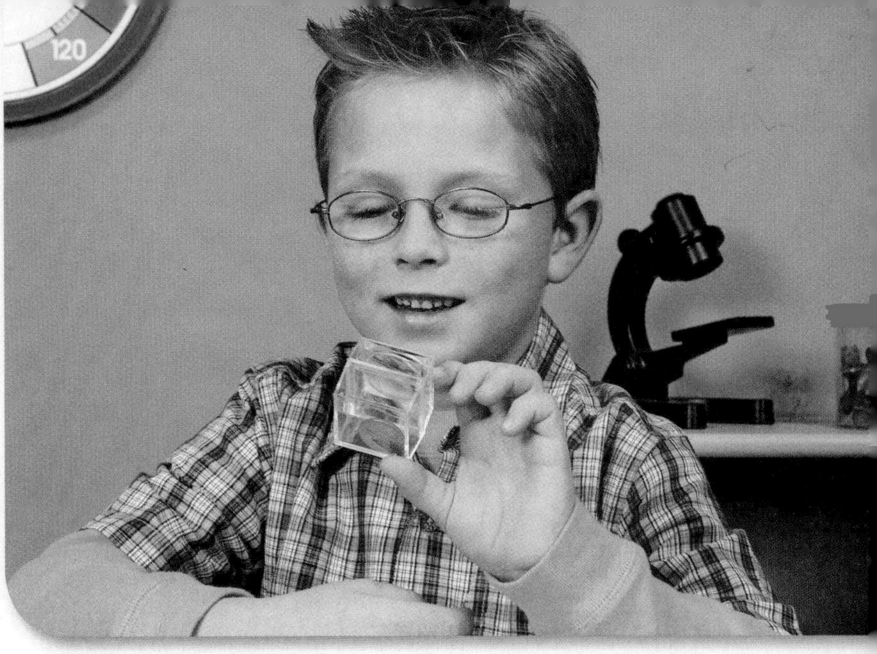

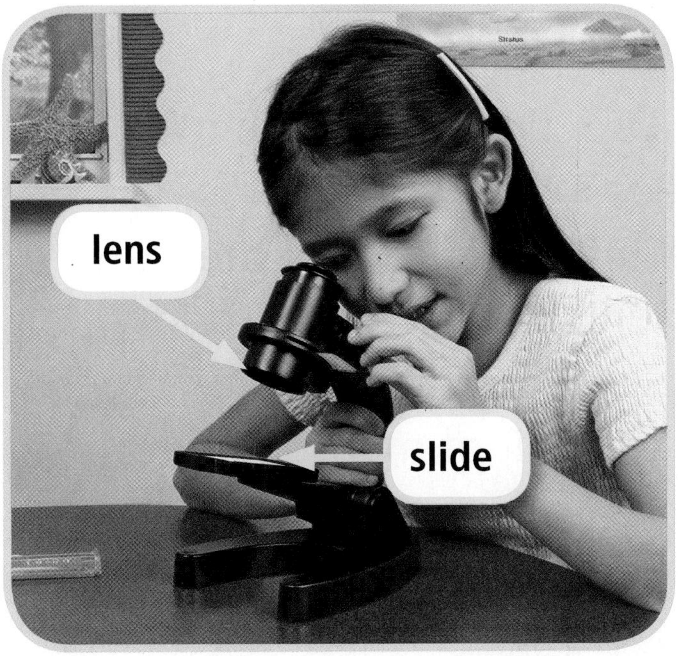

Simple Microscope

Use a microscope to make very tiny objects look larger. Put the object on the slide, and look at it through the lens.

Forceps

Use forceps to hold, move, or separate small objects.

Focus Skill MAIN IDEA AND DETAILS **How do these tools help you observe small things?**

Ruler

Use a ruler to measure how long, wide, or tall an object is. Put the first mark of the ruler at one end of the object. Read the number at the other end of the object.

Tape Measure

Use a tape measure to measure how long, wide, or tall an object is or to measure around it. Many rulers and tape measures use centimeters as the unit of measurement.

Insta-Lab

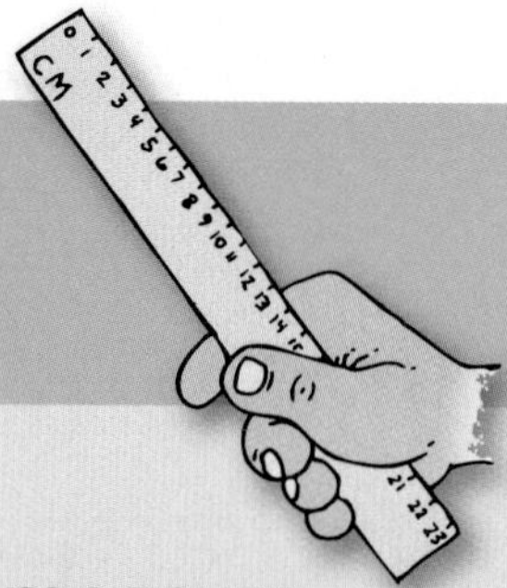

Measure Up

Use a ruler to measure in centimeters the length of this book. Then measure in centimeters to find out how wide the book is.

Dropper

Use a dropper to place small amounts of a liquid. Squeeze the bulb of the dropper. Put the dropper in the liquid and slowly stop squeezing. To drop the liquid, slowly squeeze the bulb again.

Measuring Cup

Use a measuring cup to measure a liquid. Liquids can be measured in units called liters and milliliters.

Place the cup on a table. Pour the liquid into the cup. When the liquid stops moving, read the mark on the cup.

Focus Skill **MAIN IDEA AND DETAILS** **What are some science tools people use to measure?**

Balance

Use a balance to measure the mass of an object. Mass is measured in grams and kilograms.

Place the object on one side of the balance. Place masses on the other side. Add or remove masses until the two sides of the balance are even.

Add the masses to find the mass of the object.

Scale

Use a scale to measure the weight of an object. Weight is measured in units called pounds and ounces.

Make sure the scale is at zero. Then place the object you want to weigh on the scale. Read the number.

Thermometer

Use a thermometer to measure temperature. Temperature is measured in units called degrees. Some thermometers show both Celsius and Fahrenheit degrees.

Place the thermometer where you want to measure the temperature. Wait until the line stops moving. Then read the number on the thermometer.

Focus Skill MAIN IDEA AND DETAILS **Why is a thermometer a science tool?**

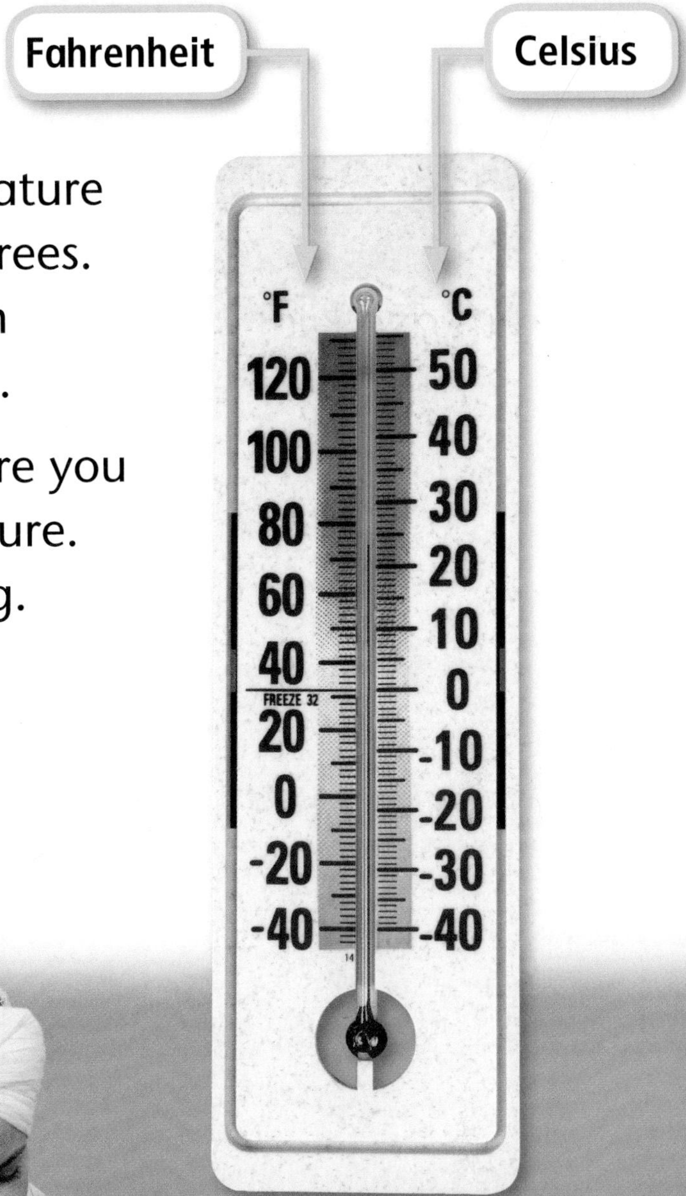

Standards Wrap-Up and Lesson Review

Essential Question

What science tools will we use?

In this lesson, you learned about science tools used to observe and measure things.

Standards in This Lesson

4.a Make predictions based on observed patterns and not random guessing.

4.b Measure length, weight, temperature, and liquid volume with appropriate tools and express those measurements in standard metric system units.

4.f Use magnifiers or microscopes to observe and draw descriptions of small objects or small features of objects.

1. Focus Skill **MAIN IDEA AND DETAILS** Make a chart like this one. Fill in details for the main idea **We use science tools.** 4.b

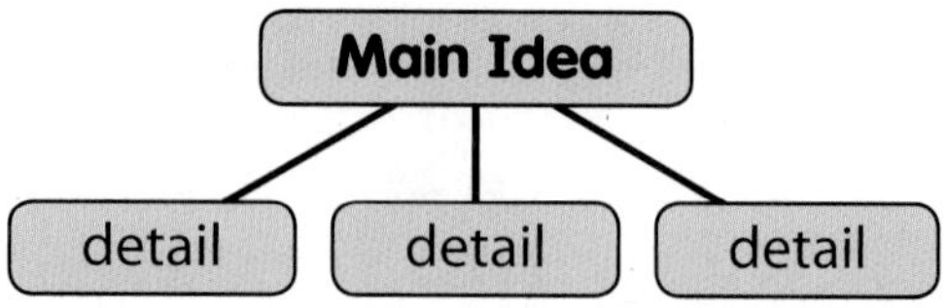

2. **DRAW CONCLUSIONS** Which is bigger—a centimeter or a meter? 4.b

3. **VOCABULARY** Use the term **science tools** to tell about how to see small things more easily. 4.f

4. **Investigation** How does observing patterns help you predict? 4.a

5. Which sentence describes a thermometer? 4.b
   - **A** It measures length.
   - **B** It measures mass.
   - **C** It measures temperature.
   - **D** It measures weight.

The Big Idea

6. Tell about science tools used to observe things and science tools used to measure things. 4.b

Writing ELA–W 1.1

Write to Describe

1. Observe some science tools.
2. Draw a picture of each tool and label it.
3. Write a sentence to describe your picture. Tell how the tool is used.
4. Share your picture and sentence with classmates.

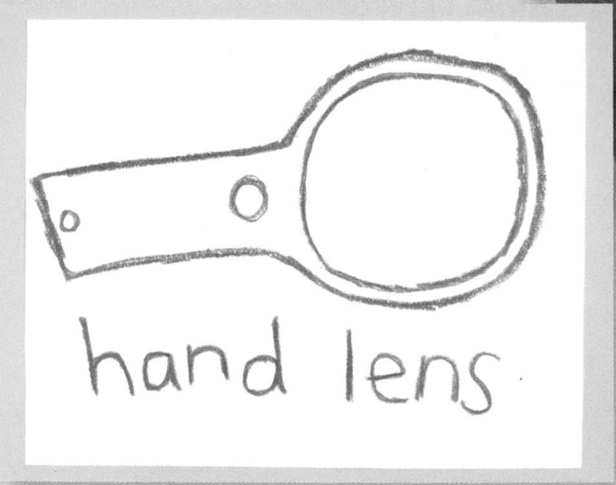

Math MG 1.1

Predict and Count

1. Predict how many pennies you would need to make a row as long as a ruler.
2. Lay the pennies beside the ruler and count them.
3. Tell how many pennies you needed.
4. Tell whether the number of pennies was more than, less than, or the same as your prediction.

For more links and activities, go to **www.hspscience.com**

California Standards in This Lesson

Investigation and Experimentation

4.e Construct bar graphs to record data, using appropriately labeled axes.

LESSON 3

Essential Question

How Do We Use Graphs?

California Fast Fact

Panning for Gold

These girls are panning for gold with a park ranger in Yuba River, California. California's Diamond Jubilee half dollar shows a gold miner panning for gold.

Vocabulary Preview

Information used in science is **data**. p. 28

My Coins	
Coin	Tally
penny	𝍸 ||
nickel	|||
quarter	𝍸 |

A **tally chart** is a diagram you use to record data. p. 28

A **picture graph** is a diagram you use to show data. Each picture stands for one thing. p. 30

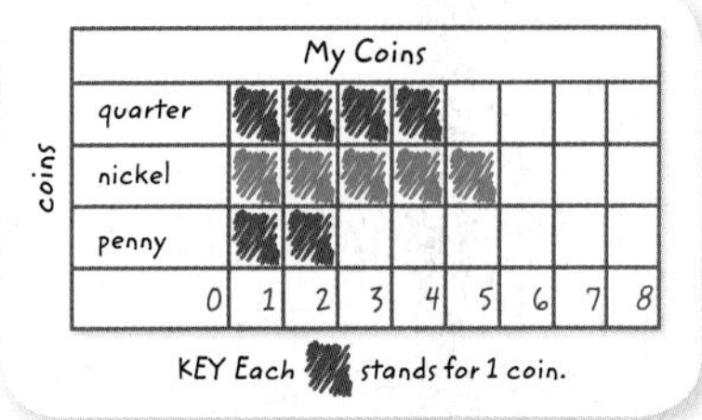

A **bar graph** is a diagram you use to show data. The bars show how much or how many. p. 32

Investigate

How to Record Data

Directed Inquiry

Ask a Question

What data, or information, about these coins might you want to record?

Get Ready

Investigation Skill Tip
You can record data by drawing pictures or making a diagram of what you observe.

You Need

dimes

pennies

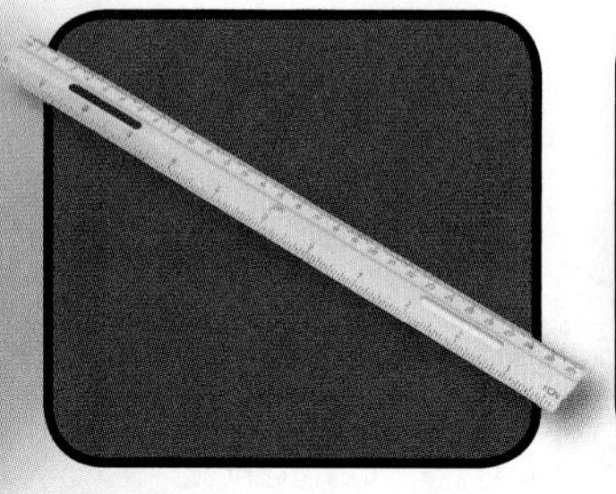

ruler

paper and pencil

What to Do

Step 1

Stand a ruler on its end. Stack pennies 2 centimeters high. Stack dimes 1 centimeter high.

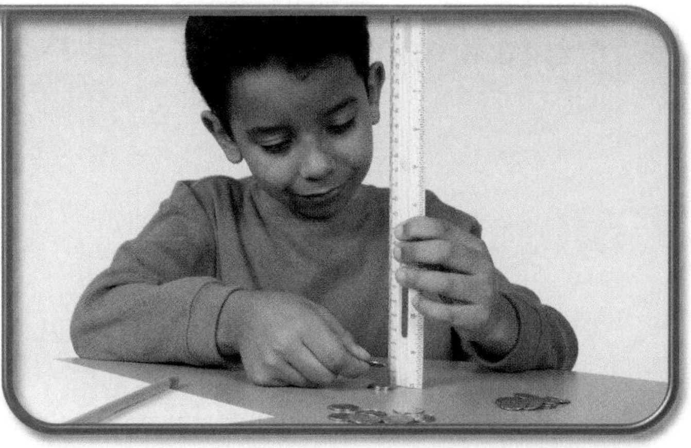

Step 2

Count the pennies and dimes. Make a tally chart to **record** the number of coins in each stack.

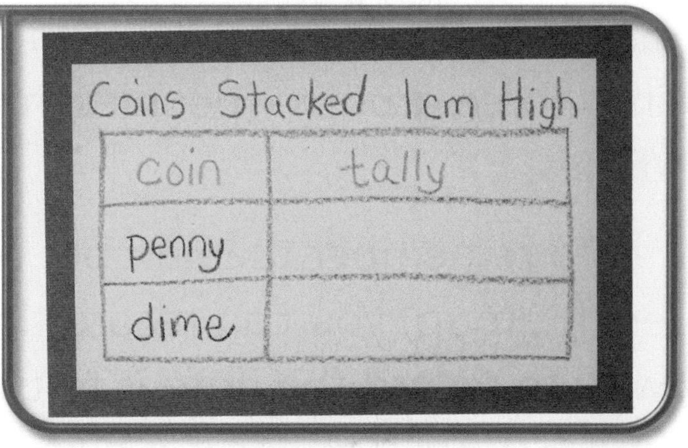

Step 3

Use the data in the tally chart to tell about the stacks of coins.

Draw Conclusions

How did the tally chart help you **record** your observations? 4.e

Independent Inquiry

Make stacks of nickels and quarters 1 centimeter high. Make a bar graph to **record** and show how many coins are in each stack. Talk about what you found out. 4.e

4.e

VOCABULARY
data
tally chart
picture graph
bar graph

Focus Skill COMPARE AND CONTRAST

Read to find out how tally charts, picture graphs, and bar graphs are alike and different.

Collecting Data

When you investigate, you collect **data**, or information. Suppose you want to find out how many pennies, nickels, and dimes are in a pile of coins. You can sort the coins into three groups—pennies, nickels, and dimes.

To remember the number of coins in each group, you can record the data. One way to record the data is to use a tally chart. A **tally chart** is a diagram you use to record data.

Focus Skill COMPARE AND CONTRAST **Compare the coins. How do you know which coins to group together?**

Using a Tally Chart

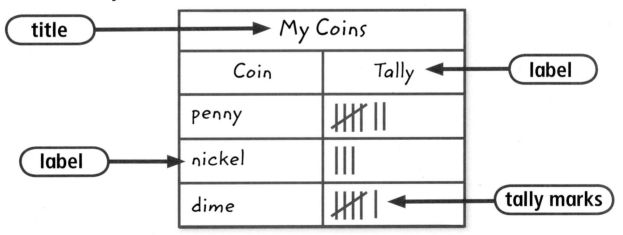

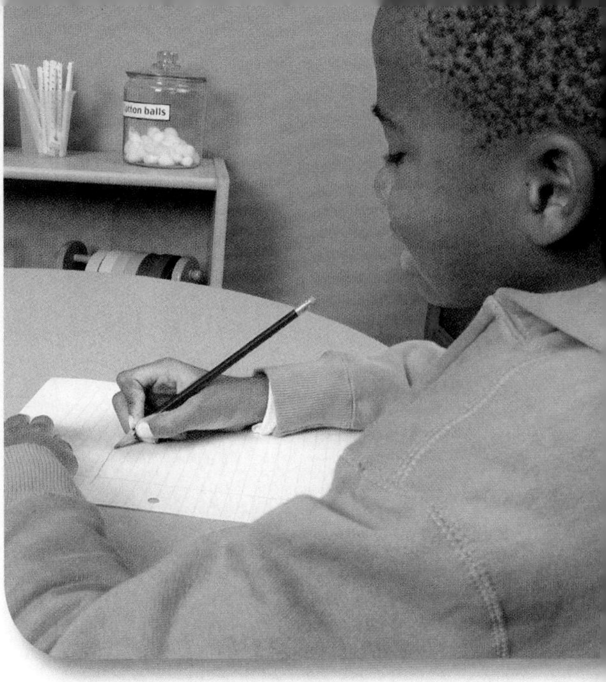

1. Draw a tally chart.
2. Write the title. It tells the kind of data.
3. Write the labels. They name the data.
4. Gather your data.
5. Record your data. Draw one tally, or mark, for each coin. Draw them in groups of five to make them easier to count. Five tallies will look like this. 卌

Practice

1. How many pennies are there?
2. How many nickels and dimes are there?

title → My Coins

My Coins	
Coin	Tally
penny	卌 ||
nickel	|||
dime	卌 |

label → Tally

label → nickel

tally marks → 卌 |

3. How many more dimes than nickels are there?

Focus Skill COMPARE AND CONTRAST **How are the rows on this tally chart alike? How are they different?**

Using a Picture Graph

You can show the data in your tally chart in different ways. A **picture graph** is a diagram that shows data. In a picture graph, one picture stands for one thing. Suppose you collected data and recorded it in this tally chart.

My Coins	
Coin	Tally
penny	𝍸 II
nickel	III
quarter	𝍸 I

Now you want to show your data in a picture graph.

How to Make a Picture Graph

1. Draw the picture graph.
2. Write the title.
3. Write the labels.
4. Write the key. The key tells what each picture in the picture graph stands for.
5. Record the data from your tally chart. Draw one circle to stand for each coin.

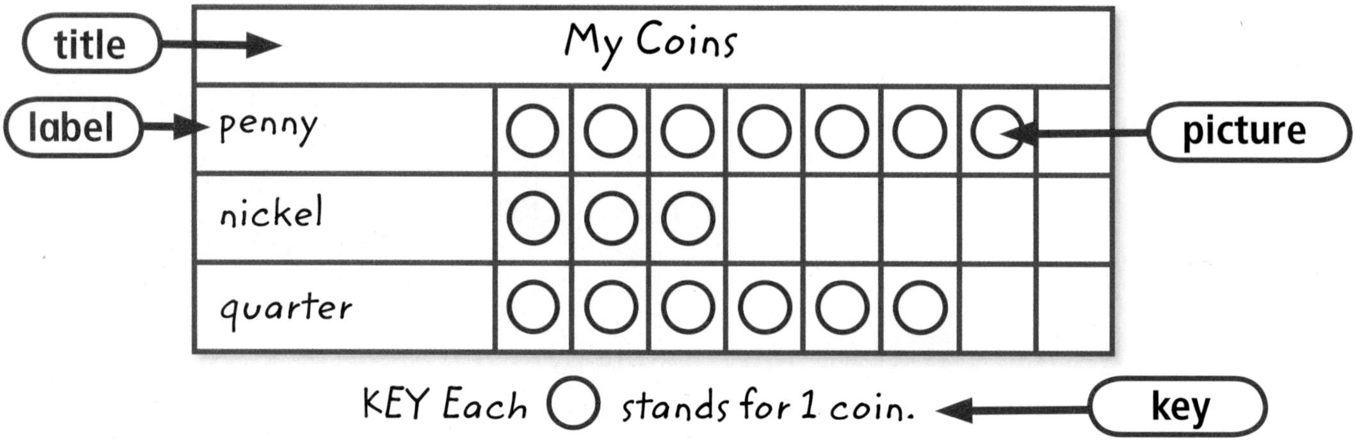

Practice

Study the picture graph on this page.
Count the number of pictures in each row.
Compare the rows.

title → My Coins

label →								
penny	○	○	○	○	○	○		
nickel	○	○	○	○	○	○	○	○
dime	○	○	○	○	○	○		

key → KEY Each ○ stands for 1 coin. picture

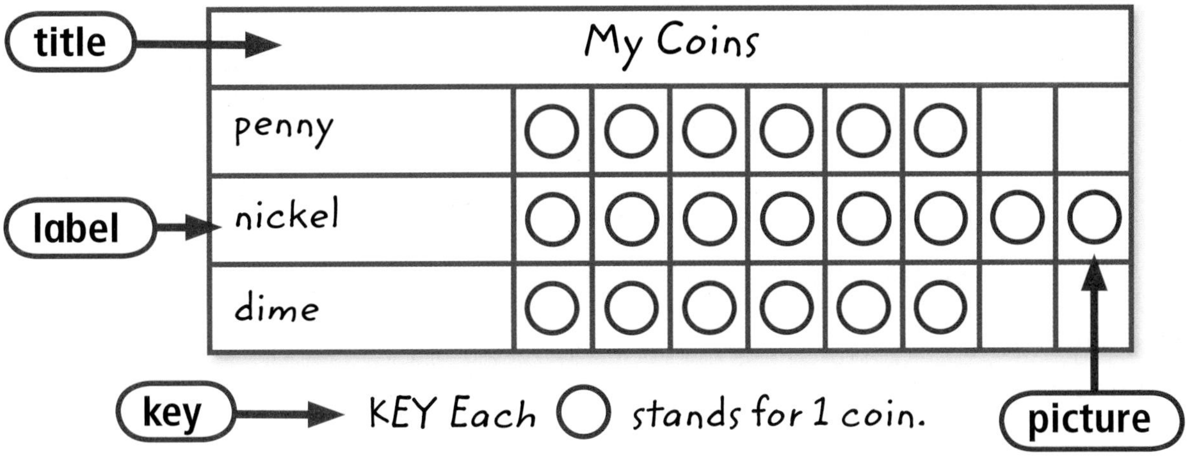

1. Which row has the most pictures?

2. Which two rows have the same number of pictures?

3. How many nickels and pennies are there?

4. How many more nickels than dimes are there?

Focus Skill **COMPARE AND CONTRAST** How are a tally chart and a picture graph alike? How are they different?

Using a Bar Graph

Using a bar graph is another way to show data. A **bar graph** is a diagram that shows data. In a bar graph, each bar shows how much or how many of one thing. Suppose you collected data and recorded it in this tally chart.

My Coins	
Coin	Tally
quarter	||||
nickel	卌
penny	||

Now you want to show your data in a bar graph.

How to Make a Bar Graph

1. Draw the bar graph.
2. Write the title.

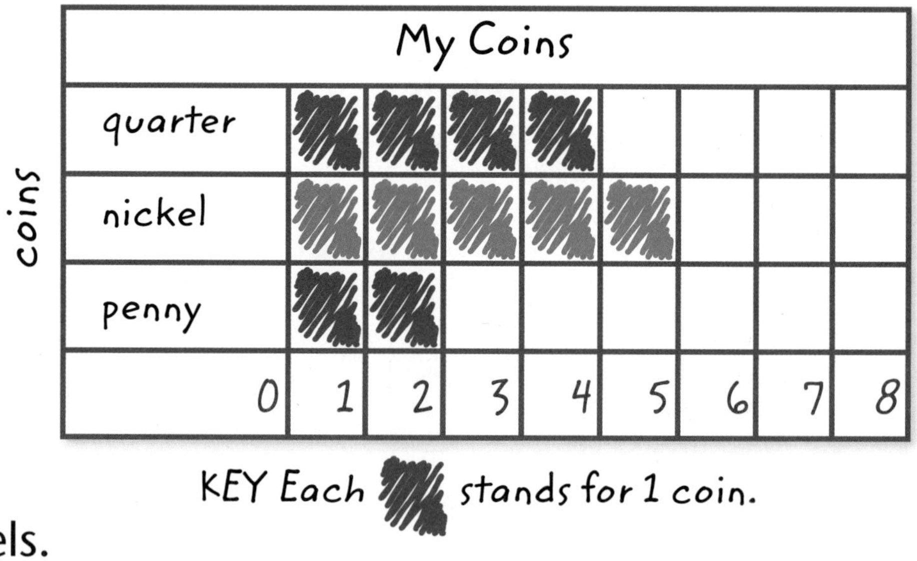

3. Write the labels.
4. Number the boxes that make up the bars. Start with zero.
5. Record the data from your tally chart. Color in one box for each number.

Practice Making a Bar Graph

1. Draw a bar graph to show the data in the tally chart on this page.
2. Write the title and all the labels.
3. Number the boxes that make up the bars of the graph.
4. Color in one box for each coin in the tally chart.

My Coins	
Coin	Tally
quarter	卌 ||||
dime	卌
nickel	卌 ||
penny	卌

Practice Reading a Bar Graph

5. How many quarters are there?
6. How many more nickels than dimes are there?
7. How many quarters, dimes, and nickels are there in all?

Focus Skill COMPARE AND CONTRAST

How are a picture graph and a bar graph alike? How are they different?

Insta-Lab

Show Data

Put a small pile of coins on your desk. Sort them into groups. Record the data in a tally chart. Then show the data in a picture graph or a bar graph. How did you decide which graph to use?

Standards Wrap-Up and Lesson Review

Essential Question

How do we use graphs?

In this lesson, you learned how to use tally charts to record data. You also learned how to use picture graphs and bar graphs to show data.

Investigation and Experimentation Standards in This Lesson

4.e Construct bar graphs to record data, using appropriately labeled axes.

1. Focus Skill **COMPARE AND CONTRAST** Make a chart like this one. Tell how tally charts, picture graphs, and bar graphs are alike and different. **4.e**

alike — different

2. **DRAW CONCLUSIONS** When might you want to show data in a picture graph? **4.e**

3. **VOCABULARY** Use the terms **data** and **graph** in a sentence. **4.e**

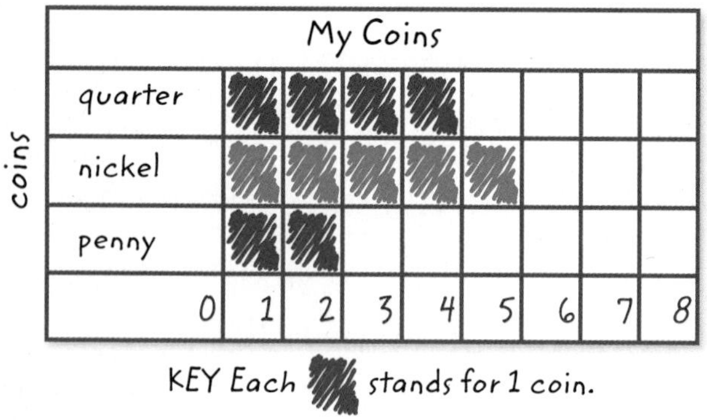

4. **Critical Thinking** Why is it useful to make a tally chart before making a bar graph? **4.e**

5. You are reading a tally chart that has data about different coins. Next to the word **nickel**, you see this. 

How many nickels are there? **4.e**

A 5 nickels
B 12 nickels
C 15 nickels
D 20 nickels

The Big Idea

6. How is knowing how to use a bar graph helpful? **4.e**

Writing — ELA–W 1.1

Write to Inform

1. Observe the tally chart. Decide which kind of graph you would use for this data.
2. Make the graph.
3. Write a sentence to explain your choice.

Coins

coin	tally
quarter	卌 ||
dime	卌
penny	卌 |||

Math — SDAP 1.1, 1.2

Coin Bar Graph

1. You have 8 pennies, 6 nickels, and 7 dimes.
2. Make a tally chart. Record how many of each coin you have.
3. Use the tally chart to make a bar graph. Label the parts of the graph.
4. Share your results.

Coins

coin	tally
penny	
nickel	
dime	

For more links and activities, go to **www.hspscience.com**

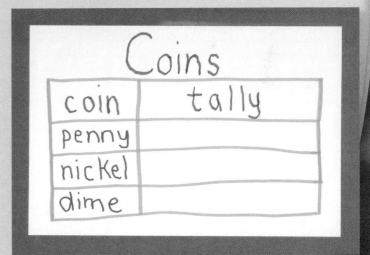

California Standards in This Lesson

Investigation and Experimentation

4.b Measure length, weight, temperature, and liquid volume with appropriate tools and express those measurements in standard metric system units.

4.d Write or draw descriptions of a sequence of steps, events, and observations.

4.g Follow oral instructions for a scientific investigation.

LESSON 4

Essential Question

How Do Scientists Work?

California Fast Fact

1984 Olympics, Los Angeles

The Olympics were held in Los Angeles in 1984. The first Olympics were held many years ago. The king shown on the coin was an Olympic winner in ancient Greece.

Vocabulary Preview

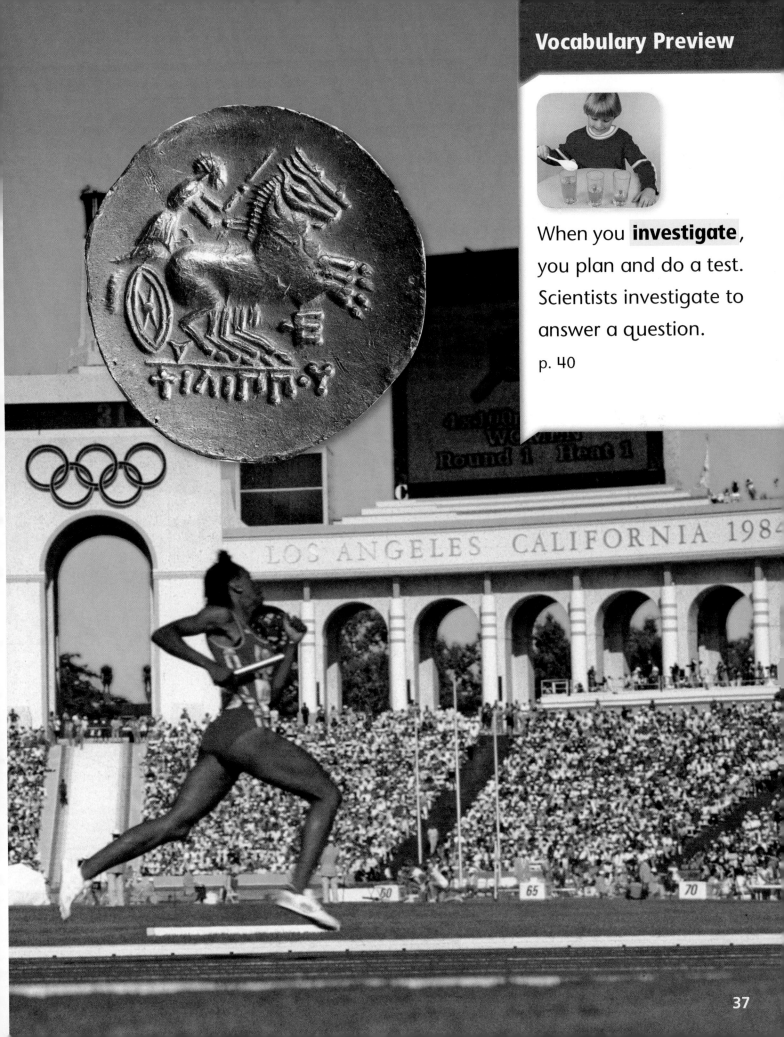

When you **investigate**, you plan and do a test. Scientists investigate to answer a question.

p. 40

Investigate

Equal Coins

Directed Inquiry

Ask a Question

How do scientists find out about things?

Get Ready

Investigation Skill Tip

When you observe two or more things, you can compare them to one another.

You Need

quarter

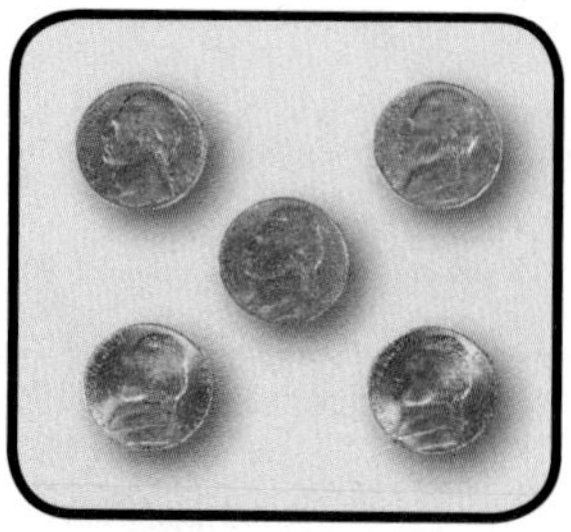

5 nickels

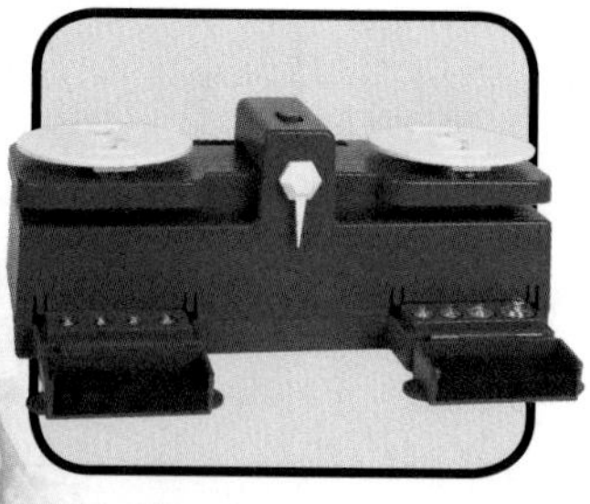

balance

What to Do

Step 1

A quarter and 5 nickels both equal 25 cents. Does a quarter have the same mass as 5 nickels? **Observe** and compare to find out.

Step 2

Make sure the balance is even. Then place the quarter on one side of the balance and the 5 nickels on the other side.

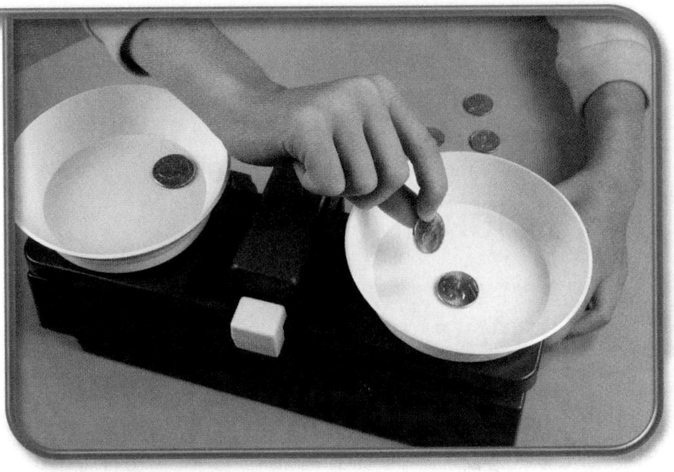

Step 3

Observe and compare the two sides of the balance. Are they even?

Independent Inquiry

Both a quarter and 2 dimes plus a nickel equal 25 cents. Use a balance. Is the mass of a quarter more than, less than, or the same as the mass of 2 dimes and a nickel?

Draw Conclusions

What did you learn about the masses of the coins? **4.b**

4.d, 4.g

VOCABULARY
investigate

SEQUENCE

Look for the order of the steps scientists use when they are investigating.

Investigating

When scientists want to answer a question, they **investigate**, or plan and do a test. Your teacher may give instructions for doing an investigation. You need to follow these instructions carefully. Or you may do your own investigation. When you investigate, you use a plan like this.

1 Observe, and ask a question.

Think of a question you want to answer. Write what you already know about the topic of your question. Figure out what information you need.

Does the mass of a real quarter equal the mass of a play quarter?

2 Form a hypothesis.

Write a hypothesis, or a scientific statement that you can test.

The mass of a real quarter is greater than the mass of a play quarter.

3 Plan a fair test.

A fair test will show what happens. List the things you need and the steps you will follow to do the test. Decide what you want to learn from the test.

Focus Skill SEQUENCE **What should you do after you form a hypothesis?**

Insta-Lab

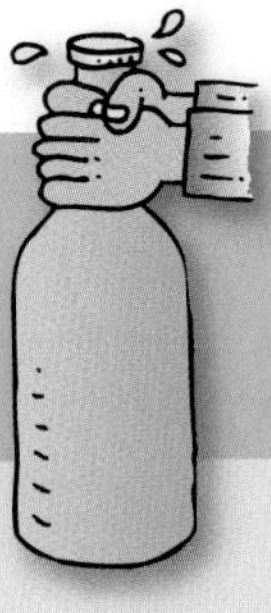

Wet Quarters

Wet a quarter. Place the quarter on the mouth of a glass bottle. Wrap your hands around the neck of the bottle. What do you observe?

4 Do the test.

Follow the steps of your plan. Observe carefully. Record everything that happens.

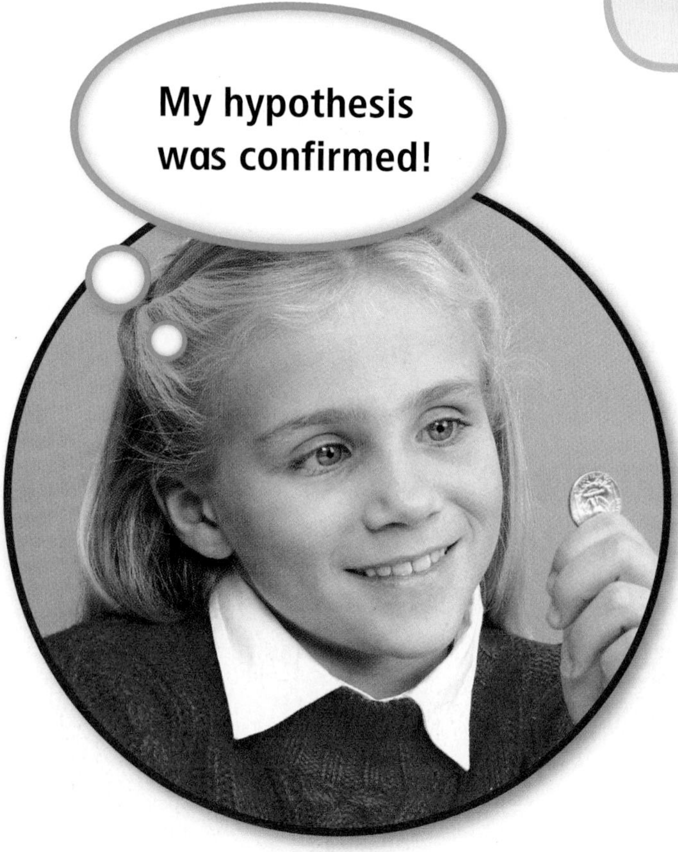
My hypothesis was confirmed!

5 Draw conclusions, and tell or show your results.

Think about what you found out. Was your hypothesis confirmed? Use what you found out to draw conclusions. Then tell or show your results to others.

Investigate more.

If your hypothesis was confirmed, ask another question about your topic to test. If your hypothesis was not confirmed, form another hypothesis and change the test.

Focus Skill **SEQUENCE** **What do you do before you draw conclusions?**

Does a real dime have the same mass as a play dime?

Standards Wrap-Up and Lesson Review

Essential Question

How do scientists work?

In this lesson, you learned the steps scientists follow when they investigate.

Investigation and Experimentation Standards in This Lesson

4.d Write or draw descriptions of a sequence of steps, events, and observations.

4.g Follow oral instructions for a scientific investigation.

1. Focus Skill **SEQUENCE** Make a chart like this one. Show the steps scientists use to investigate. **4.d**

2. **DRAW CONCLUSIONS** When might you want to record data in a tally chart? **4.d**

3. **VOCABULARY** Use the term **investigate** to tell about this lesson. **4.g**

4. **Critical Thinking** Why is it important to plan a fair test? **4.d**

5. What is the next step you should do after you form a hypothesis? **4.d**

A Observe, and ask a question.
B Plan a fair test.
C Draw conclusions.
D Investigate more.

The Big Idea

6. What are the steps scientists use to find out about things? **4.d**

Writing ELA–W 1.1

Write to Inform

1. Think of a question you would like to test.
2. Write a list of all the steps someone would need to follow to do the test.
3. Read your list to classmates.
4. Have them follow your directions.

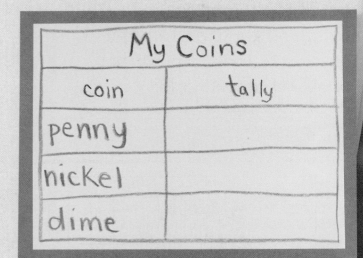

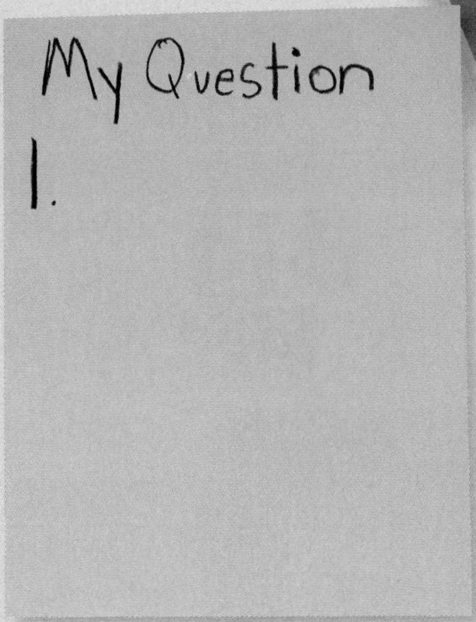

Math SDAP.1.1, 1.2

Coin Picture Graph

1. Sort a small pile of coins into pennies, nickels, and dimes.
2. Make a tally chart. Record how many of each coin you have.
3. Use your tally chart to make a picture graph. Label the parts of the graph.
4. Share your results.

My Coins

coin	tally
penny	
nickel	
dime	

For more links and activities, go to **www.hspscience.com**

Wrap-Up

Visual Summary

Tell how each picture helps explain the **Big Idea**.

The Big Idea **People learn about science by asking good questions and doing careful investigations.**

4.a, 4.g

You can do investigations to find out about things. You can use what you know and what you observe to make a prediction about what will happen.

4.b, 4.c

You can measure length, weight, temperature, and volume. You can sort objects by their properties, such as size and color.

4.d, 4.e

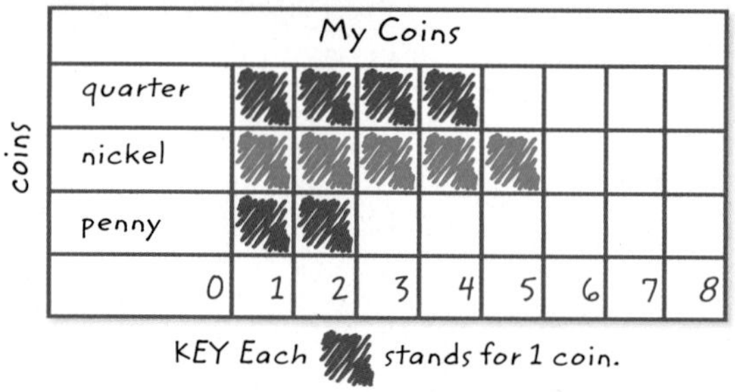

You can record your observations by drawing, writing, or using numbers in charts or graphs.

4.f

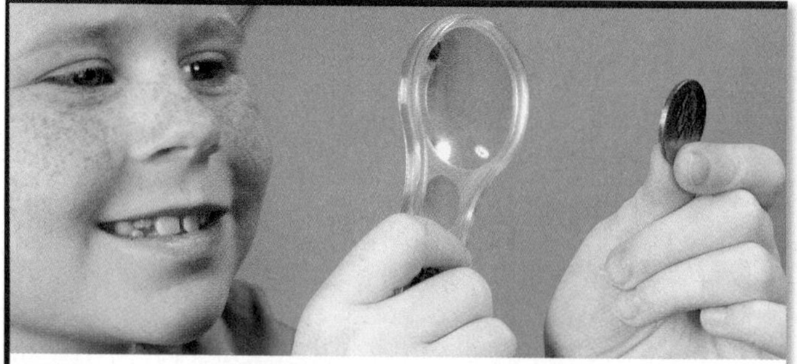

You can use a hand lens or a microscope to observe the details of very small objects.

Show What You Know

Unit Writing Activity

Write About an Inventor

Find out who invented the microscope or another science tool. Write some sentences about the inventor. Describe the science tool, and draw a picture of it. Label the parts of the tool. Share your writing and your drawing with the class.

Unit Project

Reading Bar Graph

For one week, keep track of the time you spend reading. Record in a chart the hours you read each day. Then use that data to make a bar graph. Give your graph a title, and label the parts of the graph. Share your chart and bar graph with the class.

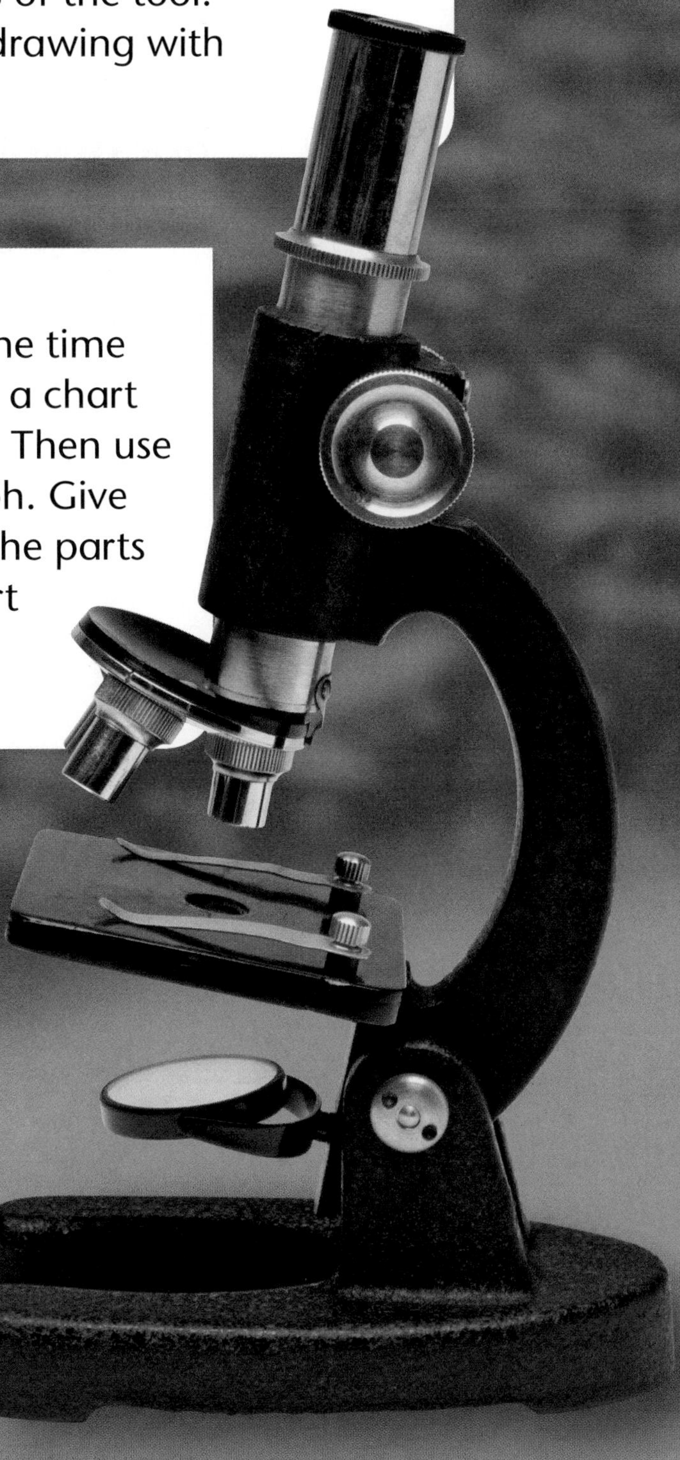

READY, SET, SCIENCE!

Review

California Science Standards in ■

Vocabulary Review

Use the terms to complete the sentences. The page numbers tell you where to look if you need help.

investigation skills p. 6
observe p. 6
science tools p. 16
data p. 28
bar graph p. 32
investigate p. 40

1. A ______ is a diagram used to show data. 4.e
2. When you plan and do a test, you ______. 4.d
3. We use ______ to observe and measure things in science. 4.f
4. Information that is used in science is ______. 4.b
5. To find out about something, you use your senses to ______ it. 4.f
6. Skills that people use to find out about things are ______. 4.c

Check Understanding

7. What science tools are in the picture? 4.b

A a thermometer and a hand lens

B a ruler and a dropper

C a measuring cup and a ruler

D a magnifying box and a balance

8. What are investigation skills? Name some investigation skills. 4.a

Critical Thinking

9. How are a tally chart and a picture graph alike? How are they different? 4.e

The Big Idea

10. How can people learn about science? 4.g

UNIT 1 PHYSICAL SCIENCE

Motion

California Standards in This Unit

1 The motion of objects can be observed and measured. As a basis for understanding this concept:

1.a *Students know* the position of an object can be described by locating it in relation to another object or to the background.

1.b *Students know* an object's motion can be described by recording the change in position of the object over time.

1.c *Students know* the way to change how something is moving is by giving it a push or a pull. The size of the change is related to the strength, or the amount of force, of the push or pull.

1.d *Students know* tools and machines are used to apply pushes and pulls (forces) to make things move.

1.e *Students know* objects fall to the ground unless something holds them up.

1.f *Students know* magnets can be used to make some objects move without being touched.

1.g *Students know* sound is made by vibrating objects and can be described by its pitch and volume.

This unit also includes these Investigation and Experimentation Standards: **4.a**, **4.b**, **4.d**, **4.e**, **4.g**

What's the Big Idea?

The motion of objects can be observed and measured.

Essential Questions

Science in California

Dear Ernesto,

Today our class went to the Cable Car Museum. Cable cars have been around for more than a hundred years. We learned that the cars are pulled on rails. They grab onto moving wires called cables. The cables get power from electricity.

Your buddy,

Rashad

Read Rashad's postcard. What did Rashad learn about how cable cars move? How does this helps explain the **Big Idea**?

Unit Inquiry

Metals and Magnets

How do magnets make things move without touching those things?
Plan and do a test to find out.

California Standards in This Lesson

Science Content

1.a *Students know* the position of an object can be described by locating it in relation to another object or to the background.

Investigation and Experimentation

4.b Measure length, weight, temperature, and liquid volume with appropriate tools and express those measurements in standard metric system units.

LESSON 1

Essential Question

How Do We Describe Position?

California Fast Fact

San Francisco–Oakland Bay Bridge

Look at all the cars on the bridge, going from one place to another! You can use a map to find distances between places.

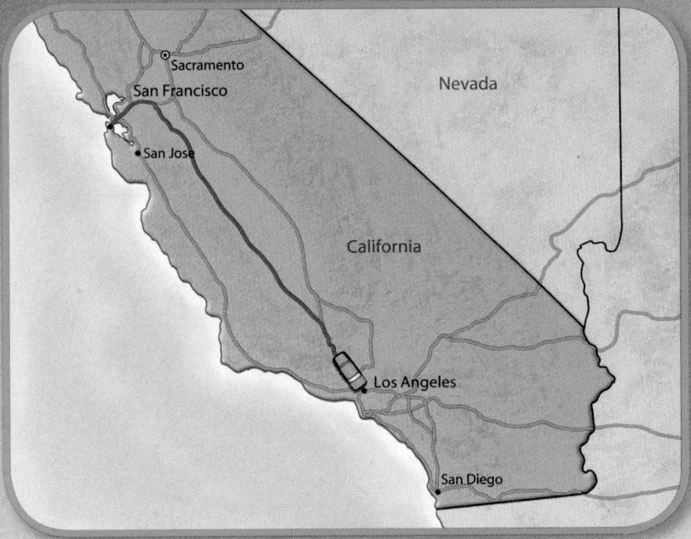

Vocabulary Preview

An object's **position** is the place where it is.
p. 56

Distance is the measure of the length between two things.
p. 60

A **centimeter** is a measure of distance or length. p. 60

A **meter** is a unit of measure for length, width, or height. One meter equals 100 centimeters. p. 60

The Distance Between Things

Directed Inquiry

Ask a Question

Why is it important to measure distance carefully?

Get Ready

Investigate Skill Tip

When you measure distance, you can use a tool such as a ruler.

You Need

stones

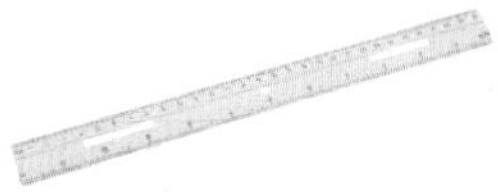

ruler

chalk

What to Do

Step 1

Put stones above and below a chalk line.

Step 2

Measure the distance from the line to one stone.

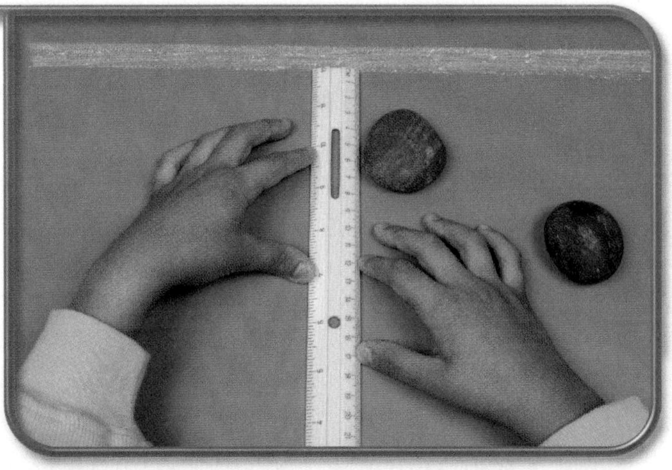

Step 3

Tell a classmate the distance. Have the classmate measure to find out which stone it is.

Draw Conclusions

How can measuring help you describe an object's location? **4.b**

Independent Inquiry

Measure and record the distance between two stones. Ask a classmate to measure the distance between the same two stones. Do your measurements agree? **4.b**

VOCABULARY
position
distance
centimeter
meter

MAIN IDEA AND DETAILS

Look for details about how to describe where something is.

Position

An object's **position** is the place where it is, compared to something else. One way to tell an object's location is to describe its position. You compare its position to the position of something that is not moving.

To compare, you can use words such as *in front of* and *behind*. In this picture, the bear is *in front of* the frog. The pail is *behind* the truck. The bear is *to the right of* the truck. The drum is *to the left of* the pail.

You can say that the doll is *on top of* the drum. The red block is *under* the green block. There are many ways to describe an object's position.

Focus Skill MAIN IDEA AND DETAILS **How can you describe an object's position?**

How can you describe the positions of objects in this picture?

Other Ways to Describe Position

There is another way to describe an object's position. Again, you compare it to the position of another object. This time, the object is far away. Remember that the second object cannot be moving.

How can you describe the position of things in this photo?

In the picture below, the hikers are *in front of* the mountain.

You can describe an object's position in another way if a row of things is behind it. Where is the lamp post in relation to the row of houses? Where is the van?

In the picture below, the older boy's body is in front of the fifth fence picket from the left.

Focus Skill **MAIN IDEA AND DETAILS**

What details are important in describing where something is?

Distance and Position

Distance is the measure of the length between two things. You can measure with a ruler. You can also use a tape measure or a meterstick.

Some rulers use **centimeters**. A mark shows each centimeter. A centimeter is the same on every ruler. One **meter** has 100 centimeters. A meter is always the same. You can use centimeters and meters to measure distance.

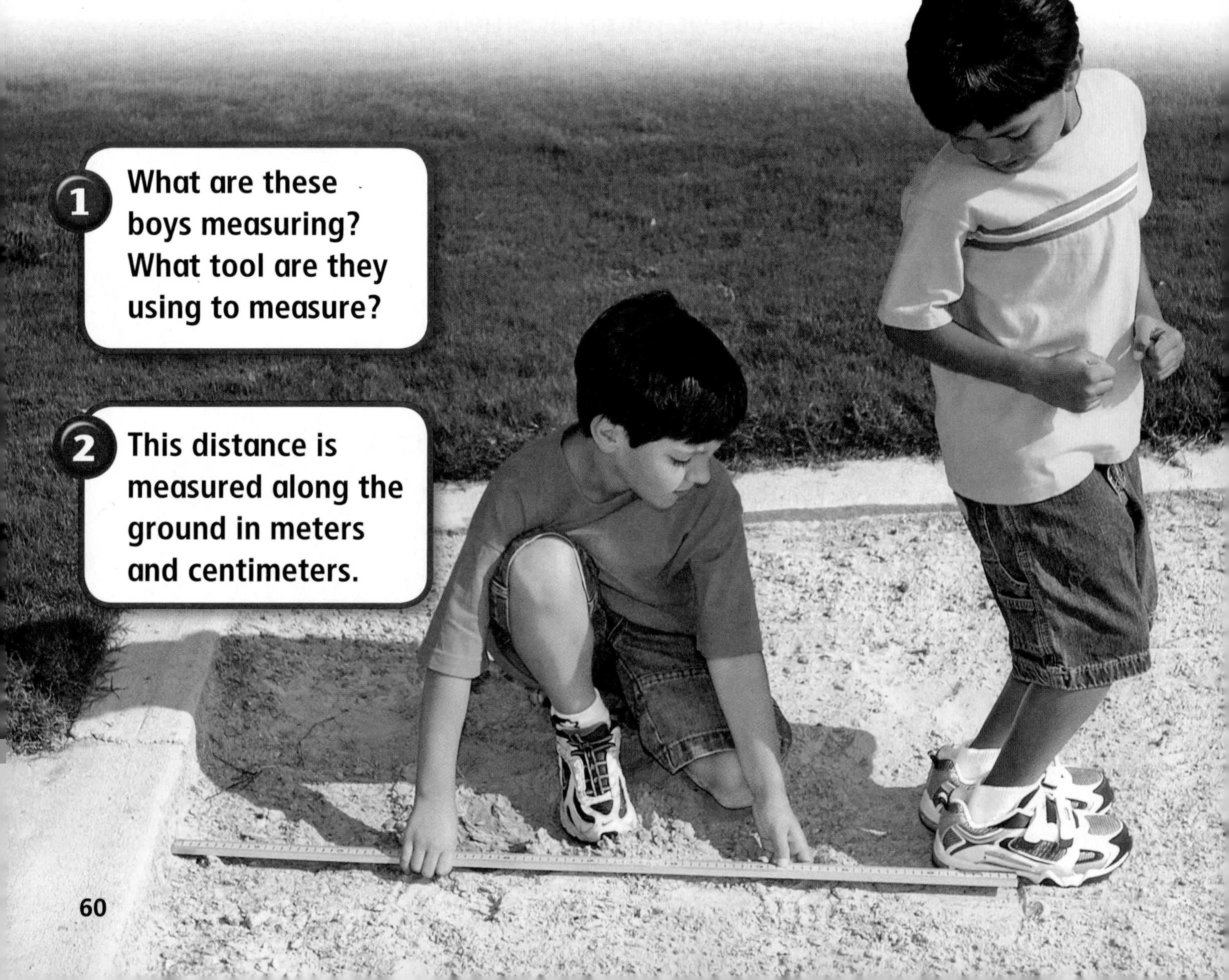

1. **What are these boys measuring? What tool are they using to measure?**

2. **This distance is measured along the ground in meters and centimeters.**

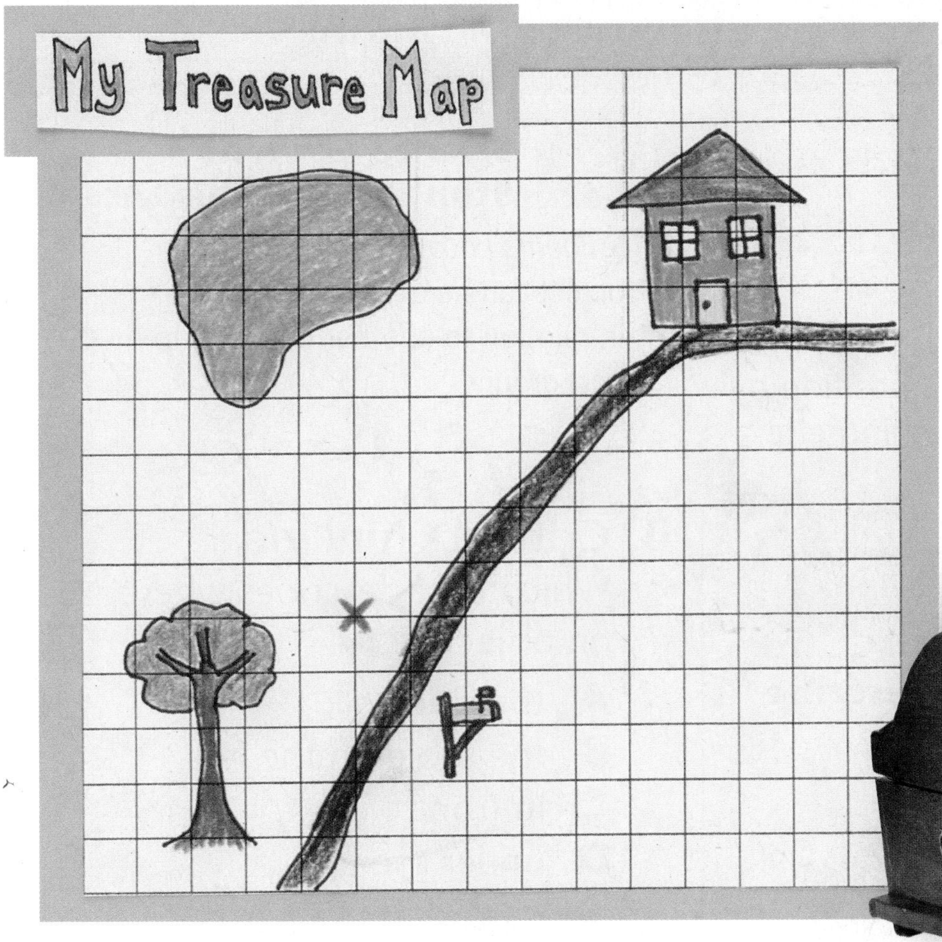

Distances can help tell a position. Use a treasure map to find the treasure.

1. Start at X.
2. Count 5 squares to the right.
3. Count 3 squares up.
4. Count 4 squares to the left.
5. Count 6 squares down.
6. Ask your teacher to check whether you found the treasure.

Insta-Lab

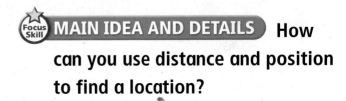

Simon Says

Play Simon Says with classmates. Simon will use distance and position words.

Focus Skill **MAIN IDEA AND DETAILS** **How can you use distance and position to find a location?**

Standards Wrap-Up and Lesson Review

Essential Question

How Do We Describe Position?

In this lesson, you learned ways you can describe an object's position by comparing it with something else.

Science Content Standards in This Lesson

I.a *Students know* the position of an object can be described by locating it in relation to another object or to the background.

1. Focus Skill **MAIN IDEA AND DETAILS** Make a chart like this one. Show details of the main idea **You can describe an object's position.** I.a

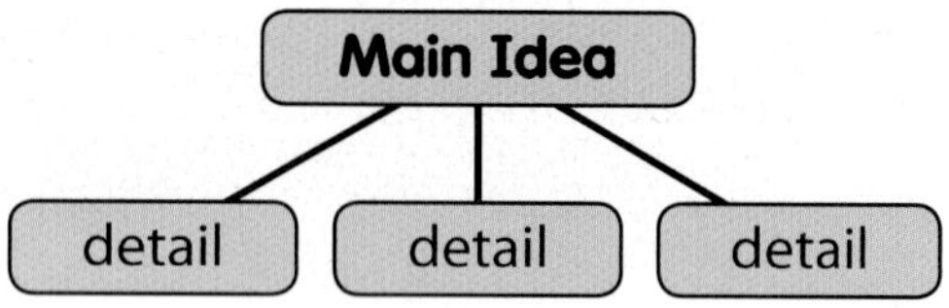

2. **DRAW CONCLUSIONS** When is it useful to measure lengths? I.a

3. **VOCABULARY** Use the term **distance** in a sentence. I.a

4. **Critical Thinking** Which best describes where an object is? I.a

- **A** the sidewalk
- **B** the table on the left
- **C** in front of
- **D** under the tree

5. What are centimeters and meters? I.a

The Big Idea

6. What is needed to describe the position of something? I.a

Writing — ELA–W 1.1

Write to Describe

1. Think of an object in the classroom. Do not tell what it is. Do not look at it.
2. Write sentences to describe the position of the object.
3. Read your sentences to your classmates. Let them guess what object the sentences describe.

Where My Object Is.

Math — SDAP 1.1, 1.2

Broad-Jump Bar Graph

1. Stand behind a line. Jump as far as you can. Draw a line where you land.
2. Measure the distance. Do this two more times.
3. Make a chart. Record your distance for each jump.
4. Use your chart to make a bar graph to show your data. Label the parts.

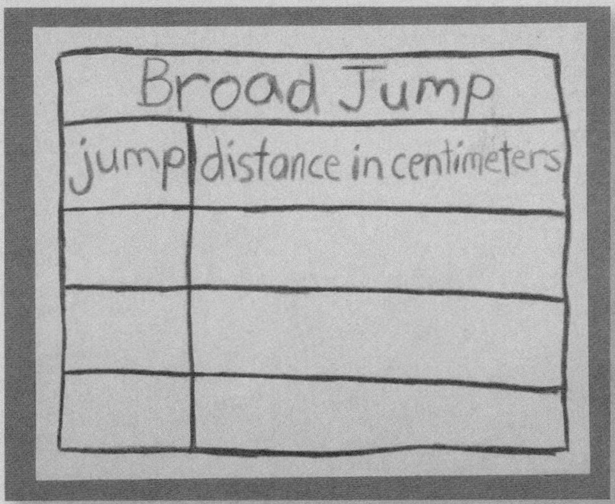
Broad Jump
jump
distance in centimeters

For more links and activities, go to **www.hspscience.com**

California Standards in This Lesson

Science Content

1.b *Students know* an object's motion can be described by recording the change in position of the object over time.

Investigation and Experimentation

4.a Make predictions based on observed patterns and not random guessing.

LESSON 2

Essential Question

How Do We Describe Motion?

California Fast Fact

Roller Coaster, Knott's Berry Farm, Buena Park

The coaster cars race through its dips and curves as fast as cars on a highway. Now that's moving!

Vocabulary Preview

Motion is a change of position. When something moves, it is in motion. p. 68

Speed describes how fast something moves. It is the distance something moves in a certain amount of time. p. 70

Investigate

Ways Things Can Move

Directed Inquiry

Ask a Question

What path do you think the bowling ball will take?

Get Ready

Investigation Skill Tip

When you predict, you use what you know to say what you think will happen.

You Need

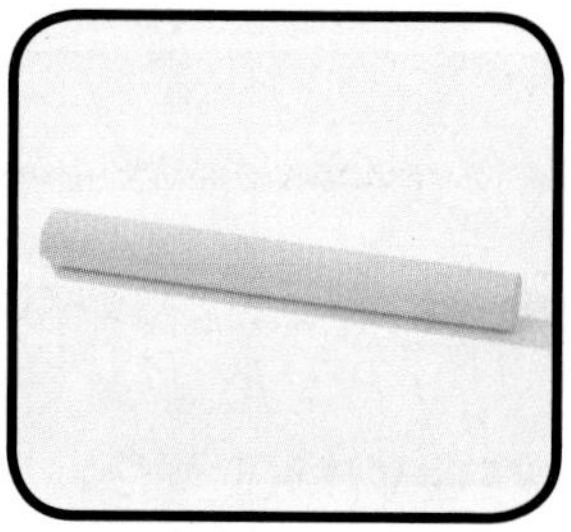

chalk

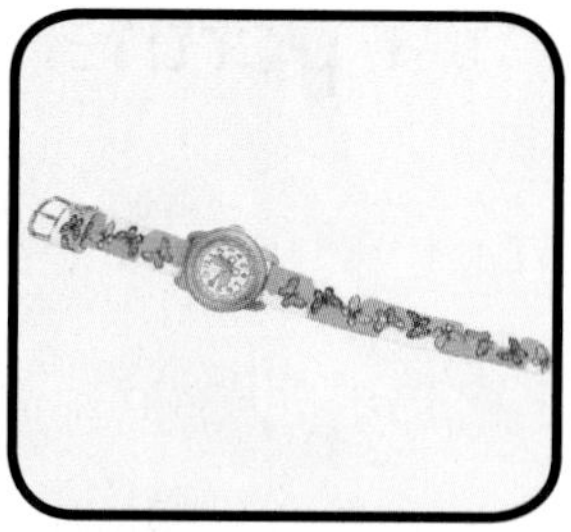

watch

What to Do

Step 1

Predict how far a partner can walk, skip, and run in 30 seconds. Mark your partner's starting point.

Step 2

Have your partner walk for 30 seconds. Mark the place where your partner stops.

Step 3

Repeat, having your partner skip instead of walk. Repeat, having your partner run.

Draw Conclusions

Were your predictions correct? In which way did your partner move the farthest in 30 seconds? **4.a**

Independent Inquiry

Think of other ways to move. **Predict** which ways will be faster and which will be slower. Observe a partner moving in each of your ways. Were your predictions correct? **4.a**

VOCABULARY
motion
speed

Focus Skill MAIN IDEA AND DETAILS

Look for details about ways to describe motion.

Motion

When something is moving, it is in motion. **Motion** is a change of position. A rolling ball is in motion.

Objects can move in many ways. A toy car can move in a straight line. A swing moves back and forth in a curved path. The hands of a clock move in a circle.

How are objects moving in this picture?

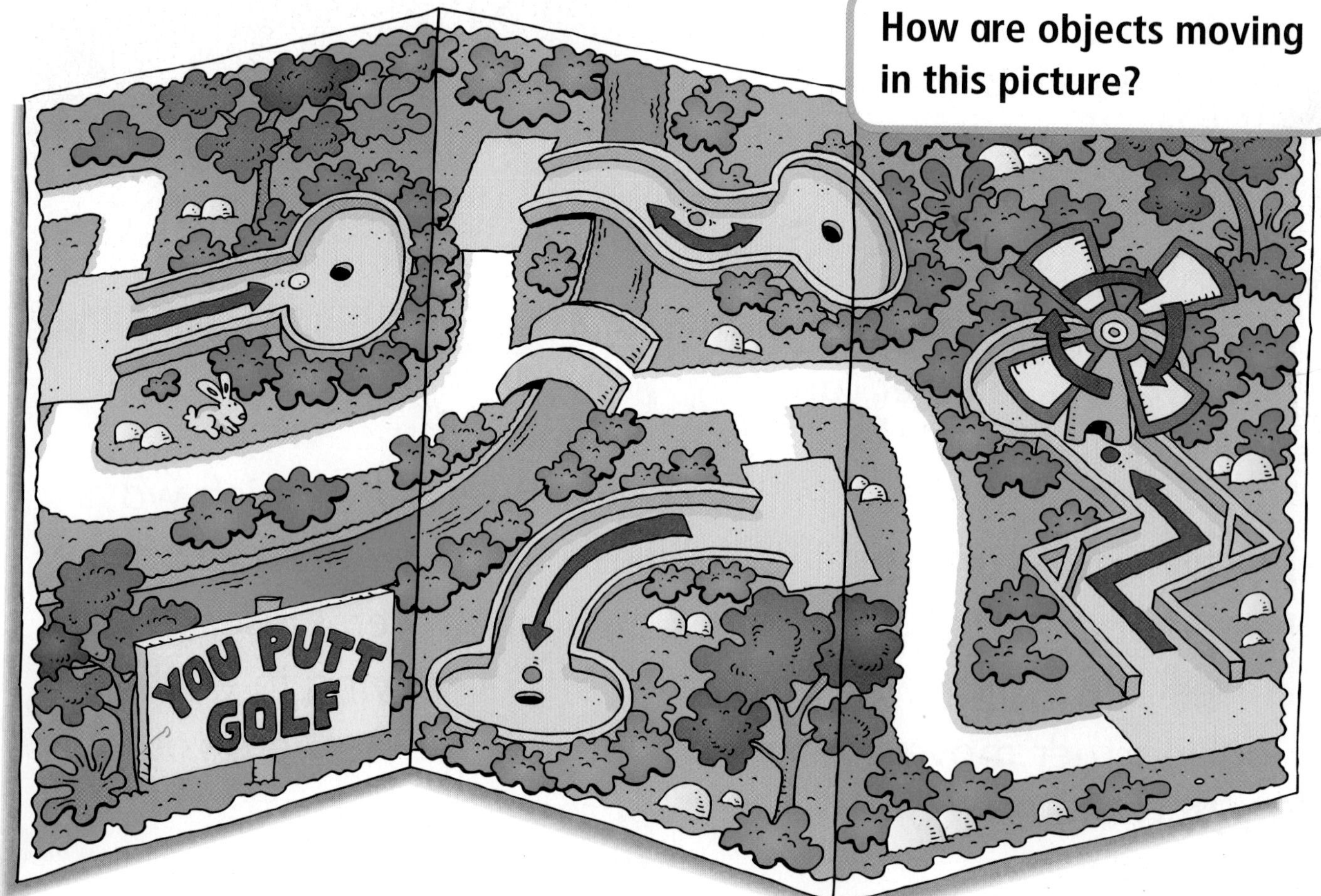

A golf ball may change direction many times on its path to a hole.

A ball moves in a straight line if it is not touched. If something touches the ball, its path can change. It can change direction.

Focus Skill **MAIN IDEA AND DETAILS** **What are some ways an object can move?**

Speed

Speed is the measure of how fast something moves. Things move at different speeds. A car moves faster than a bike. A runner moves faster than a walker.

Think of bikers riding in a race. They all start at the same time. They move along the same track for the same distance. The biker who gets to the end of the track first wins. That biker has moved the fastest, or with the greatest speed. The last biker has moved the most slowly, or with the least speed.

The bike that moves at the greatest speed will finish the race first.

Think about runners in a timed race. Each person runs for one minute. Each runner's distance is measured. The person who runs the farthest in one minute wins. This runner has moved the fastest, or with the greatest speed.

Surfers move with great speed across the water. What makes them move so fast?

Focus Skill MAIN IDEA AND DETAILS

What is speed?

Changes in Motion and Speed

Motion can be made to change. An object can begin to move, move faster, change direction, move more slowly, and then stop.

A leaf falls from a tree. The leaf moves toward the ground. It gets caught on a bush and stops moving. A wind comes along. It puts the leaf in motion again. It may change the leaf's direction.

Horses have different gaits, or ways of moving. Walking and trotting are slower than galloping.

Imagine that you go for a run. At first, you walk to warm up. Then you start running. You run faster. As you get tired, you slow down. You walk to cool down. Then you stop.

When you start moving, you change two things. You change your position. You may also change your speed.

Suppose you are at an animal park. You move from area to area. You change your position and direction many times.

You may start to walk faster if you are in a hurry to see the next area. When you get there, you stop to watch the animals. Then you start walking again.

Focus Skill **MAIN IDEA AND DETAILS** **Tell how the motion of an object can change.**

Insta-Lab

Watch It Go!

Work with two classmates. One classmate moves at different speeds and in different directions for one minute. The other two write sentences to describe what they observe. See if they both observe the same thing.

Standards Wrap-Up and Lesson Review

Essential Question

How do we describe motion?

In this lesson, you learned that you can describe an object's motion by recording the object's change in position over time.

Science Content Standards in This Lesson

1.b *Students know* an object's motion can be described by recording the change in position of the object over time.

1. **MAIN IDEA AND DETAILS** Make a chart like this one. Show details for the main idea **You can describe an object's motion.** **1.b**

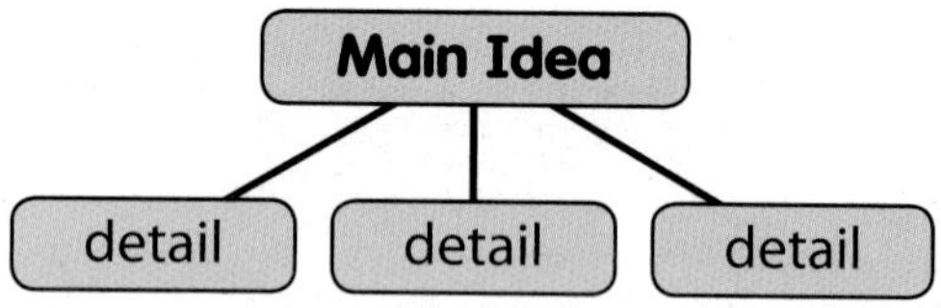

2. **SUMMARIZE** Write a sentence that tells what this lesson is about. **1.b**

3. **VOCABULARY** Use the terms **motion** and **speed** in a sentence about this picture. **1.b**

4. **Critical Thinking** Which words can describe the speed of a moving object? **1.b**
   A curved, straight
   B back, forth
   C fast, slow
   D far, near

5. **Investigation** What helps you make predictions about a ball's motion? **4.a**

The Big Idea

6. What can you observe about an object that is in motion? **1.b**

Writing ELA–W 1.1

Write to Describe

1. Think about things outside that move.
2. Write sentences that tell about the direction and speed of the moving objects.
3. Share your sentences with a classmate.

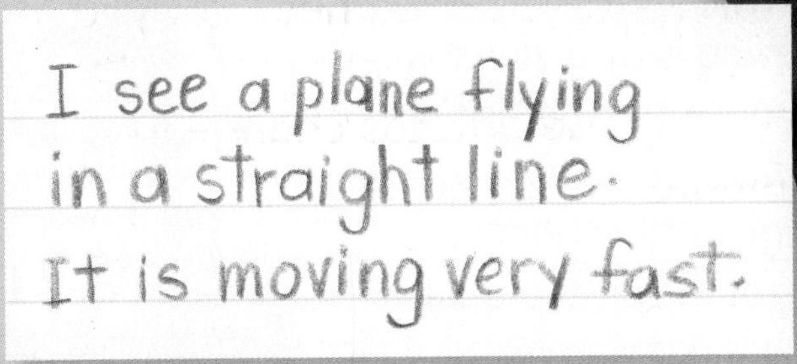

I see a plane flying
in a straight line.
It is moving very fast.

Math MG 1.3; SDAP 1.1, 1.2

Speed Bar Graph

1. Lay a line of masking tape 4 meters long on the floor.
2. Walk the length of the line. Your partner will time you. Next, skip along the line. Then hop the distance.
3. Make a chart to show your time for each way of moving.
4. Use your chart to make a bar graph. Label the parts of the graph.

For more links and activities, go to **www.hspscience.com**

California Standards in This Lesson

Science Content

1.c *Students know* the way to change how something is moving is by giving it a push or a pull. The size of the change is related to the strength, or the amount of force, of the push or pull.

Investigation and Experimentation

4.e Construct bar graphs to record data, using appropriately labeled axes.

LESSON 3

Essential Question

How Do We Move Things?

California Fast Fact

American River

The South Fork of the American River is one of the most popular places for white-water rafting in California.

Vocabulary Preview

A **force** is a push or a pull that can change how something is moving. p. 80

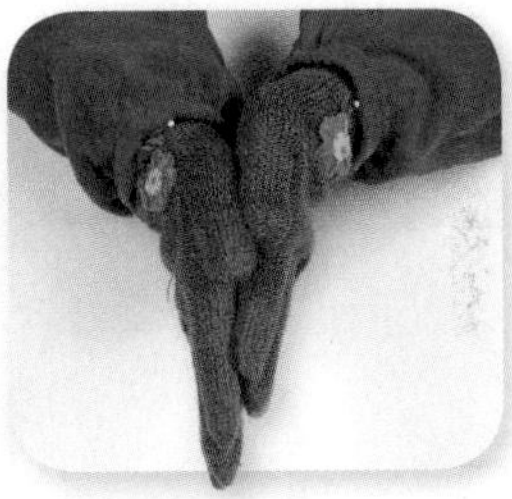

Friction is a force that slows down or stops a moving thing when it rubs against something. p. 84

Investigate

Pushes and Pulls

Directed Inquiry

Ask a Question

How do you use pushes and pulls on a playground?

Get Ready

Investigation Skill Tip

When you **record** your observations, you draw pictures or write about what you observe.

You Need

paper and pencil

What to Do

Step 1

Make a tally chart like this one.

Pushes and Pulls	
Push or Pull	Tally
pushes	
pulls	

Step 2

Move 10 objects. For each one, **record** if you used a push or a pull.

Step 3

Use your tally chart to make a bar graph. Label the parts of the graph. Compare bar graphs with classmates.

Draw Conclusions

Did you use more pushes or more pulls? **1.c**

Independent Inquiry

Make a new tally chart and bar graph to **record** and show pushes and pulls you use outside or at home. **4.e**

1.c

VOCABULARY
force
friction

Focus Skill **CAUSE AND EFFECT**

Look for the effects that forces have on objects.

Forces and Motion

You can use pushes and pulls to change an object's location. If you push a swing, it moves away from you. If you pull a swing, it moves toward you. Pushes and pulls are **forces**.

What forces are the girls using to change the ball's direction?

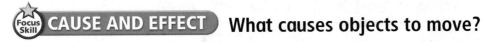

How is the juggler changing the direction of the pins?

You can use a force to change the direction of a moving object. When you play baseball, you throw the ball. You give the ball a push. The ball moves away from you.

Look at the juggler. He is throwing pins in the air and catching them. How is he changing the direction of the moving pins?

Focus Skill CAUSE AND EFFECT What causes objects to move?

Strength of Forces

You can use a small force to make a light ball move quickly. You must use more force to move a heavy ball just as quickly.

A lot of force makes an object move fast. A strong kick makes a ball move faster than a gentle kick does.

You can use a push to slow down a moving object. The ball above is moving very fast. The girl pushes the ball to stop it. Then she can pull it toward herself.

Focus Skill **CAUSE AND EFFECT** **What can change the speed of a moving object?**

Insta-Lab

Change Direction of a Ball

Show how you can change the direction of a ball by kicking it. What happens when you kick the ball on one side?

Friction

Friction is a force that slows down or stops a moving thing when it rubs against something. A bike chain rubs against the bike gears. A rusty chain makes a bike harder to pedal.

Smooth surfaces cause less friction than rough ones. Smooth surfaces do not slow down moving things as much. It is easier to ride a bike with a smooth, clean chain than a rough, rusty one.

Focus Skill **CAUSE AND EFFECT** **What effect does friction have on moving objects?**

For more links and animations, go to **www.hspscience.com**

Bike Brakes

Bike brakes use friction to stop a bike. Most of the time, the brakes do not touch the wheels. There is no friction between them.

To stop the bike, you press the brakes against the wheels. The brakes rub against the wheels and cause friction. The wheels spin more and more slowly until they stop moving.

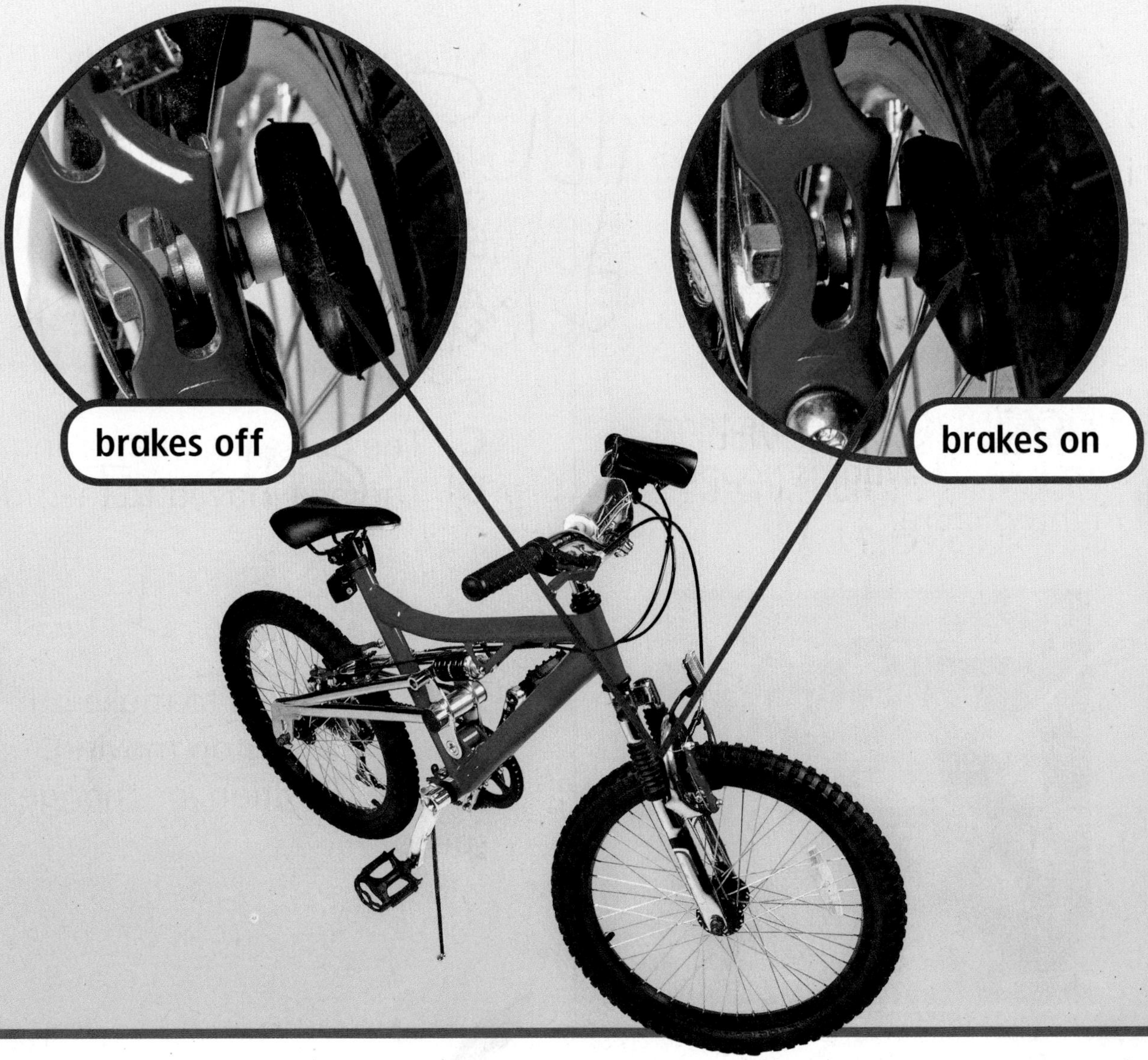

Essential Question

How do we move things?

In this lesson, you learned that we can change how things move by giving them pushes or pulls. A bigger push or pull causes a bigger change.

Science Content Standard in This Lesson

I.c *Students know* the way to change how something is moving is by giving it a push or a pull. The size of the change is related to the strength, or the amount of force, of the push or pull.

1. Focus Skill **CAUSE AND EFFECT** Make a chart like this one. Show the effects of pushes and pulls on objects. **I.c**

cause → effect

2. **DRAW CONCLUSIONS** Why does a moving thing slow down or stop? **I.c**

3. **VOCABULARY** Use the term **force** to tell what is happening in this picture. **I.c**

4. **Critical Thinking** Why does hitting a ball on the side change its direction? **I.c**

5. Mae hit a baseball lightly. Then she used more force to hit the ball. What effect did the stronger force have on the ball? **I.c**

A The ball moved more slowly.
B The ball moved faster.
C The ball stopped moving.
D The ball moved to the side.

The Big Idea

6. What is needed to make an object move, stop moving, change direction, or change speed? **I.c**

Writing ELA–W 1.1

Write to Describe

1. Think of a sport or active game you like to play.
2. How do you use forces to play it?
3. Write a description. Tell how you use forces to play the sport or game.
4. Share your description with classmates.

Math NS 2.2; MG 1.3

Measure Math

1. Roll a toy car down a ramp. Use a meterstick to measure how far the car moves after it reaches the bottom.
2. Record the distance.
3. Place a towel over the ramp. Repeat Steps 1 and 2.
4. Observe. What is the difference between the distances? Why are they different?

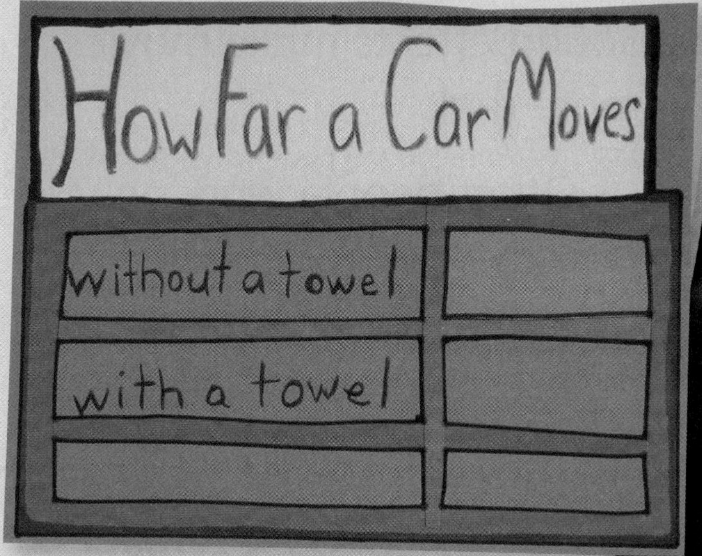

For more links and activities, go to **www.hspscience.com**

Movie Studios in Los Angeles

Do you like movies? Many people in the Los Angeles area have jobs making movies. Some people work on sound effects. Sound effects are the sounds you hear in a movie. Sound effects make movies seem more real.

Other people work on visual effects. Visual effects are what you see in a movie. Some visual effects make tiny models look life-size.

The people who work on the sound effects and visual effects make movies very exciting to watch.

entrance to a movie studio

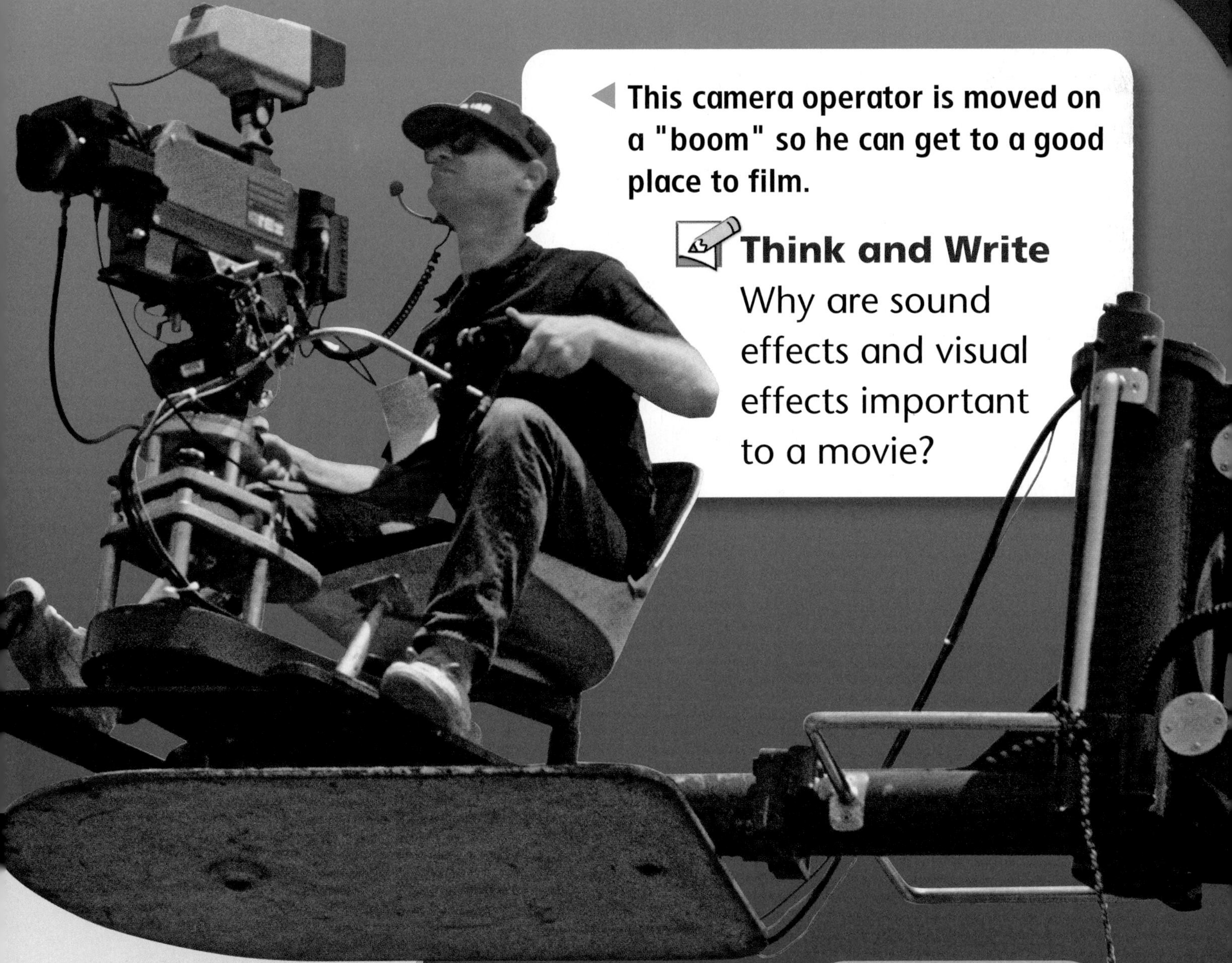

◀ **This camera operator is moved on a "boom" so he can get to a good place to film.**

Think and Write

Why are sound effects and visual effects important to a movie?

sound equipment

California Standards in This Lesson

LESSON 4

Science Content

1.d *Students know* tools and machines are used to apply pushes and pulls (forces) to make things move.

Investigation and Experimentation

4.d Write or draw descriptions of a sequence of steps, events, and observations.

4.e Construct bar graphs to record data, using appropriately labeled axes.

Essential Question

How Do Tools and Machines Move Things?

California Fast Fact

Cable Cars

San Francisco is famous for its cable cars. Each car is hooked to a cable, or wire rope, under the street. Motors pull the cable. As the cable moves, the cable car and the people in it also move.

Vocabulary Preview

A **tool** is something people use to do a certain job. A tool helps people apply more force and put the force right where they need it. p. 94

A **machine** is a device that uses power to do work. It can be used to move things. p. 96

Investigate

Tools and Machines People Use

Directed Inquiry

Ask a Question

How does using a bulldozer help people move things?

Get Ready

Investigation Skill Tip
You can record your observations by writing about them or by drawing pictures.

You Need

paper and pencil

What to Do

Step 1

Observe ways that classroom tools and machines make things move.

Step 2

Make a chart like this one. **Record** your observations in the chart.

Tools and Machines We Use	
Tool or Machine	What It Moves

Step 3

Draw and label pictures of the tools and the machines. Show how they make things move.

Draw Conclusions

How does using tools and machines help people move things? **1.d**

Independent Inquiry

Observe tools and machines outside your school. **Record** what you observe about how people are using tools and machines to help them move things. **1.d**

VOCABULARY
tool
machine

Focus Skill CAUSE AND EFFECT

Look for the effects that tools and machines have on objects.

Tools

A **tool** is something you use to help you do a job. You usually hold a tool in your hands. The tool lets you use more force. The tool also helps you put your force right where you need it. A tool can help you move things.

A rake is a tool. You use it to pull leaves to you. A hammer is also a tool. Using a hammer lets you use more force to hit a nail than you could with just your hands. The hammer also helps you apply your force right on the nail.

The boy and his grandmother are using a hammer to push nails into wood.

How does using a rake help the girl move the leaves?

How is the boy using the bat?

A baseball bat is a tool, as well. Imagine that you are a batter. As the ball comes to you, you swing the bat. The bat hits the ball and gives it a push. The push makes the ball change direction. It flies back into the field.

Insta-Lab

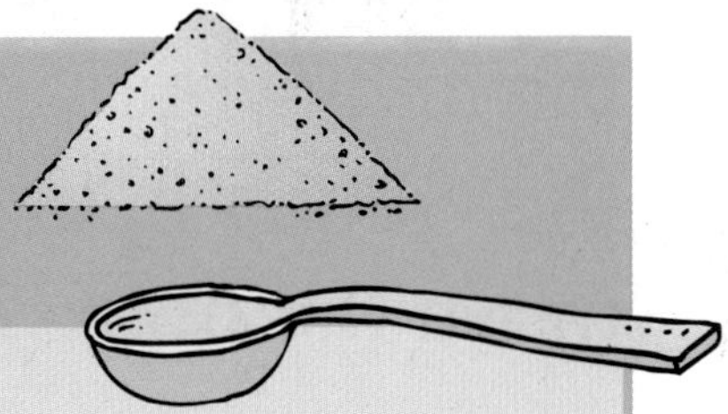

Move It!

Use your fingers to move a small pile of sand. Then move the sand with a spoon. How did using the tool help?

Focus Skill CAUSE AND EFFECT **What is the effect of using a tool to move something?**

How are the boys using a tool to move the hockey puck?

Machines

A **machine** is an object that can help people move things.

A hole punch is a machine that makes holes in many sheets of paper at one time. When you use a hole punch, you can produce a greater force than you can without a machine. You can also put your force right where you need it.

A wagon helps you move things that are too big or too heavy for you to move by yourself. How is using the wagon helping the girl move the books?

hole punch

escalator

blender

Some machines have motors. A motor uses electricity to make it work.

A blender is a machine. It has a motor. The motor uses electricity. The motor makes blades move. As the blades turn, they cut food into tiny pieces and blend them.

An escalator is a machine. It has a motor that uses electricity. What does an escalator move?

Focus Skill **CAUSE AND EFFECT** **How does a machine help people move things?**

Car Engine

The engine of a car is a machine that uses gasoline or electricity. The engine's force makes the parts of the car move. It makes the car's wheels turn. As the wheels turn, the car moves forward or backward.

Without the help of an engine, you would not be able to move a car easily.

Focus Skill CAUSE AND EFFECT **What effect does the engine have on a car?**

Essential Question

How do tools and machines move things?

In this lesson, you learned that people use tools and machines to help them do things. Tools and machines use pushes and pulls to move things.

Science Content Standard in This Lesson

1.d *Students know* tools and machines are used to apply pushes and pulls (forces) to make things move.

1. **CAUSE AND EFFECT** Make a chart like this one. Show the effects of using tools and machines. **1.d**

   cause → effect

2. **SUMMARIZE** Write a summary of this lesson. Begin with the sentence **People use tools and machines to help them move things.** **1.d**

3. **VOCABULARY** Use the terms **tool** and **machine** in a sentence. **1.d**

4. **Critical Thinking** What tools or machines could people use at home to help them move things? **1.d**

5. **Investigation** How does recording what you observe help you understand things? **4.d**

The Big Idea

6. Which of the following is true of tools and machines? **1.d**
   - **A** They always use motors.
   - **B** They always pull things.
   - **C** They always push things.
   - **D** They move things.

Writing ELA–W 1.1

Write Directions

1. Draw pictures that show how to use a shovel to move soil.
2. Number the pictures to show the order.
3. Write steps that tell how to use the shovel.
4. Share your directions with classmates.

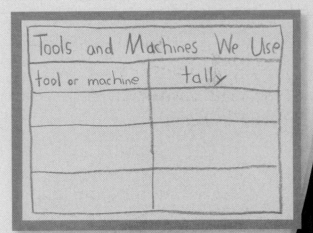

Math SDAP 1.1, 1.2

Tool and Machine Bar Graph

1. Choose 3 tools or machines in the classroom. Make a tally chart. Record the names of the tools.
2. Every time someone uses a tool or machine from your chart, make one tally mark.
3. Use your chart to make a bar graph. Label the parts.
4. Share your results with classmates.

Tools and Machines We Use

tool or machine	tally

For more links and activities, go to **www.hspscience.com**

Say Hello to ASIMO

How would you like to own a robot? It could help you with chores, such as cleaning your room. It could take out the trash. This could happen sooner than you think. Meet ASIMO, the humanoid robot.

ASIMO is 4 feet tall and weighs 115 pounds. The robot can walk, climb stairs, and even dance. Like you, it has two arms and two hands. This means that it can shake hands, hold things, open doors, and even turn on a light switch.

Engineers in Japan have spent more than 16 years making ASIMO. Their goal was to build a robot that makes people's lives better. Do you think they will meet their goal?

ASIMO stands for Advanced Step in Innovative Mobility. ▶

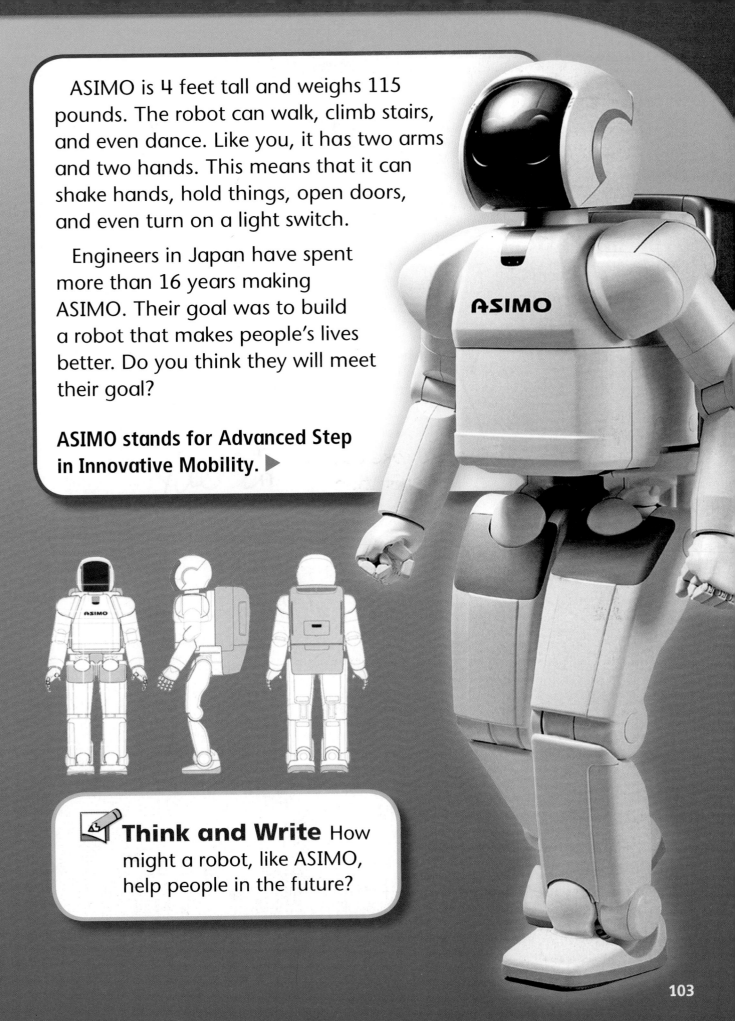

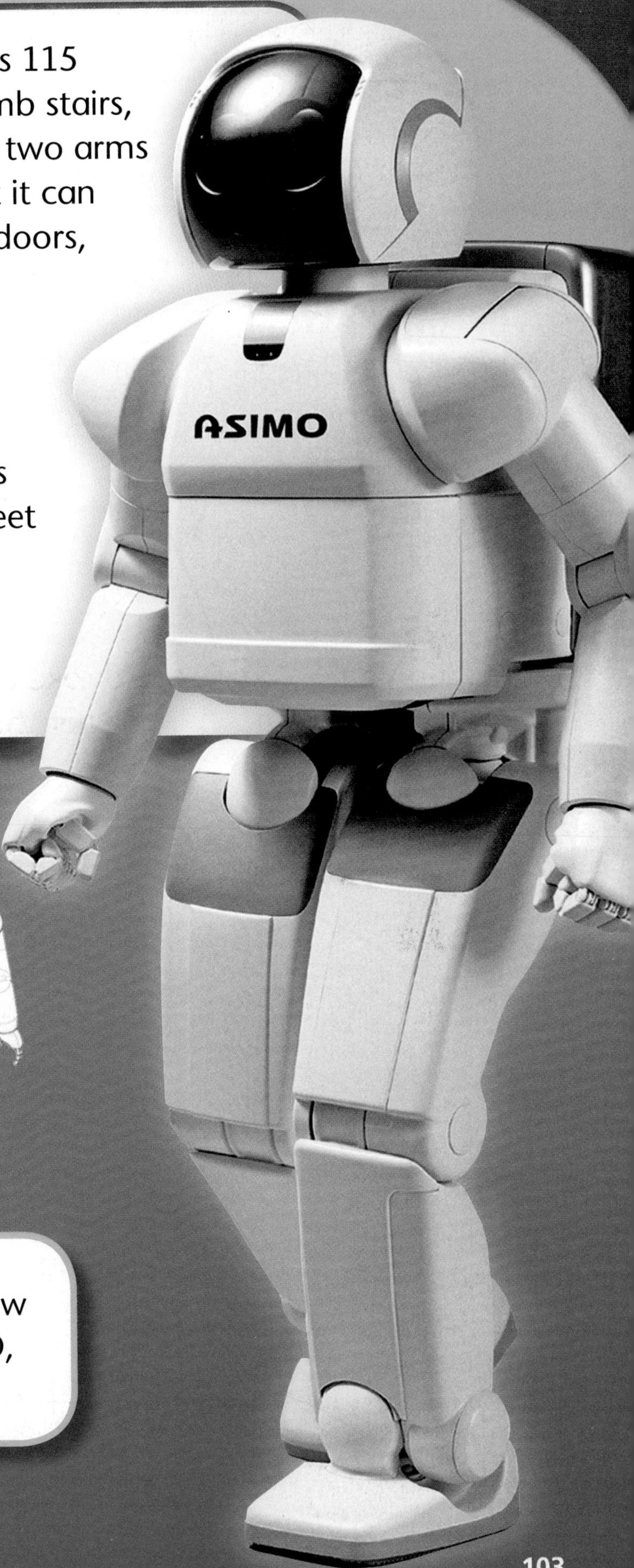

Think and Write How might a robot, like ASIMO, help people in the future?

California Standards in This Lesson

Science Content

1.e *Students know* objects fall to the ground unless something holds them up.

Investigation and Experimentation

4.a Make predictions based on observed patterns and not random guessing.

LESSON 5

Essential Question

How Does Gravity Move Things?

California Fast Fact

Skiing in the Sierra Nevadas

Skiing is a winter sport that many people in California enjoy. Skiers speed down mountains like the Sierra Nevadas.

Vocabulary Preview

Gravity is a force that pulls things toward one another. p. 108

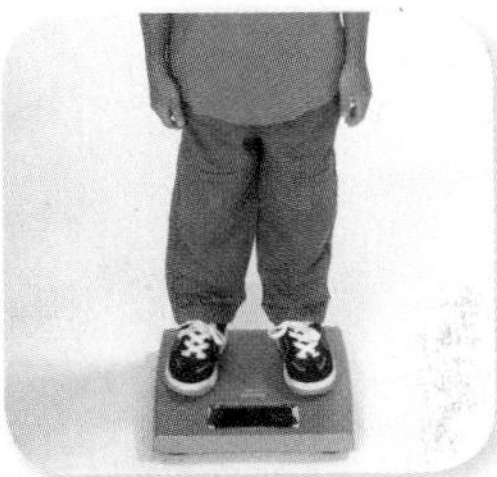

Weight is the measure of the pull of gravity. p. 109

To **float** is to move gently in the air. If an object were not pulled by Earth's gravity, it would float. p. 110

How Gravity Moves Things

Directed Inquiry

Ask a Question

What pulls your body down a slide?

Get Ready

Investigation Skill Tip
To predict what will happen, think about what you know.

You Need

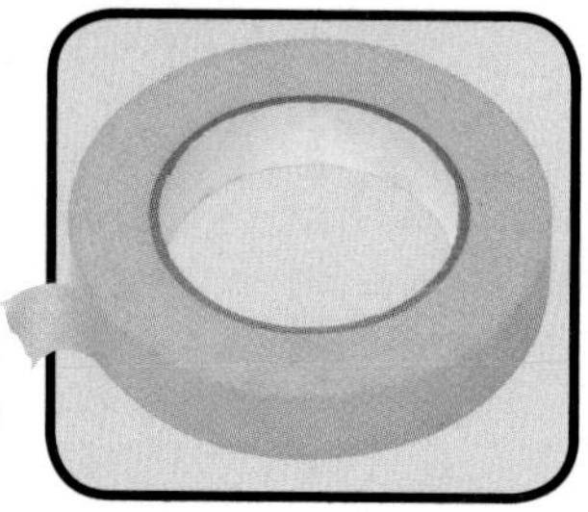

tape

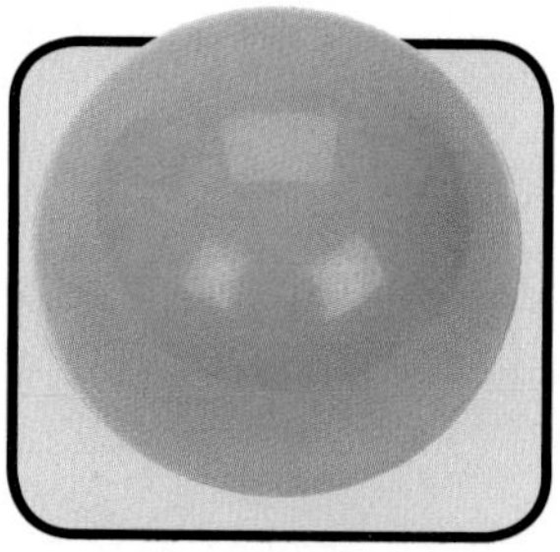

ball

ramp

books

What to Do

Step 1

Set up the ramp. **Predict** where the ball will stop when it rolls down. Mark the spot with tape.

Step 2

Let the ball roll down.

Step 3

What happens? Was your prediction correct?

Draw Conclusions

Why do you think the ball rolled the way it did? **1.e**

Independent Inquiry

Let some other objects go down the ramp. Compare their movements to that of the ball. Then make the ramp higher or lower. **Predict** what will happen. Test your prediction. **4.a**

VOCABULARY
gravity
float
weight

CAUSE AND EFFECT

Look for the causes and effects of gravity.

Gravity

Gravity is a force. It pulls all objects toward one another.

A big object has a strong pull. A small object has a weak pull. Earth is very big, so it has a very strong pull. Earth's gravity pulls everything toward the center of Earth. When you throw a ball into the air, it does not stay there. It comes back down.

Why is the ball falling?

Earth and the girl pull on each other.

Weight is a measure of the pull of gravity. Your weight is a measure of the pull of gravity between you and Earth.

You use a scale to find weight. The scale shows how strong the pull of gravity on an object is. People use scales to find out their weight. They also use scales to find the weights of foods and other things.

Focus Skill **CAUSE AND EFFECT** **What causes Earth to pull things toward its center?**

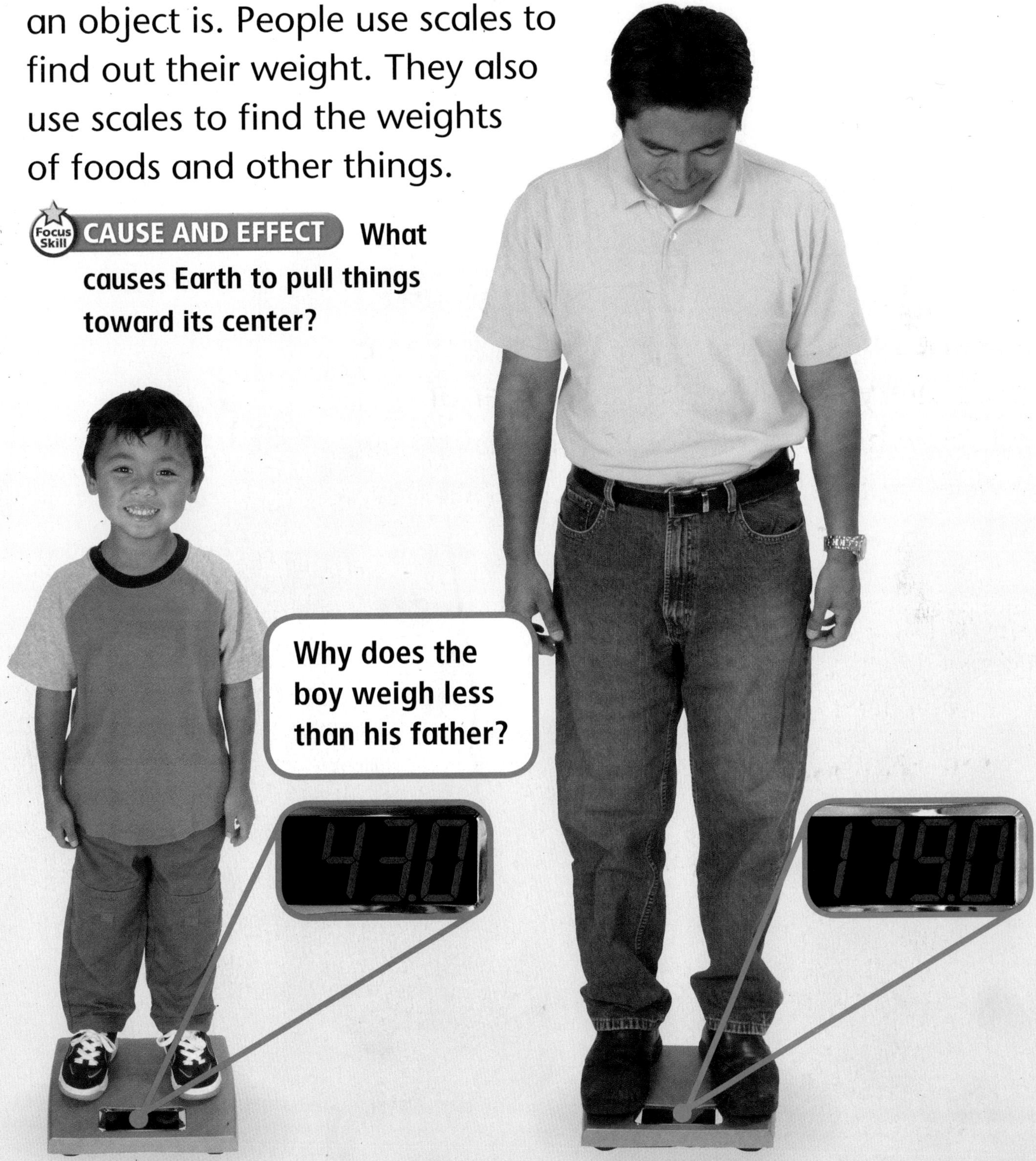

Why does the boy weigh less than his father?
43.0
179.0

What Gravity Does

Gravity makes things fall to the ground unless something holds them up. Gravity makes a ball roll down a hill. It pulls you down a slide. Gravity keeps things on the ground, too. Without gravity, they would **float**, or move gently in the air.

What is making the toy fall?

Earth's gravity is always pulling you down. But when you sit on a chair or lie on a bed, you do not fall to the floor. The chair or bed holds you up.

When you put books and toys on a bookcase, they do not fall to the floor. What keeps them from falling?

Focus Skill **CAUSE AND EFFECT** **How does gravity cause things to move?**

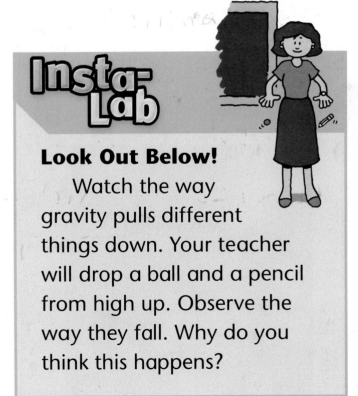

Insta-Lab

Look Out Below!

Watch the way gravity pulls different things down. Your teacher will drop a ball and a pencil from high up. Observe the way they fall. Why do you think this happens?

Standards Wrap-Up and Lesson Review

Essential Question

How does gravity move things?

In this lesson, you learned that Earth's gravity makes things fall to the ground unless something holds them up.

Science Content Standard in This Lesson

I.e *Students know* objects fall to the ground unless something holds them up.

1. **CAUSE AND EFFECT** Make a chart like this one. List the effects of gravity. **I.e**

   cause → effect

2. **DRAW CONCLUSIONS** Why does a horse weigh more than a dog? **I.e**

3. **VOCABULARY** Use the term **gravity** to tell about this picture. **I.e**

4. **Critical Thinking** You throw a ball into the air. It gets stuck in a tree. Why doesn't gravity pull the ball down to the ground? **I.e**

5. Which of these things weighs the most? **I.e**
   - **A** a ball
   - **B** a car
   - **C** a chair
   - **D** a dog

The Big Idea

6. How could you stop gravity from pulling a book to the ground? **I.e**

Writing — ELA–W 1.1

Write to Describe

1. Think of some exercises you do in which you push against gravity.
2. Draw pictures to show how you do the exercises.
3. Write sentences that describe how you push against gravity.

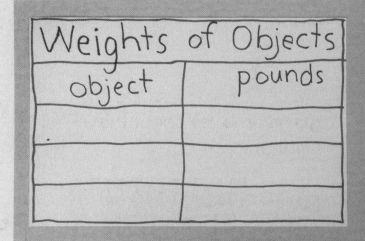

Math — SDAP 1.1, 1.2

Weight Bar Graph

1. Use a scale to weigh four classroom objects.
2. Make a chart. Record each weight to the closest pound.
3. Make a bar graph to show your data. Label the parts of your bar graph.
4. Share your bar graph with classmates.

Weights of Objects

object	pounds

For more links and activities, go to **www.hspscience.com**

California Standards in This Lesson

Science Content

1.f *Students know* magnets can be used to make some objects move without being touched.

Investigation and Experimentation

4.d Write or draw descriptions of a sequence of steps, events, and observations.

LESSON 6

Essential Question

How Do Magnets Move Things?

California Fast Fact

Bruce Gray

Bruce Gray is an artist who lives in California. He made these magnetic figures that he calls Magnanimals.

Vocabulary Preview

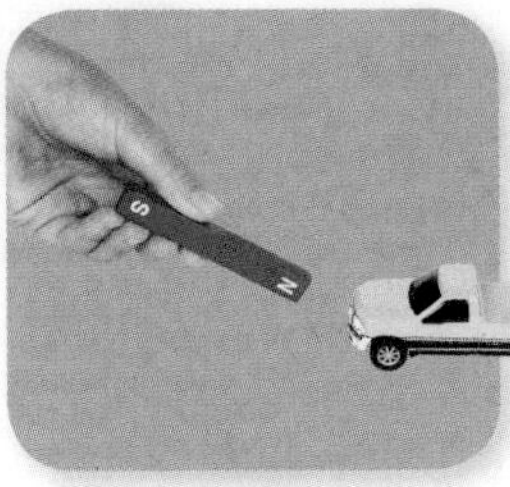

A **magnet** is an object that can move other magnets and things made of iron or steel. p. 118

The **north pole** is one of the two places on a magnet where its force is strongest. p. 120

The **south pole** is one of the two places on a magnet where its force is strongest. p. 120

To **attract** something is to pull it. p. 120

To **repel** something is to push it away. p. 120

How Magnets Move Things

Directed Inquiry

Ask a Question

What do you think is making these things stay on the board?

Get Ready

Investigation Skill Tip

When you **record** observations, you draw pictures or write about what you observe.

You Need

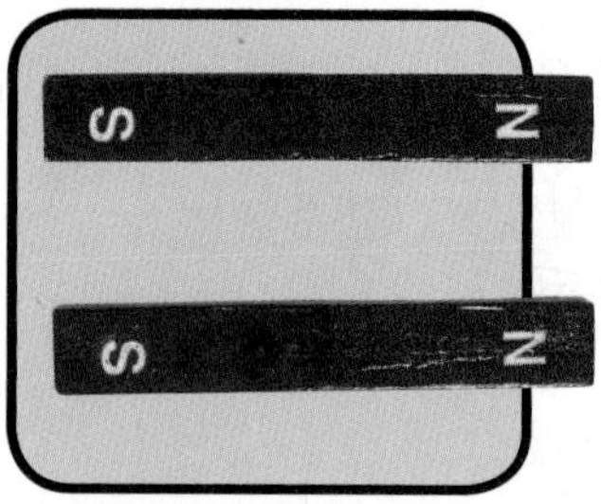

2 bar magnets

What to Do

Step 1

Make a chart like this one.

Do the Ends Attract or Repel?	
Ends	Attract or Repel
N end and S end	
N end and N end	
S end and S end	

Step 2

Bring the N end of one magnet toward the S end of the other one. Repeat with the two N ends and then the two S ends. **Record** in the chart what you observe.

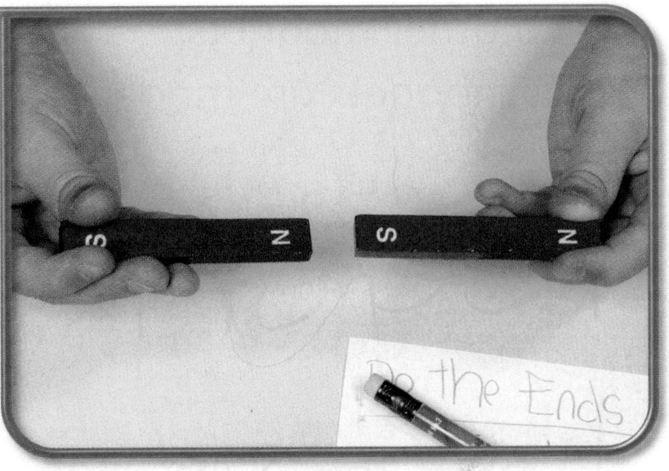

Step 3

Draw pictures or write to describe what you observed in each part of Step 2.

Draw Conclusions

What can you learn from your chart and from what you described? **4.d**

Independent Inquiry

Find some small classroom objects. Test whether a magnet can pull each object. Sort the objects into the groups *Magnet Pulls* and *Magnet Does Not Pull*. What do you **observe**? **1.f**

1.f

VOCABULARY
magnet
north pole
south pole
attract
repel

MAIN IDEA AND DETAILS

Look for details about magnets and what they can do.

Magnets

A **magnet** can pull things that are made of iron or steel. It can push or pull other magnets. Many magnets are made of metal.

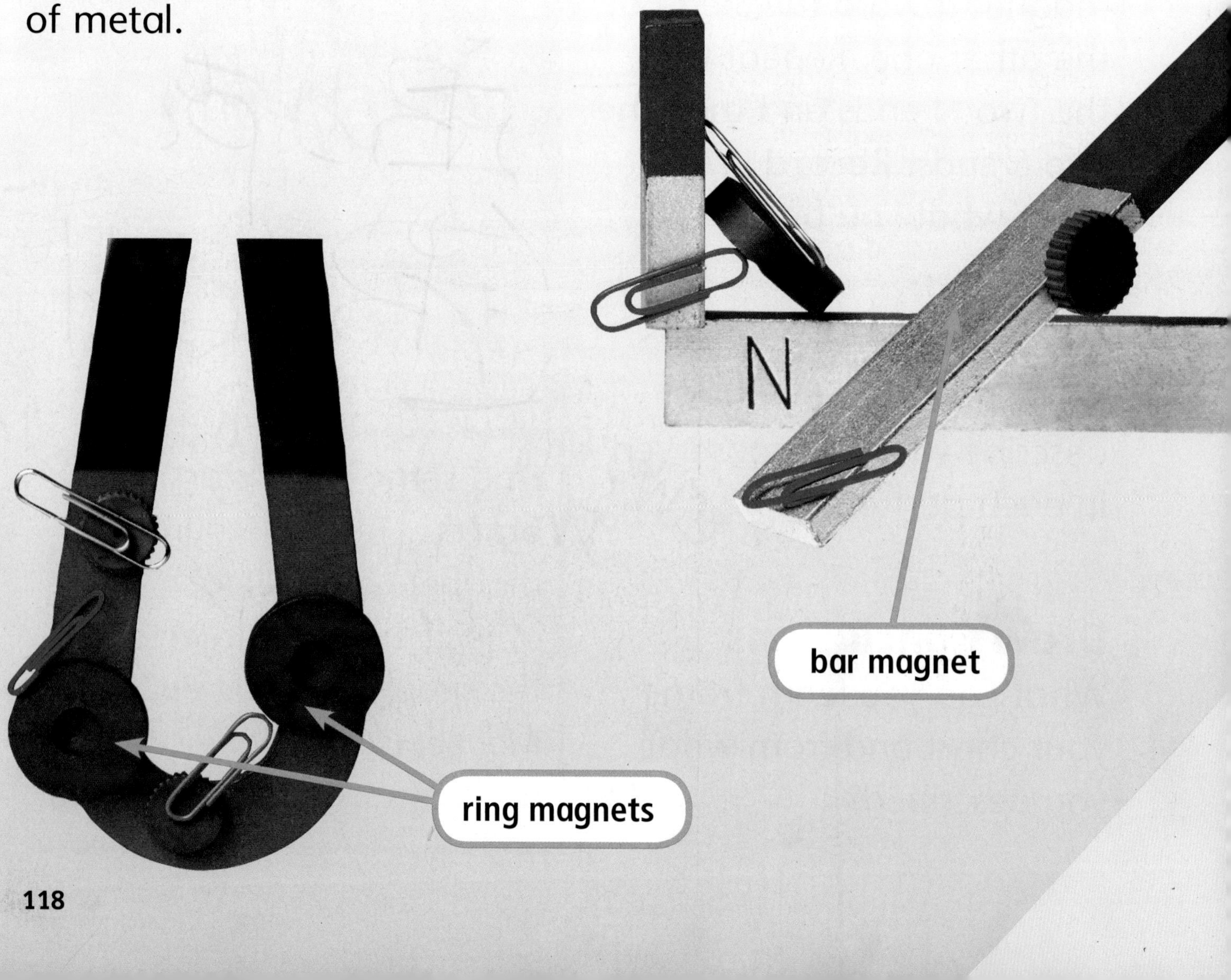

Magnets can be different sizes. They have different shapes. They can look like bars, horseshoes, or rings.

Focus Skill **MAIN IDEA AND DETAILS** **What is a magnet?**

Magnets Have Poles

Every magnet has two poles, or places where its force is strongest. One end is the **north pole**, or N pole. It may be marked with an N. The other end is the **south pole**, or S pole. It may be marked with an S.

Which two magnets attract each other? Which two magnets repel each other?

Opposite poles **attract** each other. This means that they pull each other. An N pole and an S pole attract each other.

Like poles **repel** each other. This means that they push each other away. Two N poles repel each other. Two S poles also repel each other.

These ring magnets are touching. Opposite poles face each other. They attract each other.

These ring magnets are not touching. Like poles face each other. They repel each other.

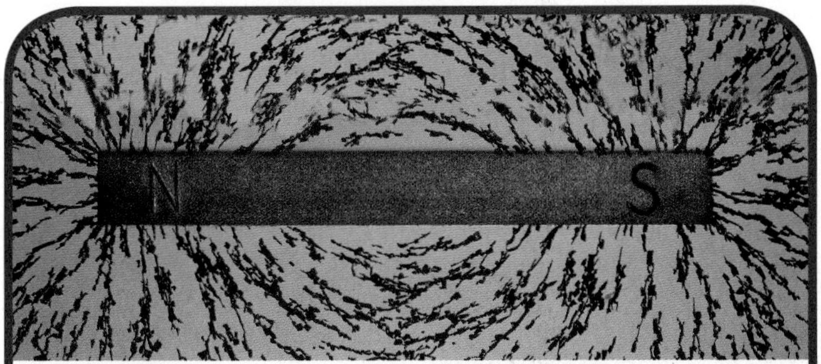

The pattern of the iron filings around the magnet shows that the magnet is the strongest at its poles.

Focus Skill **MAIN IDEA AND DETAILS**

Which poles of two magnets attract each other? Which repel each other?

What Magnets Do

Magnets do not have to touch iron and steel to attract them. They do not have to touch other magnets to attract or repel them. A magnet's force can act through air. It can also act through water and some other kinds of matter.

How does this toy work?

The magnet below pulls the toy truck. The truck has iron in it. The magnet's force acts through the air. So the magnet pulls the truck without touching it.

S
N

The paper clip is in a plastic cup with water in it. The magnet moved the paper clip. The paper clip moved from the bottom of the cup to the side. The magnet did not touch the paper clip. The magnet's pull acted through the plastic and the water.

Focus Skill **MAIN IDEA AND DETAILS** **What can the force of a magnet act through?**

Insta-Lab

Magnetic Attraction

Put iron filings in a zip-top bag. Place the bag flat on a sheet of paper. Move a magnet under the paper. What happens to the filings? Why does this happen?

Essential Question

How do magnets move things?

In this lesson, you learned that magnets can move some objects without touching them.

Science Content Standard in This Lesson

1.f *Students know* magnets can be used to make some objects move without being touched.

1. **MAIN IDEA AND DETAILS** Make a chart like this one. Show details of the main idea **Magnets can move some things without touching them.** **1.f**

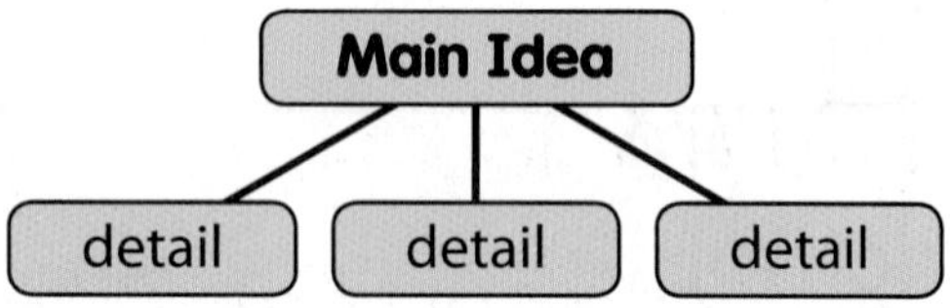

2. **SUMMARIZE** Tell what happens when you put the poles of two magnets together. **1.f**

3. **VOCABULARY** Use the terms **magnet** and **attract** to tell about the picture. **1.f**

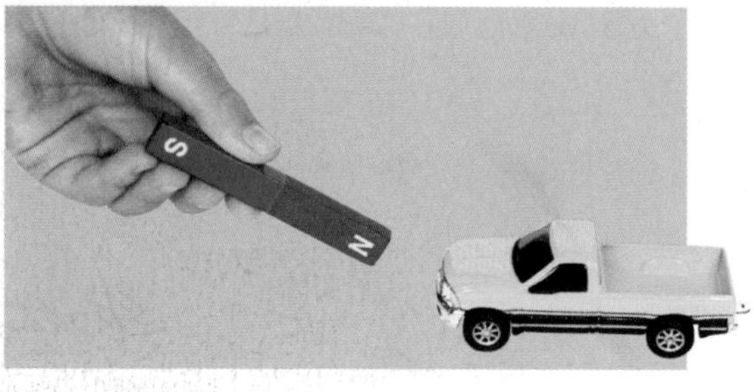

4. **Investigation** Why is it useful to record a sequence of observations? **4.d**

5. A magnet attracts a toy. What do you know? **1.f**
   - **A** The toy must be a magnet.
   - **B** The toy contains iron or steel.
   - **C** The toy does not contain iron or steel.
   - **D** The magnet pushes the toy.

The Big Idea

6. What kinds of things can a magnet move? **1.f**

Writing — ELA–W 1.1

Write to Describe

1. Invent a toy or a tool that uses a magnet.
2. Write a description of what it does and how to make it.
3. Draw a picture of it.
4. Share your invention with the class.

Paper Clip Grabber
I made a tool that picks up paper clips that fall on the floor.
I taped a magnet to the end of a ruler.

Math — SDAP 1.1, 1.2

Magnet Bar Graph

1. Hold a magnet over a pile of paper clips. Count the number of paper clips your magnet can pick up.
2. Make a tally chart. Record your result.
3. Repeat Steps 1 and 2 for a pile of pennies and a pile of safety pins.
4. Use the tally chart to make a bar graph. Label the parts.

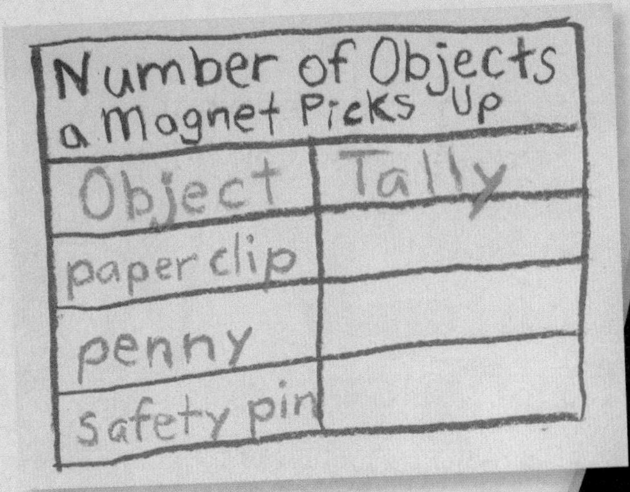

For more links and activities, go to **www.hspscience.com**

California Standards in This Lesson

Science Content

1.g *Students know* sound is made by vibrating objects and can be described by its pitch and volume.

Investigation and Experimentation

4.d Write or draw descriptions of a sequence of steps, events, and observations.

LESSON 7

Essential Question

What Causes Sound?

California Fast Fact

Walt Disney Concert Hall

This concert hall is in Los Angeles. The curved ceiling and walls make the music sound better.

Vocabulary Preview

Sound is what you hear when an object vibrates, or moves quickly back and forth. p. 130

A **vibration** is a motion back and forth. p. 131

The **volume** of a sound is how loud or soft the sound is. p. 132

Pitch is how high or low a sound is. p. 134

Investigate

How Sound Is Made

Directed Inquiry

Ask a Question

How are the people making sound?

Get Ready

Investigation Skill Tip
You can draw pictures or write sentences to record your observations.

You Need

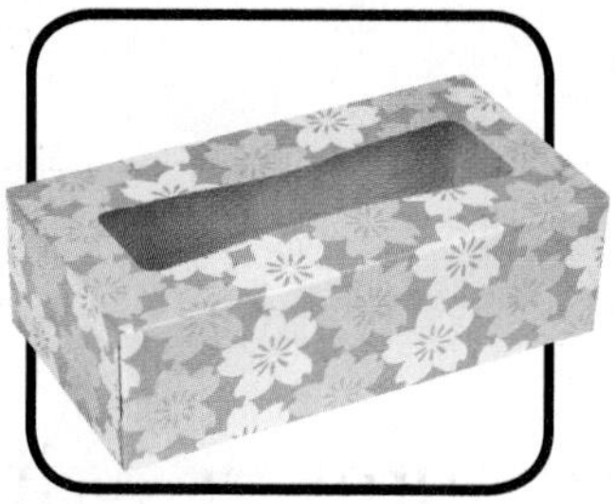
tissue box

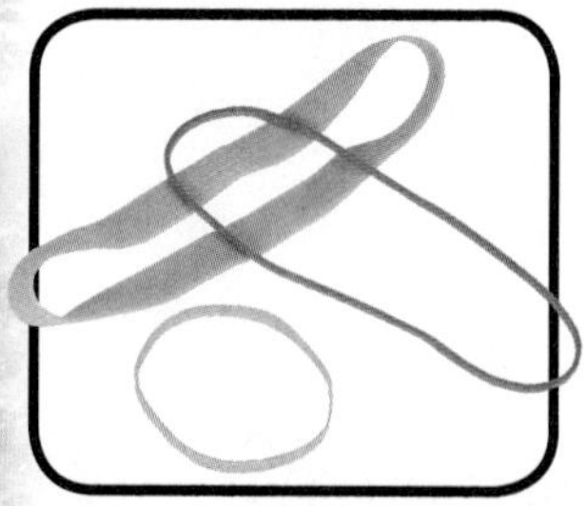
rubber bands

What to Do

Step 1

Stretch rubber bands over the box. Pluck the rubber bands. Touch them gently. What do you feel?

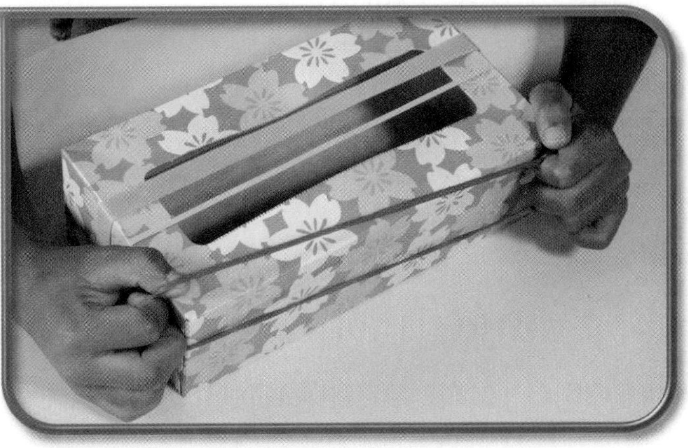

Step 2

Pluck the rubber bands more gently. Touch them. Listen to the sound. Then pluck them harder. Touch them. Listen to the sound.

Step 3

Draw pictures or write sentences to **record** what you observe.

Draw Conclusions

Why did changing the way you plucked the rubber bands change the sound? **1.g**

Independent Inquiry

Use other materials to make a different musical instrument. Find ways to make sounds with it. **Record** what you find out about how sound is made. **1.g**

1.g

VOCABULARY
sound volume
vibration pitch

Focus Skill CAUSE AND EFFECT

Look for what causes sound.

Vibrations Make Sound

Sound is what you hear. You may hear a dog barking or someone blowing a whistle. You may hear music playing or people talking.

What sounds might you hear on this street?

The sounds are different, but they are all made in the same way. All sound is made when something moves back and forth. This back and forth motion is **vibration**. When the vibration stops, or the object stops vibrating, the sound stops.

xylophone

When this boy plays the guitar, he makes the guitar strings vibrate. If you touch the strings, you can feel the vibration.

Focus Skill **CAUSE AND EFFECT** **What causes sound?**

What sound is the boy hearing?

Loud and Soft

Sounds are different. A sound may be loud, like an airplane landing. A sound may be soft, or quiet, like a whisper. The **volume** of a sound is how loud or soft it is. It takes more effort to make a loud sound than to make a soft sound.

If you are close to what is making a sound, the sound is easier to hear. Stand near some other people. You can hear them talk. Hearing them talk gets harder as you move farther away from them.

When an ambulance is far away, you may not hear the siren. As the ambulance moves closer, the sound gets louder. As the ambulance moves away, the sound gets fainter. Then you cannot hear it at all.

Focus Skill **CAUSE AND EFFECT** **What can cause the same sound to seem sometimes louder and sometimes softer?**

ambulance

High and Low

Sounds are also different in pitch. **Pitch** is how high or low a sound is. Small chimes make a sound with a high pitch. A big bell makes a sound with a low pitch.

The speed of an object's vibrations affects the pitch of its sound. Fast vibrations make a sound with a high pitch. Slow vibrations make a sound with a low pitch.

chimes

bell

A tuning fork is a tool made of steel. When you hit a tuning fork against an object, it vibrates and makes a sound. The sound has the same pitch every time. Musicians use a tuning fork to help them start playing or singing on the correct pitch.

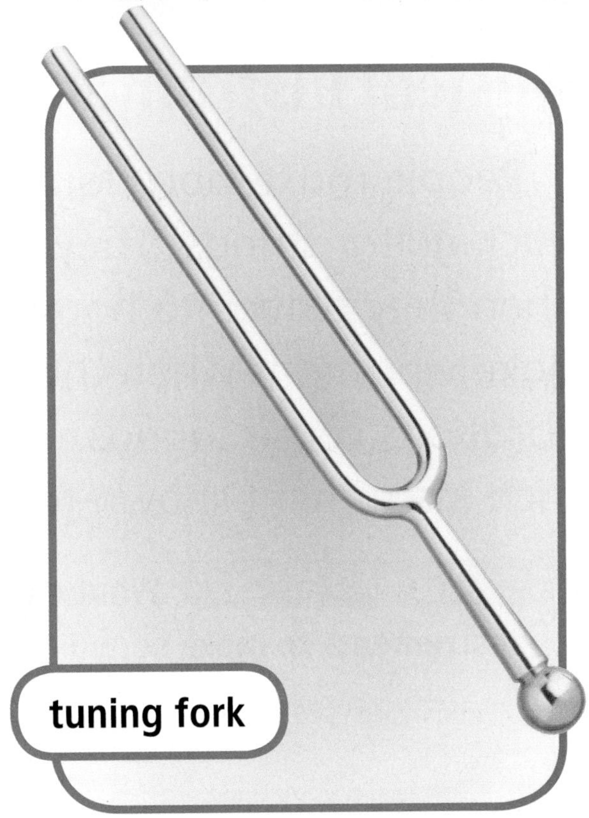

Focus Skill CAUSE AND EFFECT **What makes a sound's pitch high or low?**

Musical Instruments

People make vibrations when they pluck guitar strings. They make vibrations when they blow into horns. They also make vibrations when they hit a drum. The vibrations cause sounds. How could you use each instrument shown to make sounds?

Focus Skill CAUSE AND EFFECT **What causes musical instruments to make sounds?**

Science Up Close

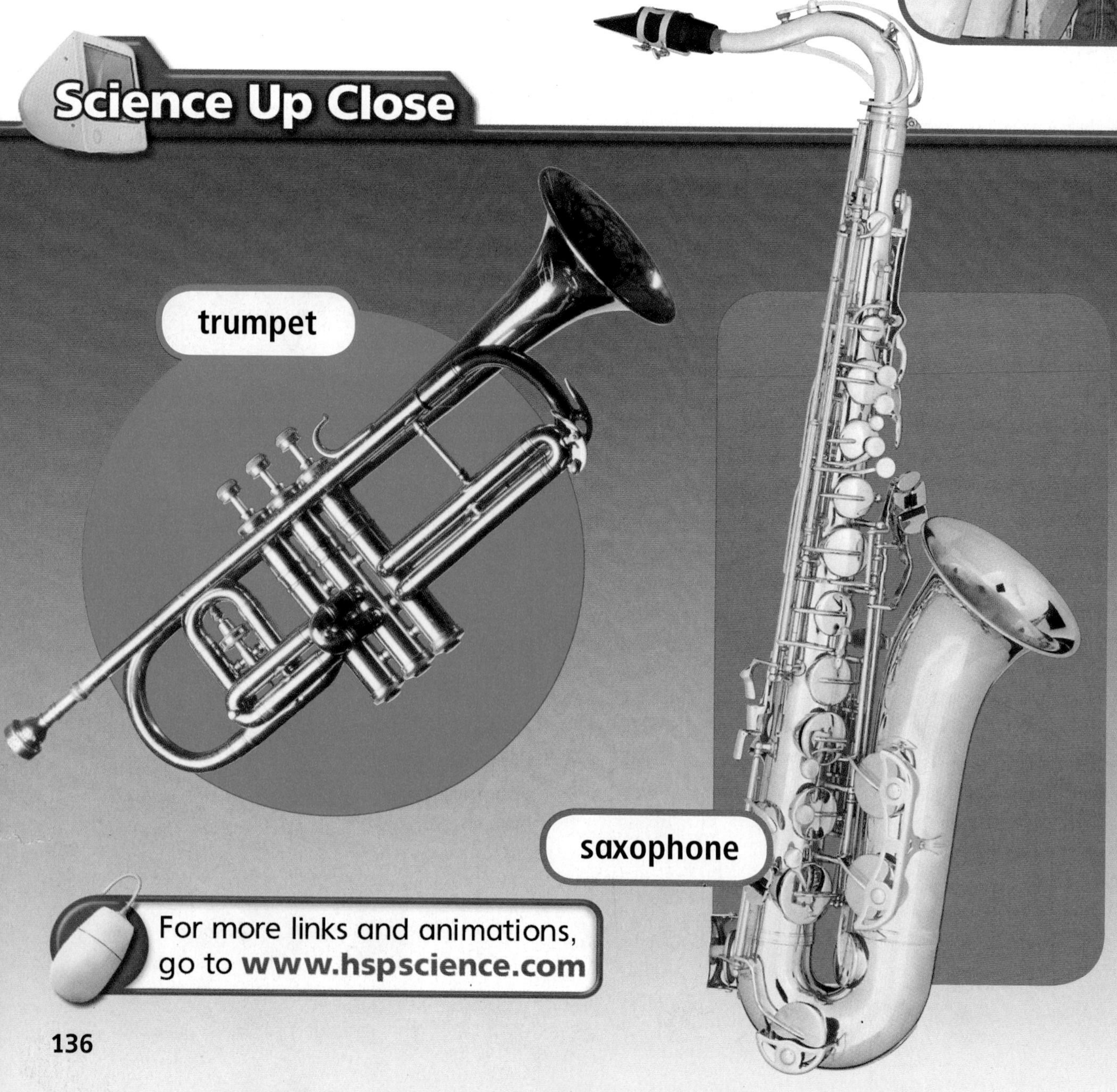

For more links and animations, go to **www.hspscience.com**

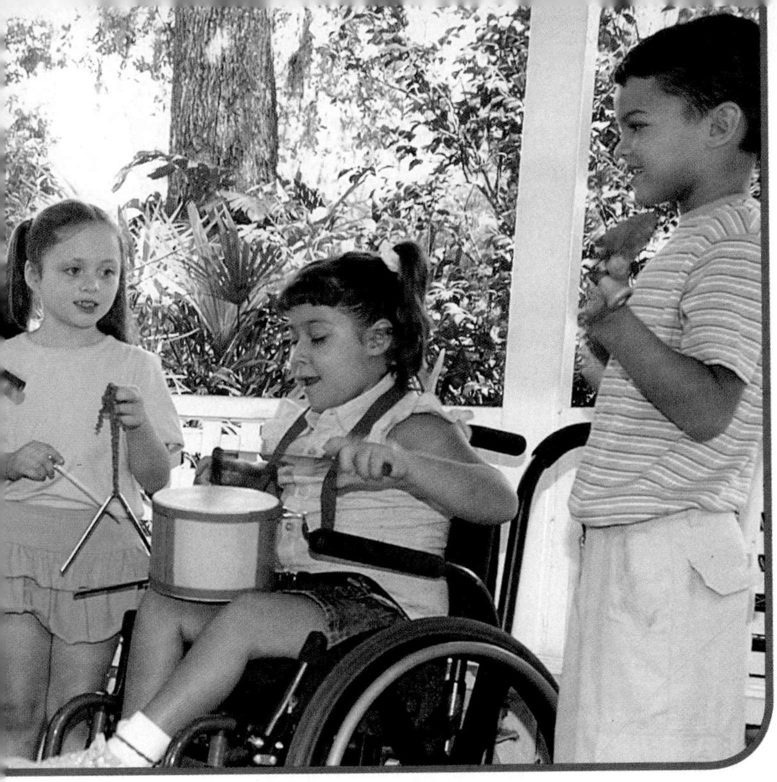

Insta-Lab

Straw Instrument

Cut a straw so the top forms a V. Pinch the top with your lips. Blow very hard. Listen. Then cut off some of the straw at the bottom. Blow again. How does the sound change?

Standards Wrap-Up and Lesson Review

Essential Question

What causes sound?

In this lesson, you learned that sound is caused by the vibrations of objects. You can describe a sound by its pitch, or how high or low it is, and its volume, or how loud or soft it is.

Science Content Standards in This Lesson

I.g *Students know* sound is made by vibrating objects and can be described by its pitch and volume.

1. Focus Skill **CAUSE AND EFFECT** Make a chart like this one. Show what causes different sounds. **I.g**

cause → effect

2. **DRAW CONCLUSIONS** Why do different musical instruments make different sounds? **I.g**

3. **VOCABULARY** Use the terms **sound** and **vibration** in a sentence about this picture. **I.g**

4. **Critical Thinking** What causes the sound a drum makes? **I.g**

5. What happens when a guitar string vibrates more quickly? **I.g**

A It makes a higher sound.
B It makes a lower sound.
C It makes no sound.
D It makes a softer sound.

The Big Idea

6. What parts of a guitar vibrate to make sounds? How do you know? **I.g**

Writing ELA–W 1.1

Write to Describe

1. Sit quietly and listen to the sounds around you.
2. Write about the sounds you hear. Describe them.
3. Compare descriptions with a classmate.

I hear a door squeak.

A dog barks outside.

Math NS 2.2; SDAP 1.0

How Long a Sound Lasts

1. Hold a triangle by its string. Tap the triangle gently. Record how many seconds the sound lasts.
2. Tap a bit harder. Record the number of seconds.
3. Hit the triangle very hard. Record the number of seconds.
4. Look at the data in your chart. Which sound lasted the longest? Why?

How Long Sounds Last

tap	seconds
gentle tap	
medium tap	
hard tap	

For more links and activities, go to **www.hspscience.com**

Alexander Graham Bell

ALEXANDER GRAHAM BELL

- **Inventor**
- Invented many things

Alexander Graham Bell was an inventor. He worked on machines that used sound. He wanted to help people who could not hear.

Alexander Graham Bell made a discovery. He found that he could send speech sounds over an electric wire. He used his discovery to invent something that is still very important today—the telephone!

Think and Write

How has Alexander Graham Bell's invention of the telephone changed our lives?

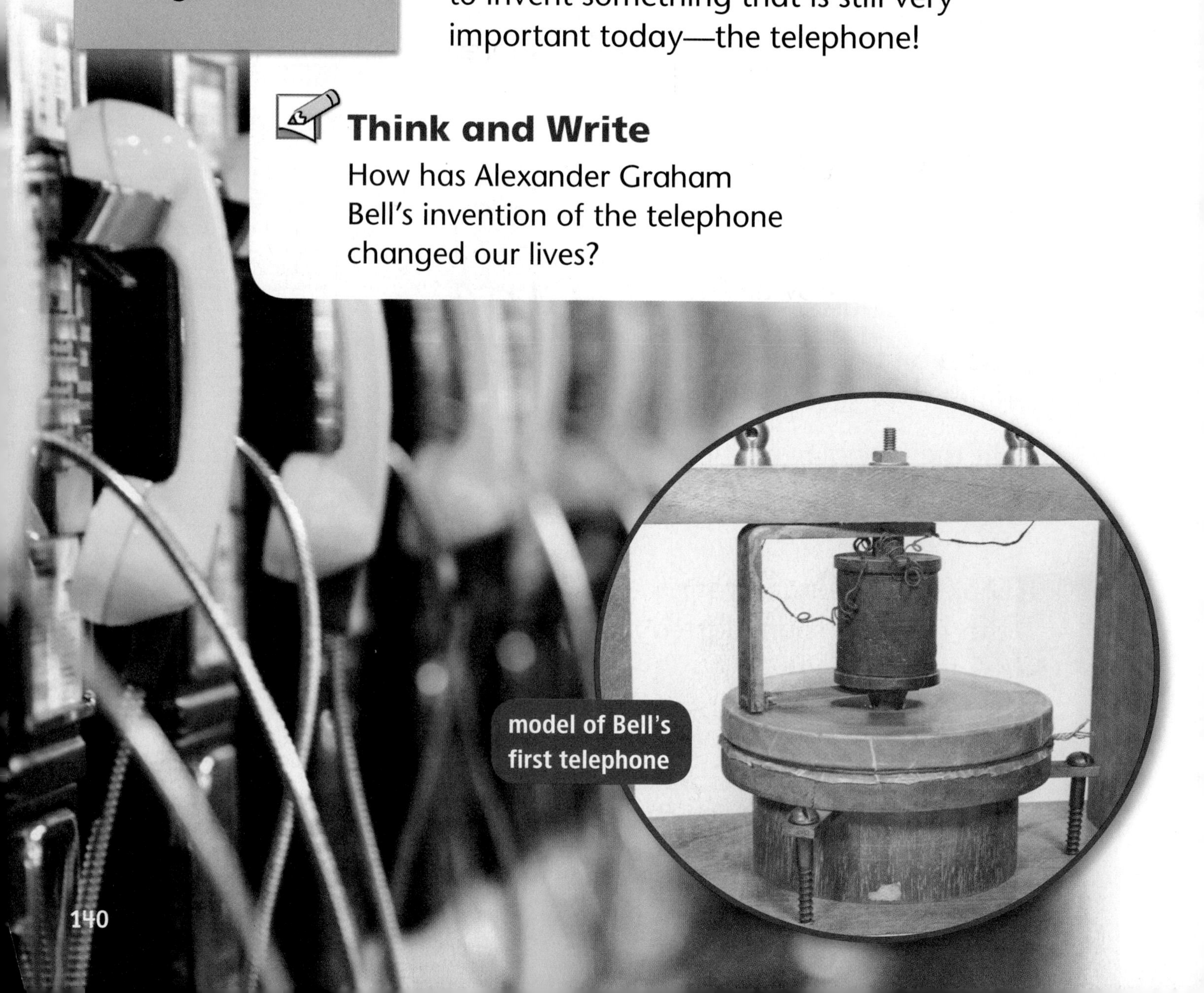

model of Bell's first telephone

Ayanna Howard

Dr. Ayanna Howard works on making robots. Some day, her robot SmartNav may walk on Mars! Dr. Howard wants it to be able to think like a human.

SmartNav can already do some things people can do. It can tell sand from stone or concrete. Doing this will help SmartNav move on Mars.

Dr. Howard also helps girls with math and science. She hopes they will share her interest in working with robots someday.

AYANNA HOWARD

- **Robotics engineer at the Jet Propulsion Lab, California Institute of Technology**
- Works on software for robots

Think and Write

How might the work of earlier space scientists help Ayanna Howard?

UNIT 1 PHYSICAL SCIENCE

Wrap-Up

Visual Summary

Tell how each picture helps explain the **Big Idea**.

The Big Idea **The motion of objects can be observed and measured.**

I.a, I.b

The position of an object can be described by comparing it to other objects that are not moving. Motion is a change of position over time.

I.c, I.d

Pushes and pulls are forces that change motion. Tools and machines help people use more force and put the force where they need it.

I.e, I.f

Gravity pulls objects toward the center of Earth. Magnets can make some objects move.

I.g

Sound is made by vibrations, or movements back and forth. Sound has pitch and volume.

Show What You Know

Unit Writing Activity

Write About an Instrument

Choose a musical instrument you like, and read about it. Then write sentences to explain how the instrument makes sound. Tell who invented the instrument and what it is made of. Draw a picture to go with your sentences. Share your writing and your picture with the class.

Unit Project

Building Tools and Machines

With a partner, invent and build a tool or a machine. Write a paragraph that tells the steps you took and the materials you used. Explain what your invention does. Share your invention and your writing with the class.

UNIT 1 PHYSICAL SCIENCE

Review

California Science Standards in

Vocabulary Review

Use the terms to complete the sentences. The page numbers tell you where to look if you need help.

meter p. 60
motion p. 68
force p. 80
gravity p. 108
attract p. 120
vibration p. 131

1. The *N* pole of a magnet will ________ the *S* pole of another magnet. **1.f**

2. A push or a pull is a ________. **1.c**

3. A motion back and forth that can make sound is a ________. **1.g**

4. ________ pulls objects toward one another and toward the center of Earth. **1.e**

5. A ________ is a unit of measure for distance or length. **1.a**

6. A change of position is ________. **1.b**

Check Understanding

7. List these objects in order from the slowest to the fastest. **1.b**

8. Which of these is usually NOT a tool? **1.d**

A a ball

B a bat

C a hammer

D a rake

Critical Thinking

9. Describe how a magnet can move some objects without touching them. **1.f**

The Big Idea

10. Describe how forces affect motion. **1.c**

UNIT 2 LIFE SCIENCE

Life Cycles

California Standards in This Unit

2 Plants and animals have predictable life cycles. As a basis for understanding this concept:

2.a *Students know* that organisms reproduce offspring of their own kind and that the offspring resemble their parents and one another.

2.b *Students know* the sequential stages of life cycles are different for different animals, such as butterflies, frogs, and mice.

2.c *Students know* many characteristics of an organism are inherited from the parents. Some characteristics are caused or influenced by the environment.

2.d *Students know* there is variation among individuals of one kind within a population.

2.e *Students know* light, gravity, touch, or environmental stress can affect the germination, growth, and development of plants.

2.f *Students know* flowers and fruits are associated with reproduction in plants.

This unit also includes these Investigation and Experimentation Standards:

4.a, **4.b**, **4.c**, **4.d**, **4.e**, **4.f**, **4.g**

What's the Big Idea?

Plants and animals change as they grow. The stages, or times, of their lives make up their life cycles.

Essential Questions

Science in California

Hi Mike,

San Diego is fun. I really liked watching the sea lions near the harbor.

A sea lion pup stays on land for just two weeks after it is born. Then it is ready to learn how to swim and fish.

Can you imagine swimming lessons when we were two weeks old? Wow!

Your friend,

Mary

Read Mary's postcard. What did Mary learn about sea lions? How do you think this helps explain the **Big Idea?**

Unit Inquiry

Plants and Gravity

How do plant roots grow and change? Plan and do a test to find out.

Science Content

2.b *Students know* the sequential stages of life cycles are different for different animals, such as butterflies, frogs, and mice.

Investigation and Experimentation

4.f Use magnifiers or microscopes to observe and draw descriptions of small objects or small features of objects.

LESSON 1

Essential Question

What Are Some Animal Life Cycles?

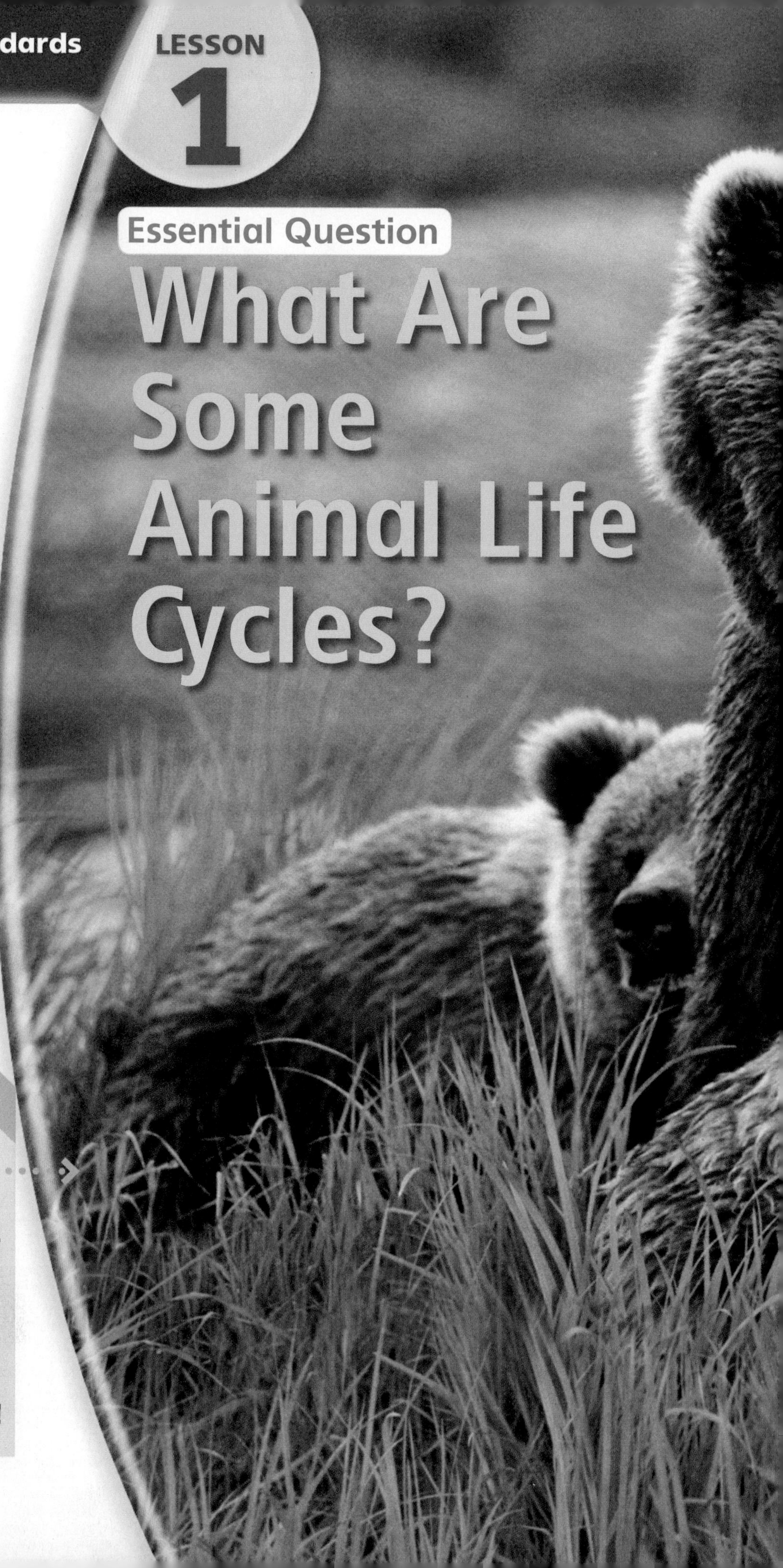

California Fast Fact

Grizzly Bears

A newborn grizzly bear weighs about as much as a can of vegetables. An adult bear can weigh as much as 25 seven-year-old children!

Vocabulary Preview

A **life cycle** is all the stages, or times, of an animal's or a plant's life. p. 152

An **adult** is a fully grown person or animal. p. 152

A **tadpole** is a young frog. p. 154

A **larva** is the young of some insects. A caterpillar is a butterfly larva. p. 156

A caterpillar becomes a **pupa** before it becomes a butterfly. p. 157

A **nymph** is the young of some insects, including grasshoppers. p. 158

How Mealworms Grow and Change

Directed Inquiry

Ask a Question

What kind of animals will these be when they are adults?

Get Ready

Investigation Skill Tip
You can use a hand lens to observe things that are very small.

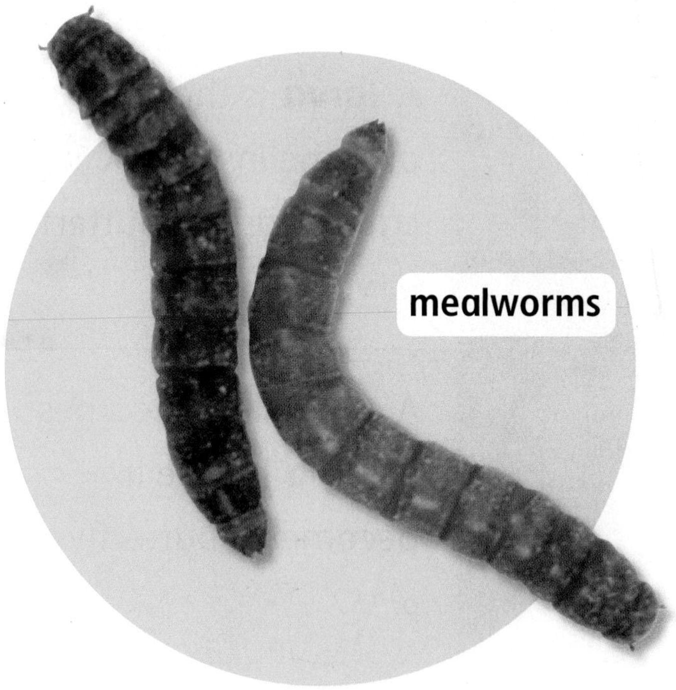

You Need

mealworms

water in bottle cap

mealworm home

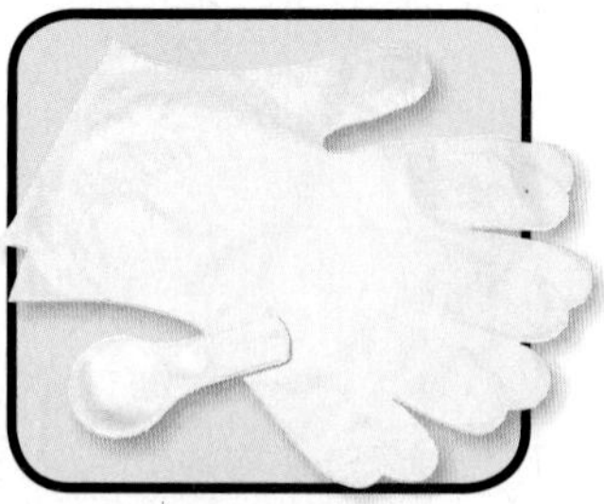
hand lens and gloves

What to Do

Step 1

Each day, give the mealworms food and water.

Step 2

Each day, use a hand lens to **observe** the mealworms. **CAUTION:** Wash your hands after you do this.

Step 3

Each day, draw a picture of what you observe. Write the date and a sentence about changes you see.

Draw Conclusions

What did you find out about how mealworms grow and change? **2.b**

Independent Inquiry

Observe caterpillars in your classroom. Find out how they grow and change to become butterflies. **2.b**

2.b

VOCABULARY
life cycle
adult
tadpole
larva
pupa
nymph

Focus Skill SEQUENCE

Look for what happens first, next, then, and last in each animal's life cycle.

Life Cycle of a Cat

Every animal has a life cycle. A **life cycle** is all the stages, or times, of an animal's life. It begins with a new animal.

The animal grows up to be an **adult**. It has its own young. A new life cycle begins.

First, kittens grow inside their mother's body. The mother cat gives birth to the kittens.

2 kitten about 3 weeks old

1 adult cat and kittens

Next, a newborn kitten begins to grow. The mother cat feeds her kittens with milk from her body. A kitten needs to have its mother keep it safe and clean.

Then, the kittens get bigger and stronger.

Last, after about one year, the cat is an adult. It can have kittens of its own.

Focus Skill SEQUENCE **What happens, first, next, then, and last as a cat grows?**

3 young cat about 6 months old

4 adult cat

Life Cycle of a Frog

Frogs have a different life cycle than most other animals. First, it starts as an egg.

Next, a **tadpole**, or young frog, hatches from the egg. The tadpole lives in water. It uses gills to take in oxygen. It has a tail and no legs. It does not look like an adult frog.

Science Up Close

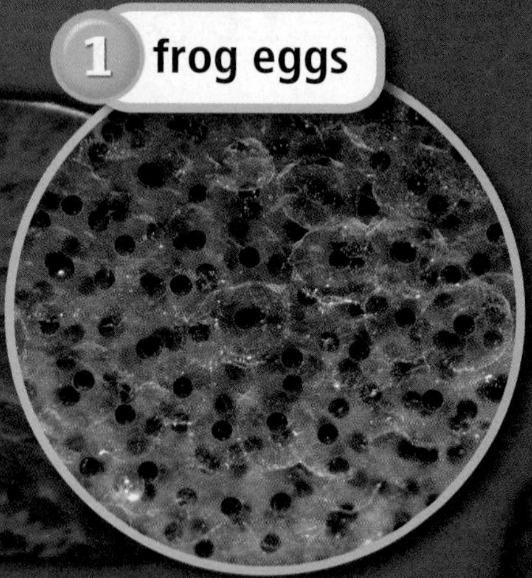

For more links and animations, go to **www.hspscience.com**

Then, the tadpole gets bigger. It grows two back legs and two front legs. It still has a tail. It starts to look more like a frog. It uses lungs to breathe.

Last, the frog is an adult and has no tail. The frog lives on land most of the time. It can have its own young.

Focus Skill SEQUENCE **What happens first, next, then, and last as a frog grows?**

Life Cycle of a Butterfly

A butterfly's life cycle has four stages. First, a butterfly begins life as an egg.

Next, a tiny **larva**, or caterpillar, hatches from the egg. The larva grows quickly. It grows a new, larger skin inside. Its old skin gets too tight. The larva molts, or gets rid of the tight skin. The growing larva molts several times.

Then, the larva becomes a **pupa**. It makes a hard covering. The pupa slowly changes inside the covering.

Last, a butterfly comes out of the covering. The adult butterfly can have its own young.

Focus Skill SEQUENCE **What happens first, next, then, and last as a butterfly grows?**

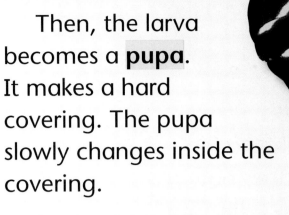

Life Cycle of a Grasshopper

A grasshopper's life cycle has three stages. First, it begins life as an egg.

Next, it hatches from the egg. The young grasshopper is called a **nymph**. It does not have wings.

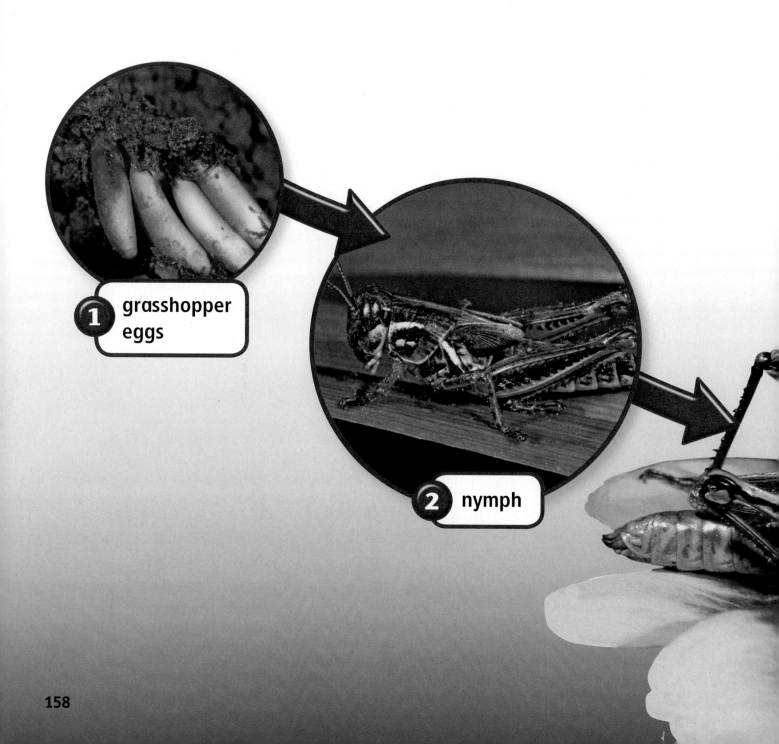

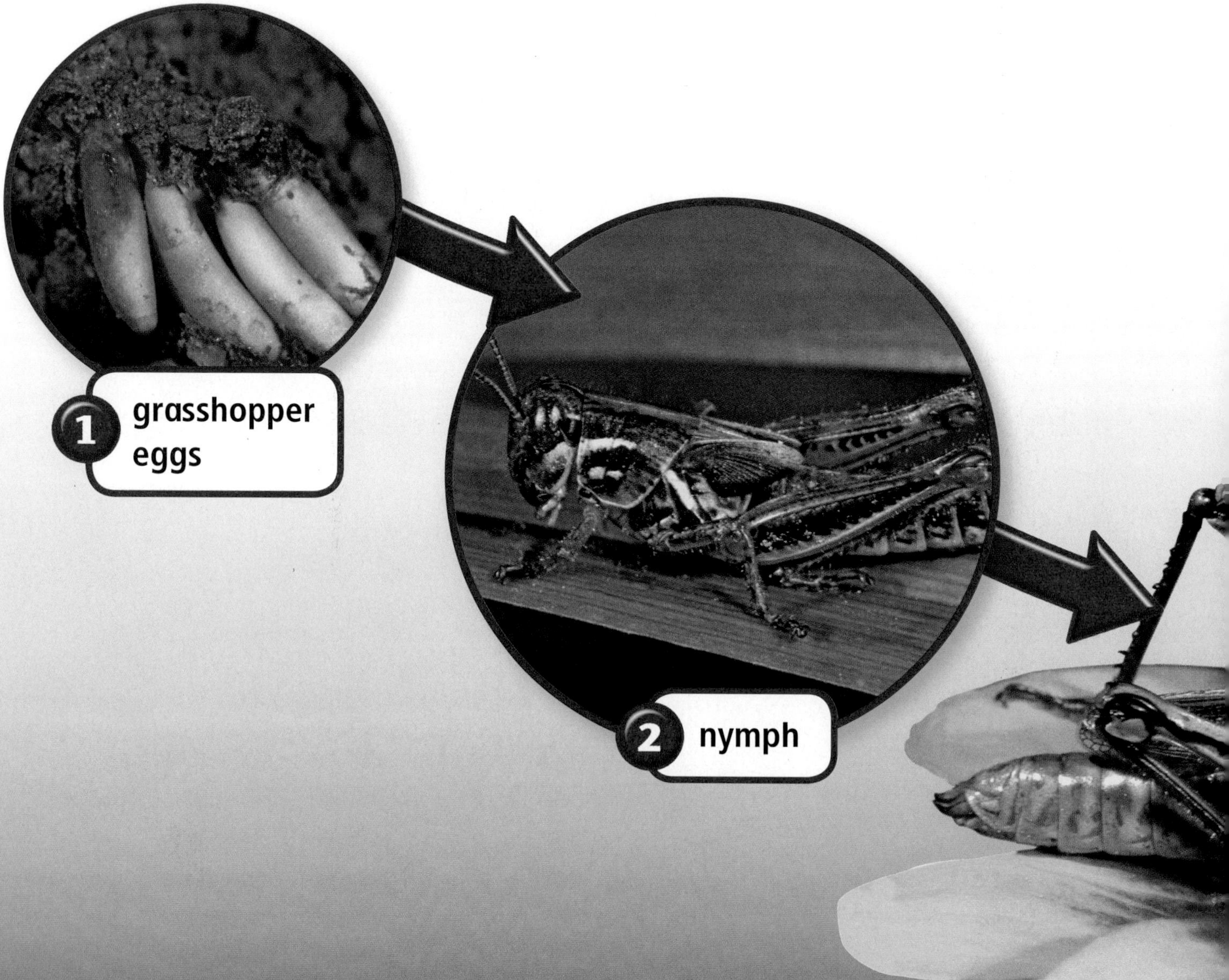

Then, the nymph grows. It gets wings. The nymph molts several times as it grows.

Last, the nymph becomes an adult grasshopper. It has wings and can fly. Soon it is able to have young.

Focus Skill SEQUENCE **What happens first, next, then, and last as a grasshopper grows?**

Insta-Lab

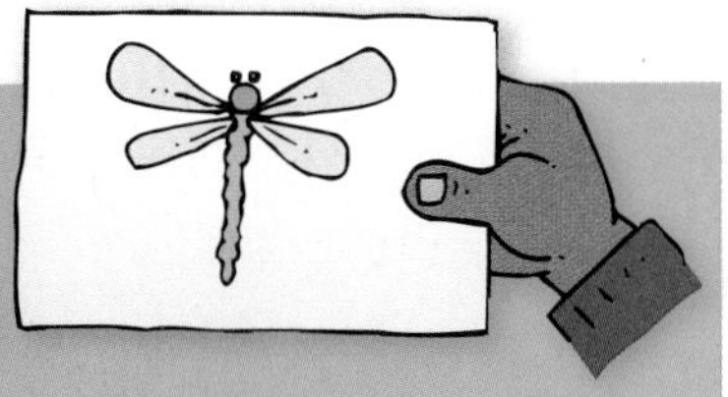

Life Cycles

Compare the Picture Cards of cats, mice, frogs, butterflies, and dragonflies. Sort them by animal. Sequence the stages of each animal's life cycle. How are the life cycles alike and different?

Standards Wrap-Up and Lesson Review

Essential Question

What are some animal life cycles?

In this lesson, you learned that animals have different life cycles.

Science Content Standard in This Lesson

2.b *Students know* the sequential stages of life cycles are different for different animals, such as butterflies, frogs, and mice.

1. **Focus Skill SEQUENCE** Make a chart like this one. Show the stages of a frog's life cycle. **2.b**

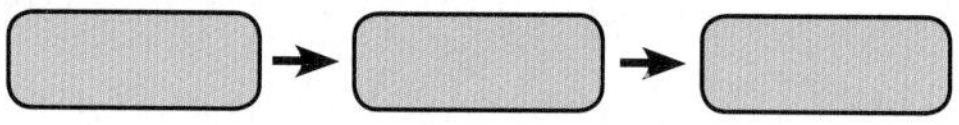

2. **SUMMARIZE** Make a chart to summarize differences between the life cycles of a butterfly and a grasshopper. **2.b**

3. **VOCABULARY** Explain the meanings of the terms **life cycle** and **tadpole**. **2.b**

4. **Critical Thinking** What animal lays the egg that a caterpillar comes from? **2.b**

5. Why do grasshoppers molt? **2.b**
   - **A** They need food.
   - **B** They need water.
   - **C** They are growing.
   - **D** They are sleeping.

The Big Idea

6. Which is the correct sequence of stages in a life cycle? **2.b**
   - **A** tadpole, egg, frog
   - **B** butterfly, egg, pupa
   - **C** egg, nymph, grasshopper
   - **D** kitten, adult cat, young cat

Writing ELA–W 1.1

Write to Describe

1. Choose two animals.
2. Draw pictures to show the stages of each animal's life cycle. Label each stage.
3. Write sentences to describe and compare the life cycles of the animals.

Math SDAP 1.1, 1.2

Life Spans Bar Graph

1. Choose three animals.
2. Find out about the life span of each animal. A life span is how long an animal usually lives.
3. Make a chart to record your data.
4. Use the chart to make a bar graph. Label the parts of the graph.

Animal Life Spans

animal	years
camel	
horse	
squirrel	

For more links and activities, go to **www.hspscience.com**

The San Diego Zoo

If you visit the San Diego Zoo, you may see Mei Sheng. Mei Sheng is a giant panda. He was born at the zoo. People have watched Mei Sheng grow since he was a small cub.

Many people like to visit the Children's Zoo. There they can pet animals or see young animals being fed.

More than 800 kinds of animals live at the San Diego Zoo. You can observe and learn about animals from all over the world!

Mei Sheng at one month old

Think and Write

How is Mei Sheng changing as he grows? **2.b**

California Standards in This Lesson

LESSON 2

Essential Question

How Are Animals Like and Not Like Their Parents?

Science Content

2.a *Students know* that organisms reproduce offspring of their own kind and that the offspring resemble their parents and one another.

2.c *Students know* many characteristics of an organism are inherited from the parents. Some characteristics are caused or influenced by the environment.

2.d *Students know* there is variation among individuals of one kind within a population.

Investigation and Experimentation

4.f Use magnifiers or microscopes to observe and draw descriptions of small objects or small features of objects.

California Fast Fact

California Pumas

Puma cubs have dark spots on their bodies. They also have dark rings on their tails. These markings fade as the cubs get older.

Vocabulary Preview

The **appearance** of something is the way it looks. p. 169

An animal's **environment** is made up of everything around the animal. p. 172

How Earthworms Are Alike and Different

Directed Inquiry

Ask a Question

What are some ways these chickens are alike and different?

Get Ready

Investigation Skill Tip
When you observe, you can use a hand lens, a magnifying box, or a microscope to help you see small things.

You Need

earthworms

bowl with soil

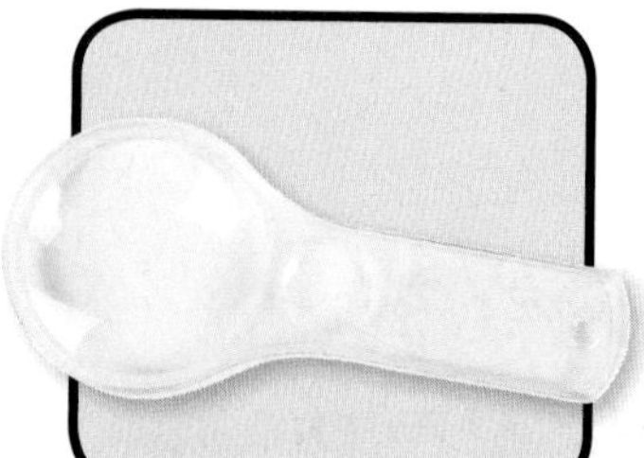

hand lens

paper and pencil

What to Do

Step 1

Carefully place some earthworms in soil.
CAUTION: Wash your hands after you do this.

Step 2

Use a hand lens to **observe** the way the earthworms look. Also observe what they do.

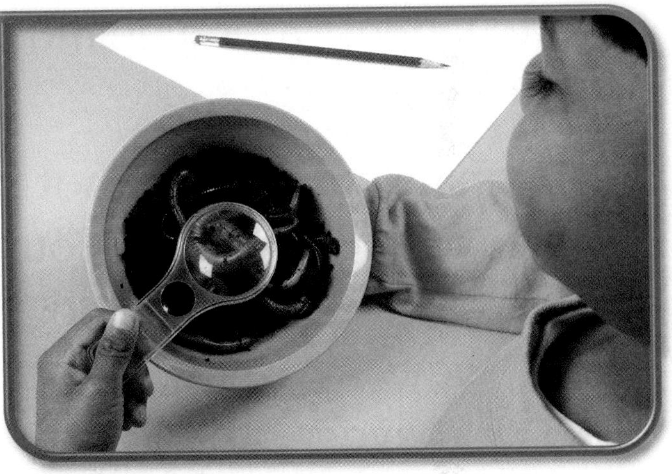

Step 3

Record what you observe.

Draw Conclusions

How are the earthworms alike? How are they different? **2.d**

Independent Inquiry

Use a hand lens to **observe** ladybugs or other insects. Write or draw pictures to show what you observe about the ladybugs. **4.f**

2.a, 2.c, 2.d

VOCABULARY
appearance
environment

COMPARE AND CONTRAST

Look for ways animals are like their parents and ways they are different from their parents.

Animals Are Like Their Parents

Animals have young that are the same kind of animal they are. For example, a mother dog has puppies. It cannot give birth to kittens. Young animals look and act like their parents.

Dolphins are animals that live in water. They have a tail and fins. Young dolphins look like their parents. All dolphins act in certain ways. They swim, and they breathe air to get oxygen. They eat fish and make sounds. Young dolphins act in the same ways their parents do.

mother dolphin and her young

Giraffes have a certain **appearance**, or way they look. They have four legs and a tail. Their fur has a pattern. Giraffes eat the leaves of trees. Young giraffes have an appearance like that of their parents. They act as their parents do.

Penguins have feathers, two legs, and two wings. They cannot fly. How is the young penguin like its parents?

Focus Skill **COMPARE AND CONTRAST** **How are young animals like their parents?**

parent penguins and their young

mother giraffe and her young

Animals Are Different from Their Parents

Young animals are like their parents. But they are not exactly like them. Their fur may look different. They are smaller but may grow to be larger than their parents. They may become stronger or faster. The young animals may not act exactly as their parents do. They may eat more or run more.

How are these cows alike and different? ▼

An animal's parents may be very different from each other. Dog parents may be different kinds of dogs.

Their puppies may be like both parents. Or they may be more like just one parent. Also, the puppies may not be like one another.

Focus Skill COMPARE AND CONTRAST **How may puppies be like their parents and like one another? How may they be different?**

Animals and the Environment

Animals look and act like their parents. But the environment also affects how animals look and act. The **environment** of an animal is everything around it.

A cold environment affects animals. Some animals grow thicker fur in fall. The thicker fur keeps them warm in winter. Other animals eat more in fall or store food. This helps them live in winter, when there is less food.

Arctic fox in summer

▲ Arctic fox in winter

The fur of some animals changes colors with the seasons. In spring, new brown fur matches the color of the environment. It helps these animals hide in summer. In fall, white fur grows. It matches the color of snow. The white fur helps the animals hide in winter.

Focus Skill COMPARE AND CONTRAST How are some animals different in the summer and in the winter?

More Animals, More Differences

Animals are a little different from their parents. Sometimes, many animals of one kind and their young live in a large group. The animals in a large group have even more differences.

The fish above are koi. The koi have differences in their appearance. Many koi in a school, or a group, have even more differences.

The horses below are also different from one another. Their young will be a little different from their parents. They will be different from one another. There will be even more differences in a large group of horses and their young.

COMPARE AND CONTRAST

How do the horses look alike? How do they look different?

Insta-Lab

Cats and Kittens

Draw a mother cat, a father cat, and two or more kittens. Compare your drawing with drawings your classmates make. How are all the cats alike? How are they different?

wild horses

Standards Wrap-Up and Lesson Review

Essential Question

How are animals like and not like their parents?

In this lesson, you learned that the way an animal looks and acts is affected by its parents and the environment.

Science Content Standards in This Lesson

2.a *Students know* that organisms reproduce offspring of their own kind and that the offspring resemble their parents and one another.

2.c *Students know* many characteristics of an organism are inherited from the parents. Some characteristics are caused or influenced by the environment.

2.d *Students know* there is variation among individuals of one kind within a population.

1. **COMPARE AND CONTRAST** Make a chart like this one. Tell how a puppy and its parents look alike and different. **2.c**

   alike — different

2. **DRAW CONCLUSIONS** A mother dog has five puppies. Will they all look the same? Explain your answer. **2.a**

3. **VOCABULARY** Use the term **appearance** in a sentence. **2.d**

4. **Critical Thinking** You see an animal that can swim. What do you know about its parents? **2.c**

   A The parents are dolphins.
   B The parents can swim.
   C The parents cannot swim.
   D The parents have brown eyes.

5. **Investigation** Why is it helpful to use a hand lens to look at very small things? **4.f**

The Big Idea

6. How will a squirrel's parents and its environment affect the way it looks and acts? **2.c**

Writing ELA–W 1.1

Write to Describe

1. Find or draw a picture of a family.
2. Describe ways the children look like their parents and like one another.
3. Describe ways the children look different from their parents and one another.

Math SDAP 1.1, 1.2

Puppy Color Bar Graph

1. A mother dog has 9 puppies. There are 3 brown puppies, 2 black puppies, and 4 tan puppies.
2. Make a tally chart. Record how many puppies are each color.
3. Use your tally chart to make a bar graph. Label the parts of the graph.

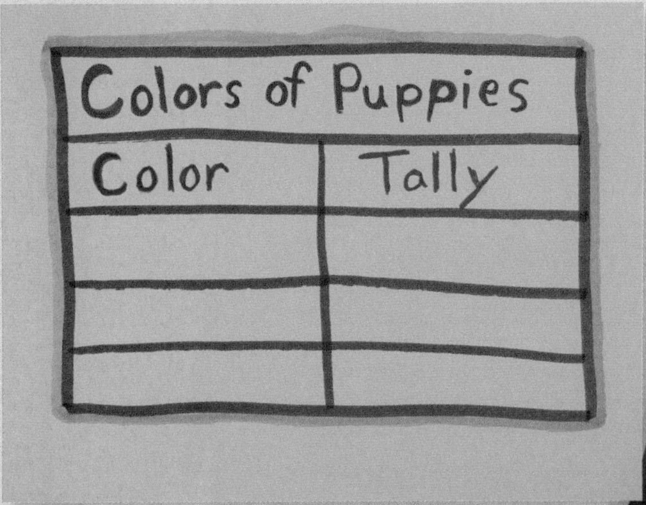

For more links and activities, go to **www.hspscience.com**

California Standards in This Lesson

Science Content

2.f *Students know* flowers and fruits are associated with reproduction in plants.

Investigation and Experimentation

4.d Write or draw descriptions of a sequence of steps, events, and observations.

4.f Use magnifiers or microscopes to observe and draw descriptions of small objects or small features of objects.

LESSON 3

Essential Question

What Are Some Plant Life Cycles?

California Fast Fact

Dandelion Seeds

The dandelion plant has a fluffy ball of seeds at the top. The wind can blow away the seeds. Then the seeds land. They may grow into new dandelions.

Vocabulary Preview

A **seed** is a plant part that new plants grow from. p. 182

Roots are plant parts that hold the plant in place and take in things the plant needs. p. 183

A **stem** is a plant part that holds up the leaves. A stem carries food and water through the plant. p. 183

A **flower** is a plant part that makes fruits. p. 184

A **fruit** is a plant part that holds and protects the seeds. p. 184

Investigate

The Life Cycle of a Bean Plant

Directed Inquiry

Ask a Question

Where do the beans people eat come from?

▼ pinto beans

Get Ready

Investigation Skill Tip

You can write about or draw things you observe changing. Sequence your notes or drawings, or put them in order. This shows the order in which things happened.

You Need

water

cup filled with soil

bean seeds

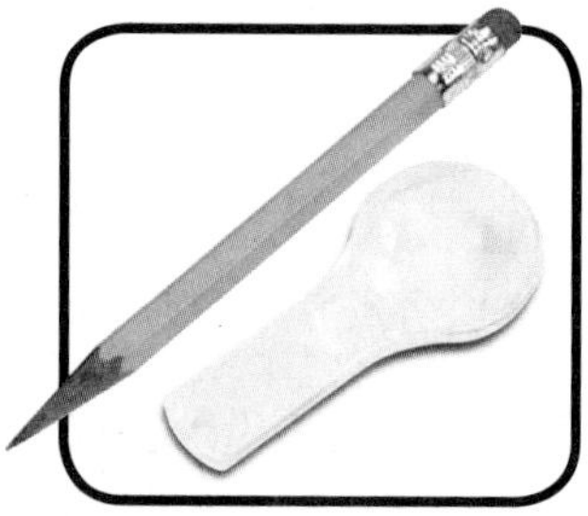

pencil and hand lens

What to Do

Step 1

Make holes in the soil. Put a bean in each hole. Cover the beans with soil. **CAUTION:** Wash your hands after you do this.

Step 2

Water the beans. Each day, use a hand lens to observe them.

Step 3

Each day, write and draw what you observe. **Sequence** your pictures.

Draw Conclusions

What did you find out about how beans grow and how they change? 4.d

Independent Inquiry

Soak a bean overnight. Open it carefully. Look at the parts of the bean. Use a hand lens or a microscope. Tell what you **observe**. Use a hand lens or a microscope to observe small parts of other plants. 4.f

2.f

VOCABULARY
seed
roots
stem
flower
fruit

Focus Skill SEQUENCE

Look for the order of the stages of a plant's life cycle.

Life Cycle of a Bean Plant

All the stages of a plant's life are its life cycle. First, a bean plant's life cycle begins with a seed. The **seed** is the plant part that a new plant grows from.

Next, a small plant starts to grow from the seed.

Inside each bean seed is a tiny plant and some stored food. The plant uses the food when it begins to grow.

When a seed gets water, warmth, and oxygen, it may germinate, or sprout. The roots grow down.

Then, the young plant keeps growing. **Roots** grow down into the soil or water. They hold the plant in place. They take in water and other things the plant needs. A stem begins to grow. The **stem** holds up the leaves. It carries food and water through the plant.

Last, the plant makes seeds that may grow into new plants. A new life cycle begins. This will happen over and over.

Focus Skill **SEQUENCE** **What happens to a bean seed?**

The stem of the small plant breaks through the ground. It grows up toward the light. Some stems start to make food for the plant.

More leaves and stems grow. In time, flowers will grow on the bean plant and make seeds.

▲ orange blossoms, or flowers

▲ orange

Flowers, Fruits, and Seeds

Some plants, such as orange trees, have flowers. **Flowers** are plant parts that make seeds.

When a plant has flowers, part of each flower becomes a fruit. The **fruit** grows around the seeds. The fruit holds and protects the seeds.

Focus Skill **SEQUENCE** **What happens to a flower?**

Parts of a Flower

Insta-Lab

Observe a Flower

Carefully take apart a flower. Use a hand lens or a microscope to observe the parts of the flower. Draw a picture of what you observe.

For more links and animations, go to **www.hspscience.com**

Life Cycle of an Oak Tree

An oak tree's life cycle is like that of many other plants. It begins with a seed. The seed is in a hard fruit, or nut. This nut is called an acorn.

First, the acorn starts to grow.

Next, a small plant grows. The small plant starts to look like a small oak tree.

1
acorn

2
tiny oak tree

Then, over time, the oak tree gets taller. The trunk gets thicker. More branches and leaves grow. Flowers grow on the branches.

Last, each flower forms an acorn. A new life cycle begins.

Focus Skill SEQUENCE **What happens to an acorn?**

3
fully grown oak tree

Standards Wrap-Up and Lesson Review

Essential Question

What are some plant life cycles?

In this lesson, you learned that plants look like their parents and one another. The flowers and fruits of a plant help it make new plants of the same kind.

Science Content Standards in This Lesson

2.f *Students know* flowers and fruits are associated with reproduction in plants.

1. **Focus Skill SEQUENCE** Make a chart like this one. Show the stages of a bean plant's life cycle. **2.f**

   [ ] → [ ] → [ ]

2. **DRAW CONCLUSIONS** Why is an acorn a fruit? **2.f**

3. **VOCABULARY** Use the terms **fruit**, **flower**, and **seed** in a sentence. **2.f**

4. **Investigation** How can sequencing pictures of what you observe help you understand how things change? **4.d**

5. How do flowers help plants make new plants? **2.f**

   A by getting water from soil
   B by making food
   C by making fruits and seeds
   D by holding up the plant

The Big Idea

6. What will a seed grow into in the second stage of its life cycle? **2.f**

Writing ELA–W 1.1

Write to Describe

1. Stick toothpicks in a sweet potato to hold it partly in a jar of water.
2. Observe the sweet potato for a month.
3. Write to describe how it changes.

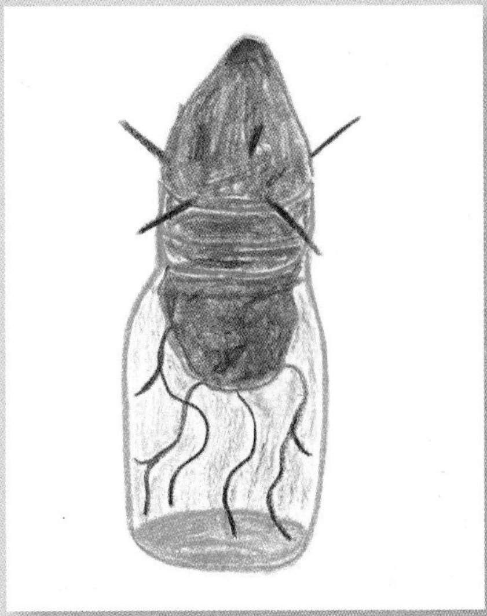

Math SDAP 1.1, 1.2

Seed Bar Graph

1. Watch as your teacher cuts open three apples.
2. Count the seeds in each apple. Make a tally chart. Record the number of seeds in each apple.
3. Use your tally chart to make a bar graph. Label the parts of the graph.
4. Talk with your classmates about what you found out.

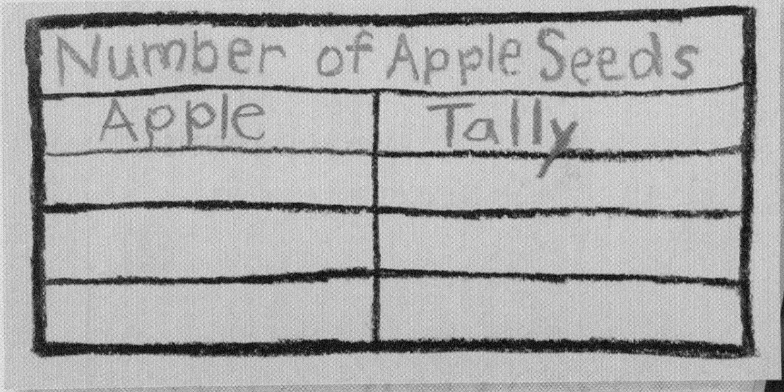

For more links and activities, go to **www.hspscience.com**

Irene Wibawa

IRENE WIBAWA

- **California Plant Scientist**
- Finds what is wrong with sick plants

You have probably used clues to find answers to your questions. Irene Wibawa uses clues in her work. She finds out what is wrong with sick plants.

Irene Wibawa works in a laboratory. She observes ways insects and diseases harm plants. She uses what she observes and what she knows to figure out what is wrong with sick plants. Irene Wibawa helps keep California's plants healthy.

Think and Write

Why is Irene Wibawa's work with plants important?

George Washington Carver

Dr. George Washington Carver was a plant scientist. He worked with farmers who grew crops. He showed them a way to plant that would keep their soil healthy. When they did this, they had bigger and better crops.

Dr. Carver did experiments with plants such as sweet potatoes, cotton, soybeans, and peanuts. He thought of more than 300 things to make with peanut plants!

GEORGE WASHINGTON CARVER

1860–1943

- **Plant Scientist**
- Invented many things using peanuts.

Think and Write

Why is it important for farmers to keep their soil healthy?

peanuts

California Standards in This Lesson

Science Content

2.a *Students know* that organisms reproduce offspring of their own kind and that the offspring resemble their parents and one another.

2.c *Students know* many characteristics of an organism are inherited from the parents. Some characteristics are caused or influenced by the environment.

2.d *Students know* there is variation among individuals of one kind within a population.

Investigation and Experimentation

4.f Use magnifiers or microscopes to observe and draw descriptions of small objects or small features of objects.

LESSON 4

Essential Question

How Are Plants Like and Not Like Their Parents?

California Fast Fact

Sequoia Trees

This giant sequoia is in Sequoia National Park. Some sequoias are more than 3,000 years old.

Vocabulary Preview

A **characteristic** is a feature or a trait that a plant or an animal has. p. 196

Investigate

How Plants Are Alike and Different

Directed Inquiry

Ask a Question

What are some ways flowers are alike and different?

Get Ready

Investigation Skill Tip
You can compare two things when you observe them carefully.

You Need

2 plants of the same kind

papers and markers

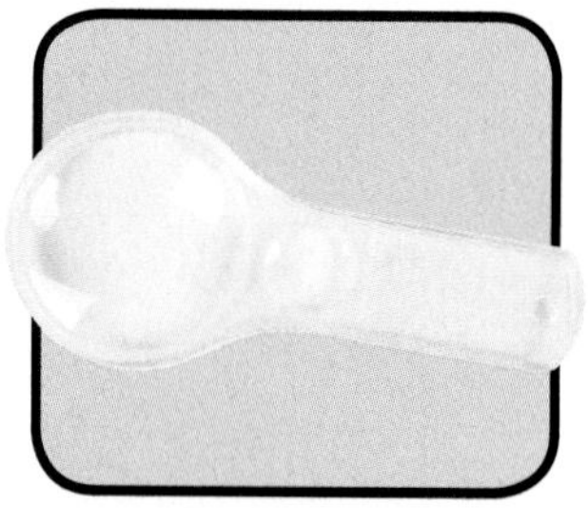

hand lens

What to Do

Step 1

Observe each plant. What color is it? How tall is it? How many leaves does it have? Use a hand lens to observe small parts of the plants.

Step 2

Make a chart like this one.

	Plant 1	Plant 2
color of plant		
number of leaves		
shape of leaves		

Step 3

Compare charts with a classmate.

Draw Conclusions

What are some ways plants are alike and different? **2.c**

Independent Inquiry

Observe other plants. Look at the colors, shapes, textures, and sizes of the leaves. Compare and sort their leaves by two or more characteristics. **4.f**

2.a, 2.c, 2.d

VOCABULARY
characteristic

Focus Skill **CAUSE AND EFFECT**

Look for reasons that plants are like and not like their parents.

Plants Look Like Their Parents

Plants make new plants. At first, the new plants are smaller than their parents. They may not get flowers, even if the parent plants do.

The young plant grows to look like its parents. This is because the parent trees pass on **characteristics**, or traits, to the new plant.

orange trees

Plants get most of their characteristics from their parents. They have the same shape of leaves. A parent plant may grow cones or fruits. Then the young plant also grows cones or fruits.

Focus Skill **CAUSE AND EFFECT** **Why do plants look like their parents?**

grand fir trees

Plants Look Different from Their Parents

Most new plants gets characteristics from two parents. This is why plants look like their parents but not exactly like them.

One parent plant may be tall. The other may be short. Some of the new plants may be tall and some may be short.

The two parent plants may have flowers of different colors. Some of the new plants may have flowers of one color. Other new plants may have the other color.

Plants of one kind may grow in a group. The plants are not all alike. They are different sizes. They have flowers of different colors.

The plants make new plants. The new plants also have different sizes and colors. Each time parent plants make new plants, there will be more differences.

sweet peas

Focus Skill **CAUSE AND EFFECT** **What may cause new plants to look different from their parents?**

snapdragons

Plants and the Environment

The environment affects plants. Water is part of the environment. A plant may get too little water. It may get too much water. If so, the plant will not grow well. So, the wrong amount of water can make a plant different from its parents.

These corn plants do not get enough water. They may grow few or no ears of corn.

These corn plants get all the water they need. They will grow many ears of corn.

cress grown with the right amount of light

cress grown with no light

If a plant gets too much or too little light, it will not grow well. It may not make flowers. So, getting the wrong amount of light can make a plant different from its parents.

The environment can affect the growth of plants in other ways, too. The soil affects how well a plant grows. Insects can harm plants.

Focus Skill CAUSE AND EFFECT How does the environment affect a plant's characteristics?

Insta-Lab

Observe a Leaf

Closely observe a leaf. What can you tell about the environment of the plant the leaf came from? Did it get the right amount of food, water, and light?

Standards Wrap-Up and Lesson Review

Essential Question

How are plants like and not like their parents?

In this lesson, you learned that a plant gets characteristics from its parents. The environment can also affect a plant's characteristics.

Science Content Standards in This Lesson

2.a *Students know* that organisms reproduce offspring of their own kind and that the offspring resemble their parents and one another.

2.c *Students know* many characteristics of an organism are inherited from the parents. Some characteristics are caused or influenced by the environment.

2.d *Students know* there is variation among individuals of one kind within a population.

1. Focus Skill **CAUSE AND EFFECT** Make a chart. Show what causes a plant to look a certain way. **2.a**

   cause → effect

2. **SUMMARIZE** Write a summary of the lesson. Begin with the sentence **Plants look like and different from their parents.** **2.c**

3. **VOCABULARY** Use the term **characteristic** in a sentence. **2.c, 2.d**

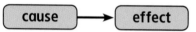

4. **Investigation** What can you learn by using a hand lens to look at parts of a plant? **4.f**

5. Both parents of a plant have yellow flowers. What color will the new plant's flowers probably be? **2.c**

   A orange
   B red
   C white
   D yellow

The Big Idea

6. If you see a tree, what would you infer, or figure out, about its parents? **2.c**

Writing ELA–W 1.1

Write to Describe

1. Draw pictures of two flowers of the same kind.
2. Write sentences to tell how they are alike.
3. Write sentences to tell how they are different.
4. Share your sentences with classmates.

Math SDAP 1.1, 1.2

Plant Growth Picture Graph

1. Put sandy soil in one pot and potting soil in another. Plant grass seeds in both pots. Water the seeds. Measure the grass plants on the same day each week.
2. Make a chart. Record your data.
3. Use your chart to make a picture graph. Label the parts of the graph.

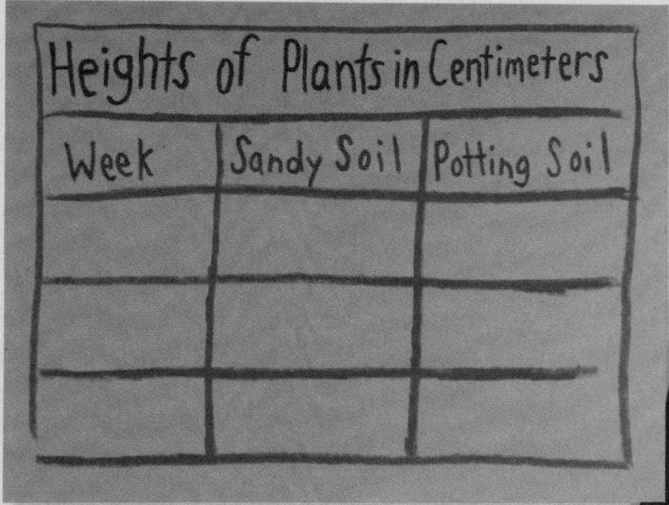

For more links and activities, go to **www.hspscience.com**

California Agricultural Technology Institute

Grapes are an important crop in California.

This scanner gives farmers information about the grapes. It is used in different parts of a field.

Farms in California are very large. How can farmers know if the crops in the middle of a field are healthy? How can they know if the crops have enough water or the right nutrients? Scientists at the California Agricultural Institute are working on ways to help.

This is one way scientists are helping. Pictures of a field are taken from an airplane. The pictures show how well the crops are growing. Some pictures show whether the crops need water. Others show how the soil affects the crops. This information is helping California farmers. They can grow larger and better crops.

Think and Write

How can science help farmers grow better crops?

Find out more. Log on to **www.hspscience.com**

California Standards in This Lesson

Science Content

2.c *Students know* many characteristics of an organism are inherited from the parents. Some characteristics are caused or influenced by the environment.

2.e *Students know* light, gravity, touch, or environmental stress can affect the germination, growth, and development of plants.

Investigation and Experimentation

4.a Make predictions based on observed patterns and not random guessing.

LESSON 5

Essential Question

What Can Affect How a Plant Grows?

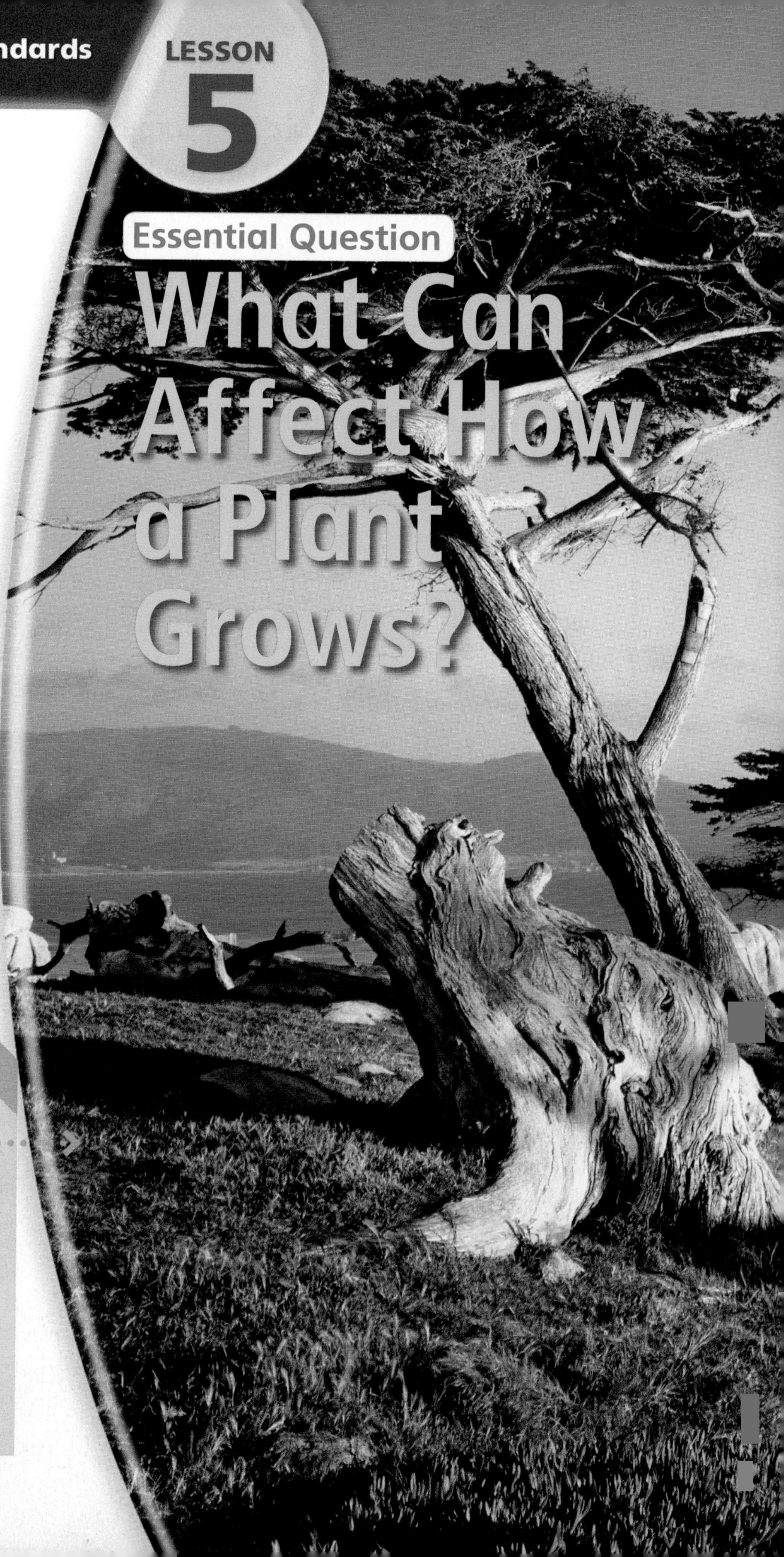

California Fast Fact

Monterey Cypress Trees

These Monterey Cypress trees grow along the coast in Monterey. The strong winds make the trees grow to one side.

Vocabulary Preview

Nutrients are things that plants and animals take in to help them survive. Plants get nutrients from the soil. p. 215

Investigate

How Light Changes a Plant

Directed Inquiry

Ask a Question

Why is the plant bending toward the window?

Get Ready

Investigation Skill Tip

When you predict, you tell what you think will happen. You use what you have seen before to make your prediction.

You Need

2 plants

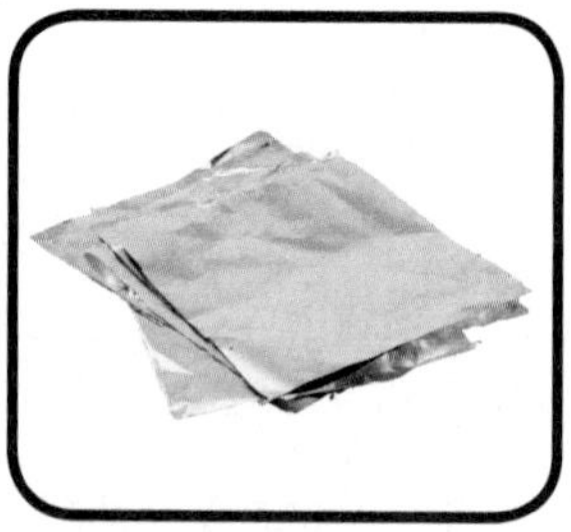

foil

What to Do

Step 1

Cover the leaves of one plant with foil. **Predict** what will happen.

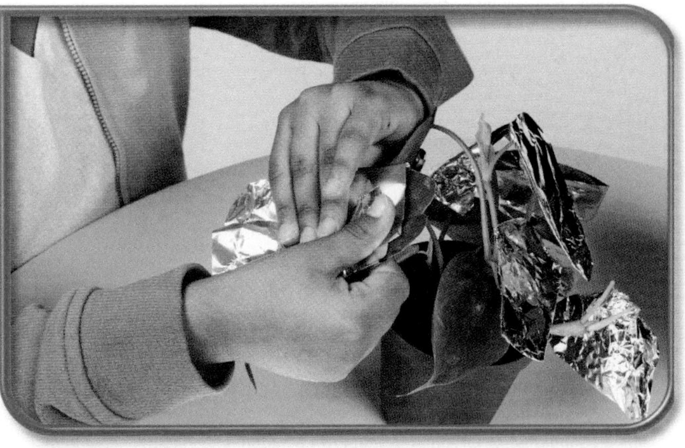

Step 2

Put both plants in a sunny place. Water them both when the soil is dry. Wait one week.

Step 3

Remove the foil. Observe and compare the plants. Was your prediction correct?

Draw Conclusions

Why are the two plants different? **2.c**

Independent Inquiry

Predict what other things besides light can affect the way plants grow. Investigate. See whether your predictions are correct. **4.a**

2.c, 2.e

VOCABULARY
nutrients

MAIN IDEA AND DETAILS
Look for details about things that can affect the way a plant grows.

Light

Plants need light to grow. They grow toward a source of light. Sunflowers turn their heads to follow the sun during the day. In the morning, when the sun is in the east, they face east. In the afternoon, when the sun is in the west, they face west.

A source of light may be on only one side of a plant. For example, the light may be coming through a window. When this happens, the plant's stems and leaves turn toward the light source.

MAIN IDEA AND DETAILS **How does light affect the way a plant grows?**

sunflowers

impatiens

Gravity

A plant's roots grow down because of gravity. The stem and leaves grow up to find sunlight.

If a plant is placed on its side, the roots will turn and grow down. The stems and leaves will turn and grow up.

Focus Skill MAIN IDEA AND DETAILS **Why do a plant's roots grow down?**

germinating runner bean seed ▼

stem on side, turning to grow upward ▼

Touch

Touch affects some plants. The stems of a vine, such as morning glory, grow up. When they touch something, they curl around the object. The leaves of the mimosa plant close when they are touched.

morning glory vine

Some plants, such as the Venus' flytrap, use insects for food. These plants have special hairs on them. When an insect touches the hairs, the leaves snap shut. They trap the insect inside.

Venus' flytrap

Focus Skill **MAIN IDEA AND DETAILS** **How does touch affect some plants?**

mimosa leaves

Water

Many seeds need water to germinate, or sprout. Plants need water to live, but too much water will harm them. The roots will rot, and the plants will die.

If plants do not get enough water, their leaves and stems droop. Then they dry out and turn brown. Soon the plant dies.

Focus Skill **MAIN IDEA AND DETAILS** **What will happen if a plant gets too much or too little water?**

Insta-Lab

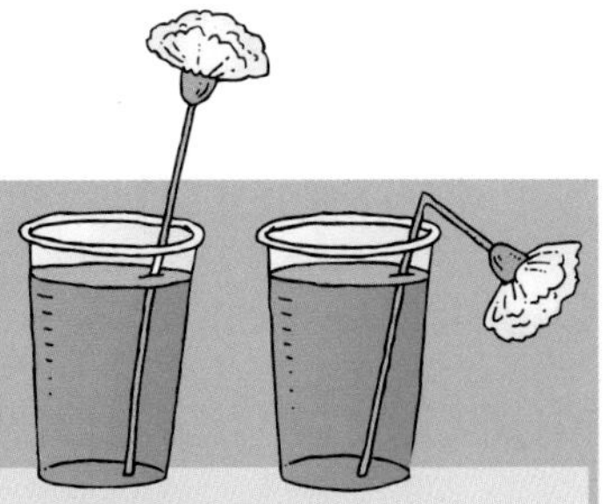

Compare Carnations

Take two white carnations of the same size. Bend the stem of one. Then place each carnation in a cup of colored water. Observe the carnations for two days. What changes do you see?

▲ **begonia plant after being watered**

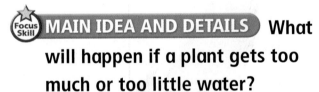

▲ **begonia plant with no water**

Temperature

Temperature also affects the germination of seeds and plant growth. Many seeds need the temperature to be just right to germinate.

Some plants, such as palm trees, grow better in warmer temperatures. Other plants grow better in cooler temperatures. Lilacs need cold winters.

lilac tree

Other Parts of the Environment

Nutrients are things in soil that plants need to grow and stay healthy. If the soil does not have the right nutrients, the plant may not grow well.

Plants may not have enough space to grow well. Insects and other animals may eat the plants. Things in the soil or water may also harm the plants.

Focus Skill MAIN IDEA AND DETAILS **What things in the environment can affect plants?**

These plants grow in dark soil.

This plant grows in the sandy desert.

Essential Question

What can affect how a plant grows?

In this lesson, you learned how light, gravity, touch, water, and other things in the environment affect how a plant grows.

Science Content Standards in This Lesson

2.c *Students know* many characteristics of an organism are inherited from the parents. Some characteristics are caused or influenced by the environment.

2.e *Students know* light, gravity, touch, or environmental stress can affect the germination, growth, and development of plants.

1. Focus Skill **MAIN IDEA AND DETAILS** Make a chart like this one. Show details about things that affect the way a plant grows. **2.e**

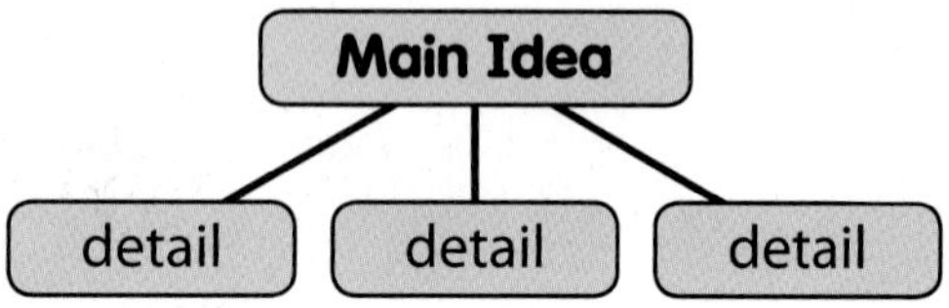

2. **SUMMARIZE** Write a summary of the lesson. Begin with the sentence **Many things affect plant growth.** **2.c**

3. **VOCABULARY** Use the term **nutrients** in a sentence. **2.e**

4. **Critical Thinking** You touch a plant's leaves, and the leaves close up. What can you infer, or figure out, about this plant? **2.e**

5. How does gravity affect plants? **2.e**

The Big Idea

6. Imagine that someone gives you a plant. What do you need to know to keep it healthy? **2.e**

Writing ELA–WA 2.1.a

Write to Inform

1. Put five seeds and a very wet paper towel in a zip-top bag. Zip the bag shut.
2. Put five seeds and a dry paper towel in another bag. Zip the bag shut.
3. Observe for one week.
4. Write about what happens. Explain why it happens.

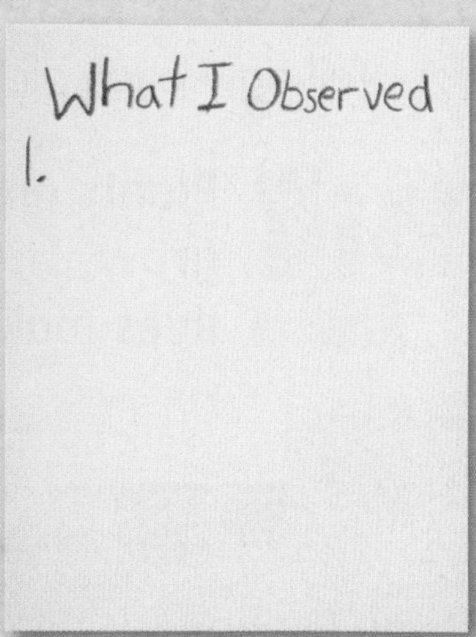

Math SDAP 1.1, 1.2

Watering Plants Bar Graph

1. Three plants got different amounts of water. Plant A grew 3 centimeters, Plant B grew 4 centimeters, and Plant C grew 2 centimeters.
2. Make a chart. Record your data.
3. Use your chart to make a bar graph. Label the parts.
4. Share your results with classmates.

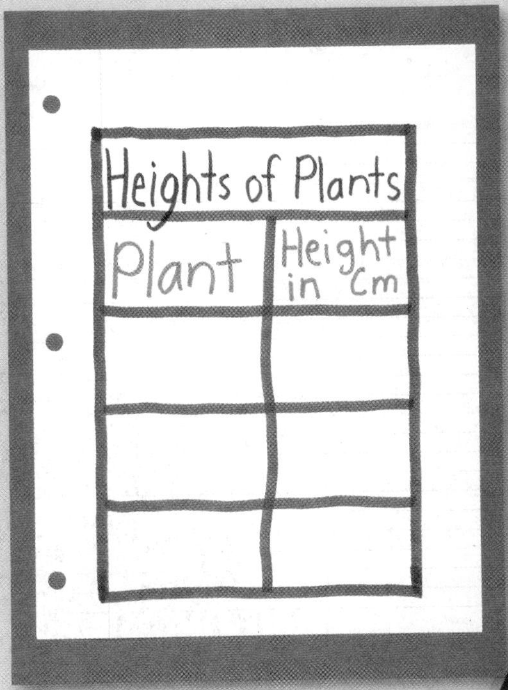

For more links and activities, go to **www.hspscience.com**

UNIT 2 LIFE SCIENCE

Wrap-Up

Visual Summary

Tell how each picture helps explain the **Big Idea**.

The Big Idea **Plants and animals change as they grow. The stages, or times, of their lives make up their life cycles.**

2.a, 2.f

All plants and animals have life cycles. Animals and plants look like their parents. This is because they get their characteristics from their parents.

2.b

Animals have different life cycles. Some, such as cats and mice, have live young. Other animals, such as frogs, butterflies, and grasshoppers, lay eggs.

2.c, 2.d, 2.e

Plants and animals get some characteristics from one parent and some from the other. The environment affects how they grow and change.

2.f

Many plants have flowers and fruits that help them make new plants.

Show What You Know

Unit Writing Activity

Write About a Life Cycle

Monarch butterflies come to California each winter. Find out about the life cycle of monarch butterflies. Write sentences to describe it. Then draw pictures to go with your sentences. Your pictures should show the stages of the butterfly's life cycle in sequence.

Unit Project

Fact Book About California's Living Things

Find out about plants and animals that live in California. Make pages with facts about the plants and animals. Tell how each living thing changes as it grows. Draw pictures to go with your facts. Put your pages together to make a book.

UNIT 2 LIFE SCIENCE

Review

California Science Standards in

Vocabulary Review

Use the terms to complete the sentences. The page numbers tell you where to look if you need help.

life cycle p. 152 **fruit** p. 184

tadpole p. 154 **characteristic** p. 196

environment p. 172 **nutrients** p. 215

1. Everything around an animal is the animal's _______. **2.a**

2. A trait, or feature, of a plant or an animal is a _______. **2.c**

3. A _______ holds and protects seeds. **2.f**

4. A young frog is a _______. **2.b**

5. All the stages, or times, of a plant's or an animal's life make up its _______. **2.b**

6. _______ are things that plants and animals must take in to live and grow. **2.e**

Check Understanding

7. Write *first*, *next*, *then*, and *last* to show the sequence. **2.f**

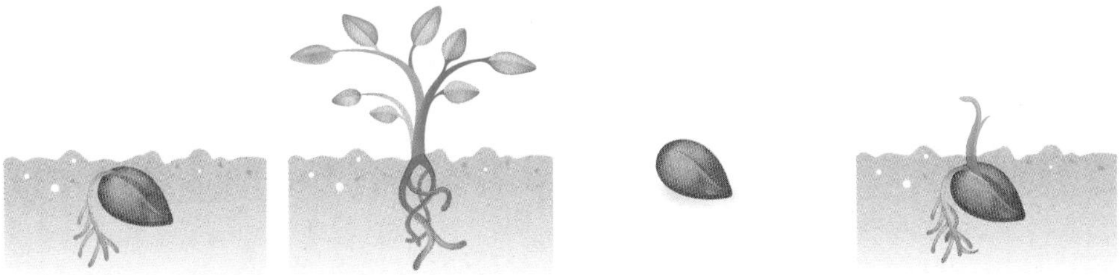

__________ __________ __________ __________

8. Which of these is a correct life cycle? **2.b**

A egg, nymph, grasshopper

B acorn, oak tree, small plant

C larva, butterfly, pupa, egg

D tadpole, egg, frog

Critical Thinking

9. Describe how some young animals look different from their parents. **2.d**

The Big Idea

10. Describe the life cycles of one plant and one animal. **2.b**

UNIT 3 EARTH SCIENCE

Earth Materials

California Standards in This Unit

3 Earth is made of materials that have distinct properties and provide resources for human activities. As the basis for understanding this concept:

3.a *Students know* how to compare the physical properties of different kinds of rocks and know that rock is composed of different combinations of minerals.

3.b *Students know* smaller rocks come from the breakage and weathering of larger rocks.

3.c *Students know* that soil is made partly from weathered rock and partly from organic materials and that soils differ in their color, texture, capacity to retain water, and ability to support the growth of many kinds of plants.

3.d *Students know* that fossils provide evidence about the plants and animals that lived long ago and that scientists learn about the past history of Earth by studying fossils.

3.e *Students know* rock, water, plants, and soil provide many resources, including food, fuel, and building materials, that humans use.

This unit also includes these Investigation and Experimentation Standards:

4.b, 4.d, 4.e, 4.f, 4.g

What's the Big Idea?

Earth is made up of materials that are different from one another. People use these materials.

Essential Questions

Science in California

Hi Luis,

We went to Red Rock Canyon! Rain and wind have weathered the rocks into interesting shapes.

We saw fossils in the rocks! Fossils are what is left of plants and animals that lived a long time ago.

I'll tell you more when I see you.

Christine

Read Christine's postcard. What did Christine learn about rocks? How do you think that helps explain the **Big Idea**?

Unit Inquiry

Soil Holds In Water

How much water can different kinds of soil hold in? Plan and do a test to find out.

California Standards in This Lesson

Science Content

3.a *Students know* how to compare the physical properties of different kinds of rocks and know that rock is composed of different combinations of minerals.

Investigation and Experimentation

4.c Compare and sort common objects according to two or more physical attributes (e.g., color, shape, texture, size, weight).

4.f Use magnifiers or microscopes to observe and draw descriptions of small objects or small features of objects.

LESSON 1

Essential Question

What Are Rocks and Minerals?

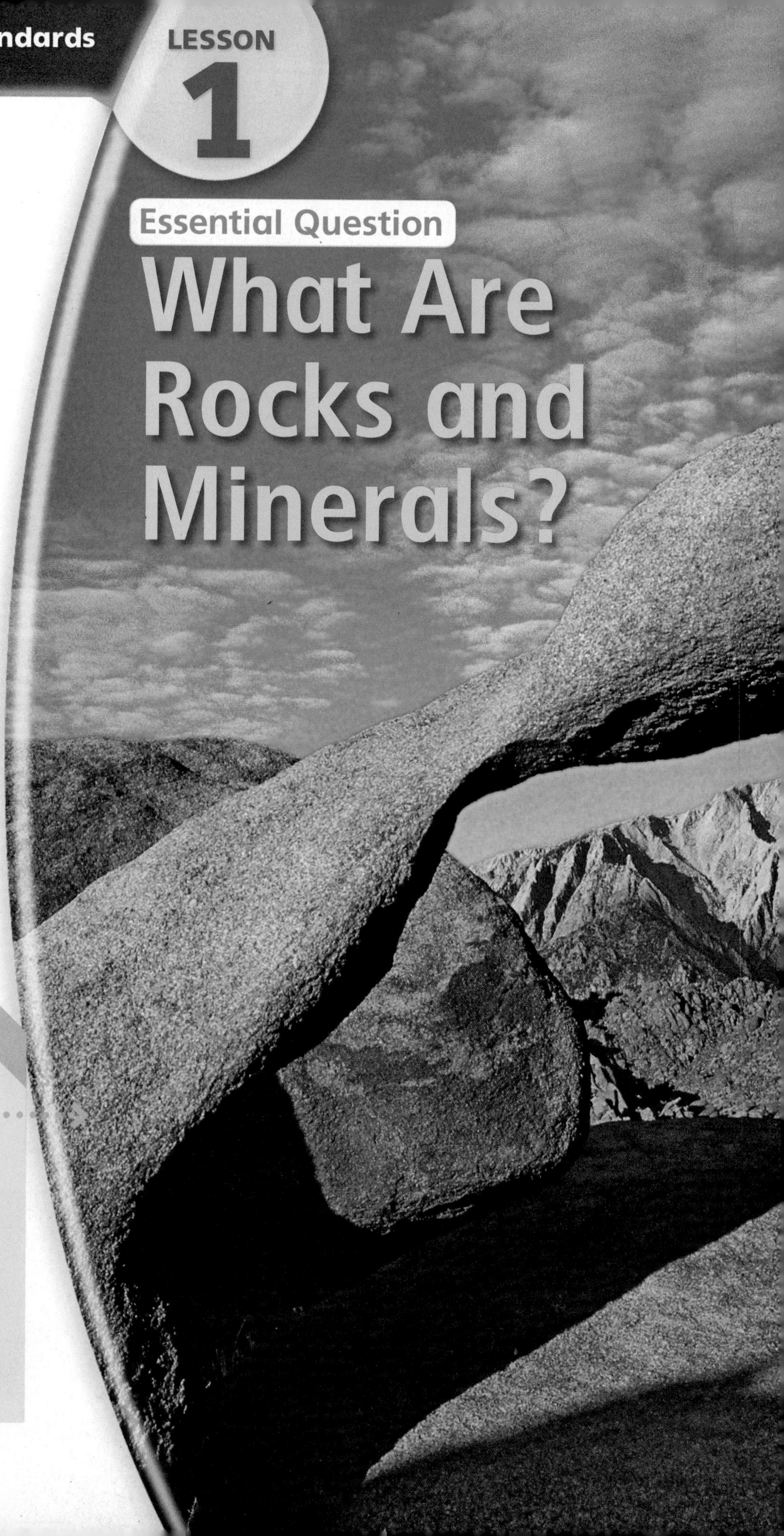

California Fast Fact

Alabama Hills

The Alabama Hills are in the Owens Valley, east of the Sierra Nevada Mountains. They have unusual granite rock formations.

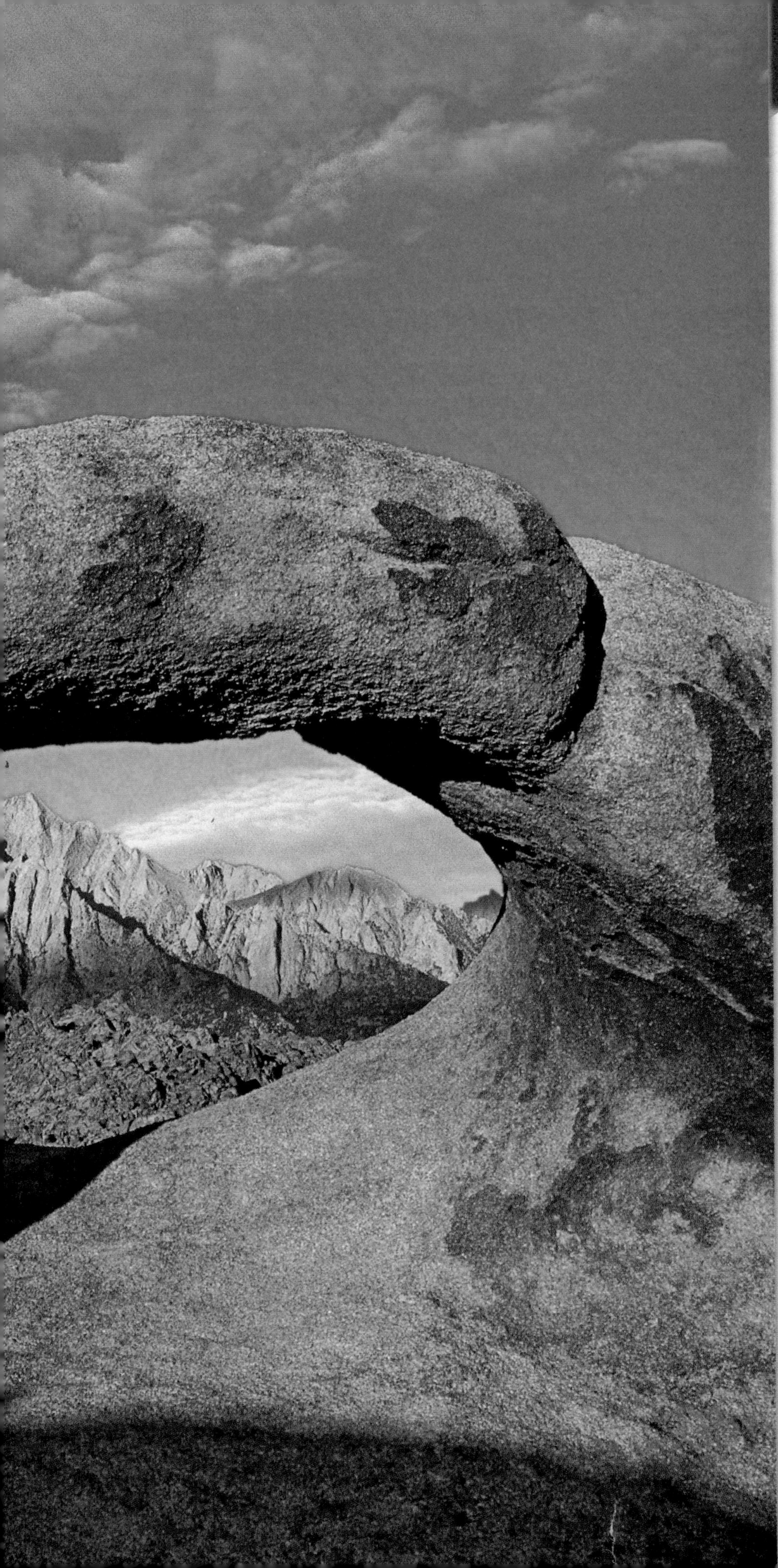

Vocabulary Preview

Rock is a hard material found in nature. Rock is made up of one or more minerals. p. 228

A **mineral** is a solid material that is found in nature. A mineral was never living. p. 229

A **property** is a characteristic that something has. p. 230

Texture is the way an object feels when you touch it. p. 230

Hardness of Minerals

Directed Inquiry

Ask a Question

How is the natural diamond different from the cut and polished diamond? Why do you think diamonds are used in jewelry?

Get Ready

Investigation Skill Tip

You can **observe** some things by touching them.

You Need

minerals

copper penny

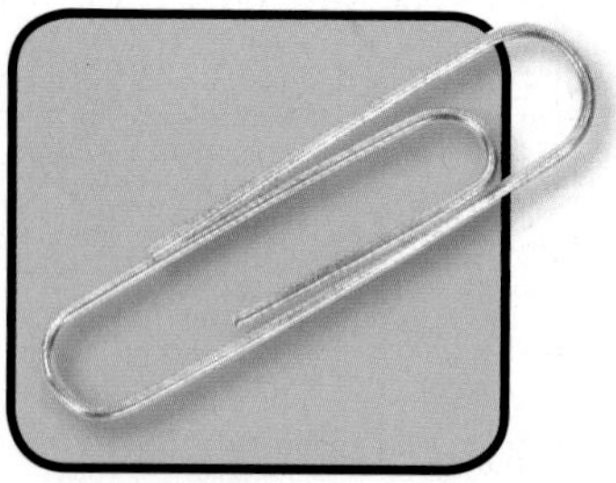

steel paper clip

What to Do

Step 1

Make a hardness chart.

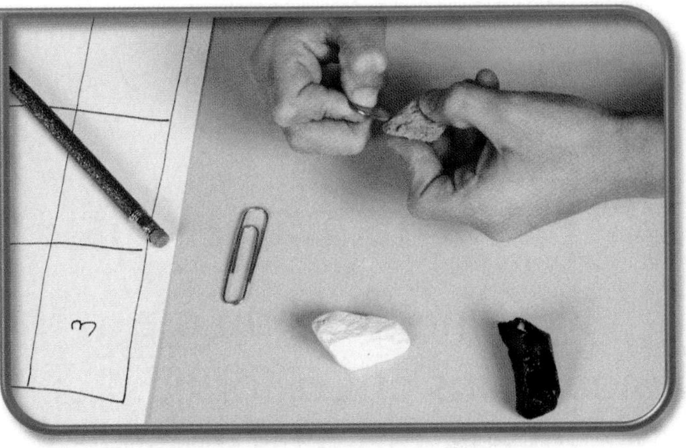

Step 2

Scratch each mineral with your fingernail, a penny, and a paper clip. **Observe** what happens.

Which Objects Leave Marks on Minerals?

	fingernail	penny	paper clip
1			
2			
3			

Step 3

Record in your chart which objects make a mark on each mineral.

Draw Conclusions

Objects that are harder than a mineral make a mark on it. Which objects are harder than each mineral? **3.a**

Independent Inquiry

Observe some rocks with a hand lens. What properties do they have? Sort the rocks into groups by two or more of these properties. **4.c, 4.f**

3.a

VOCABULARY
rock
mineral
property
texture

MAIN IDEA AND DETAILS

Look for details about rocks and minerals.

Rocks and Minerals

Imagine that you are in the mountains of California. Rocks are all around you. **Rock** is a hard, solid material found in nature.

Some rocks are very large. Some are so small that you need a hand lens or a microscope to see them clearly.

Sierra Nevada mountains

limestone, a rock

rhodochrosite, a mineral

Rock is made up of minerals. A **mineral** is a solid material found in nature. A mineral was never living.

Some kinds of rock have only one mineral. Most kinds are made up of two or more minerals.

Focus Skill MAIN IDEA AND DETAILS **What is rock made of?**

Insta-Lab

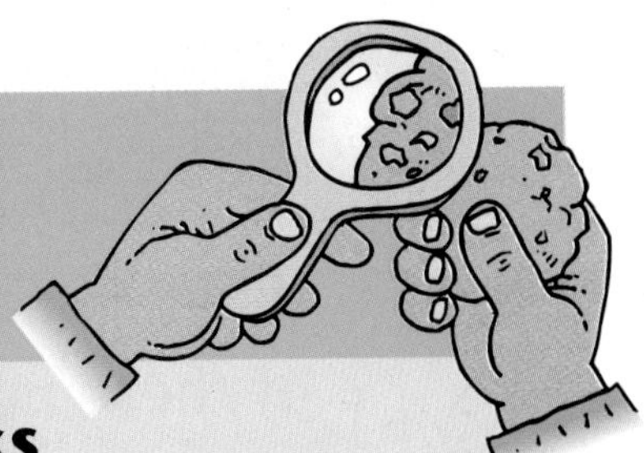

Sorting Rocks

Use a hand lens to look for minerals in rocks. Sort the rocks by the minerals you find in them.

Properties of Minerals

Minerals are different from one another. They have different properties. A **property** is a characteristic that something has. Minerals look different. They have different colors and lusters. Luster is shininess. Some minerals are shinier than others.

Minerals have different textures, too. **Texture** is the way something feels when you touch it. Some minerals feel rough. Others feel smooth.

Some minerals are harder than others. You learned that you can test a mineral's hardness by trying to scratch it.

Mineral Color
What color is each of these minerals?

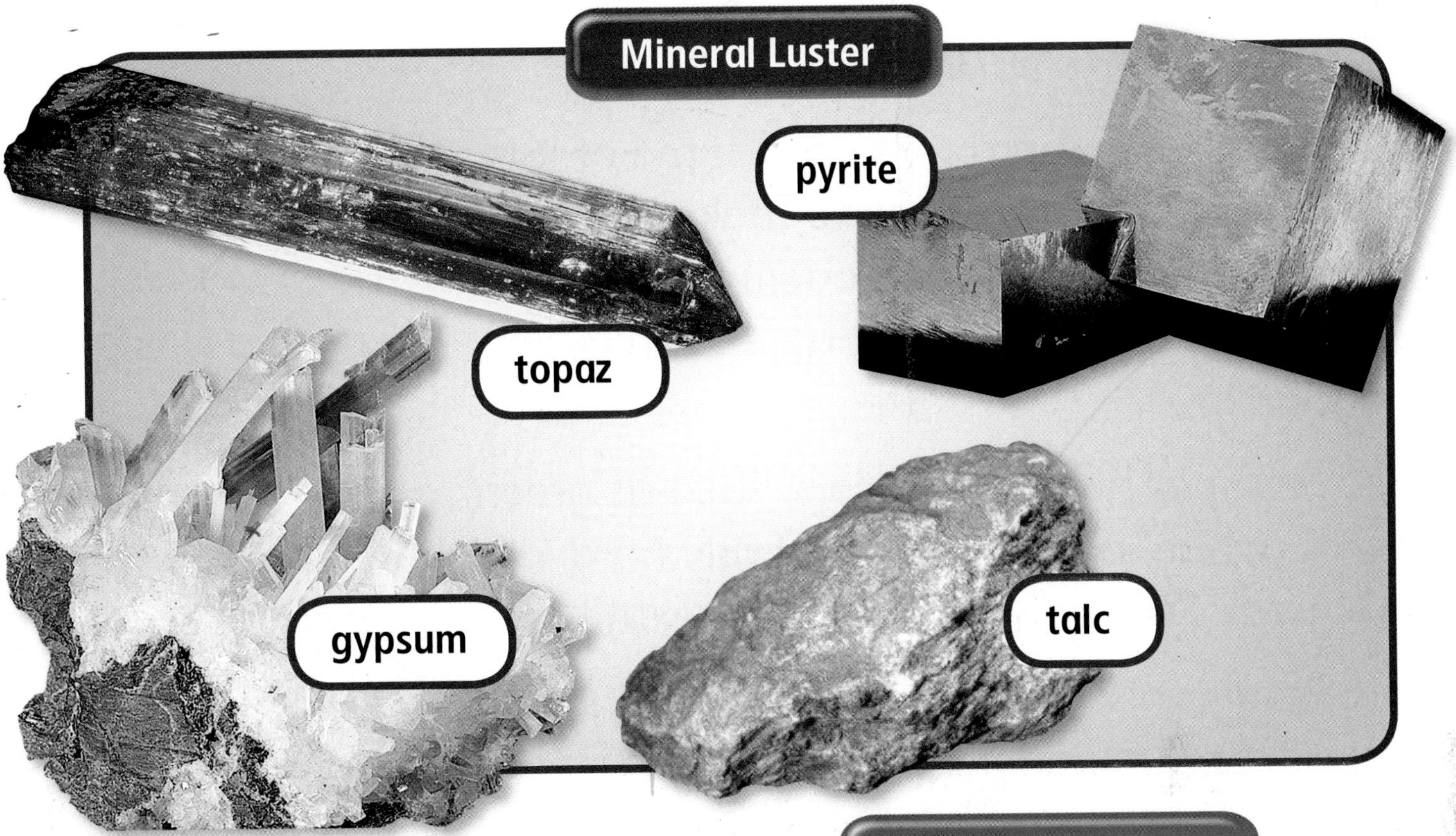

Some minerals have more mass than others. Same-size pieces of different minerals may look as if they would have the same mass. When you check with a balance, you may find that one has more mass.

Mineral Hardness
Talc is the softest mineral.
Diamond is the hardest mineral.

One rock on the balance has more mass than the other rock. Why is this so?

MAIN IDEA AND DETAILS

What are some properties of minerals?

Comparing Minerals

Granite is a hard rock, and some of it is beautiful. It is often used to make buildings and statues. Granite is made up mostly of the minerals feldspar, quartz, hornblende, and mica.

Feldspar has many colors, such as green, pink, white, and gray. It is a fairly hard mineral. Feldspar has a smooth texture.

Quartz also has many colors, and it looks glassy. It is a little harder than feldspar. Quartz has a smooth texture.

Science Up Close

Different Textures

Some rocks feel smooth. Other rocks feel rough. You can compare the textures of rocks by looking at them and feeling them. A hand lens lets you see more details. How are the textures of these rocks different? How can you tell?

For more links and animations, go to **www.hspscience.com**

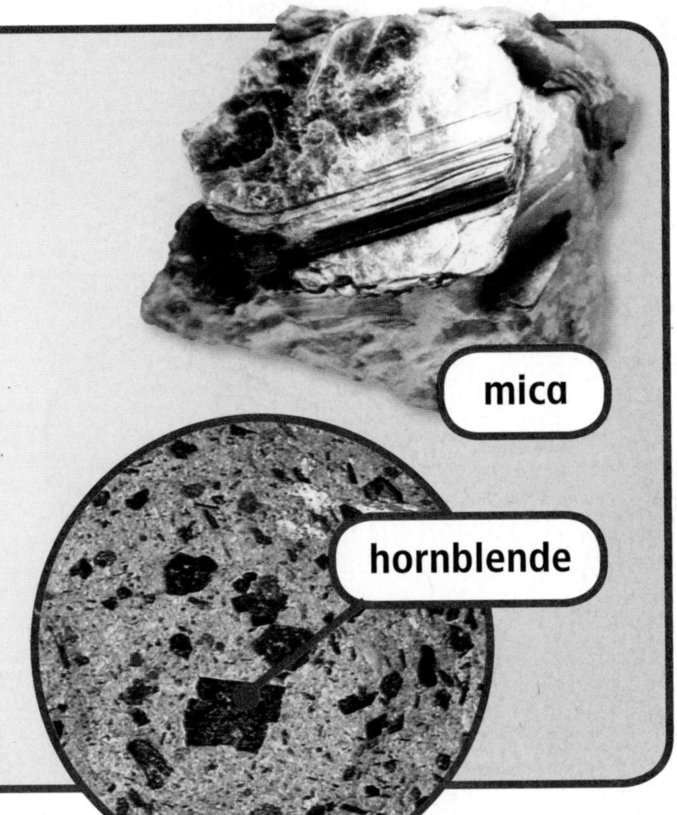

Mica can be clear, as well as black, green, red, and other colors. It is soft. Some mica feels smooth, and some feels rough. It is flaky.

Hornblende can be shiny black or dark green. It is about as hard as feldspar. It is smooth. It is not flaky.

Focus Skill MAIN IDEA AND DETAILS What are some properties of the minerals found in granite?

Standards Wrap-Up and Lesson Review

Essential Question

What are rocks and minerals?

In this lesson, you learned that different kinds of rock have different properties. You also learned that rock is made up of different minerals.

Science Content Standards in This Lesson

3.a *Students know* how to compare the physical properties of different kinds of rocks and know that rock is composed of different combinations of minerals.

1. Focus Skill **MAIN IDEA AND DETAILS** Make a chart like this one. Show details for the main idea **Minerals have different properties.** **3.a**

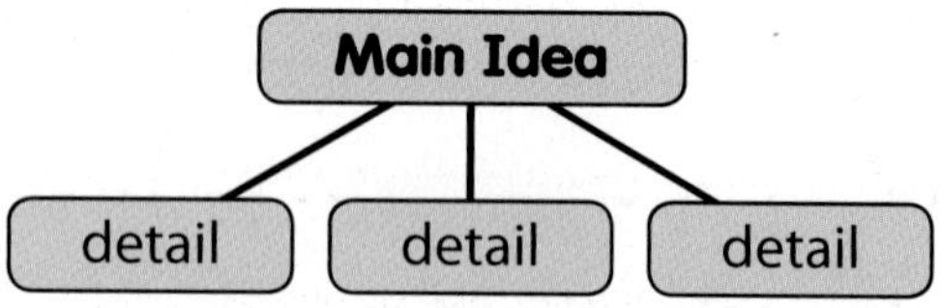

2. **DRAW CONCLUSIONS** Observe a mineral. What are its properties? **3.a**

3. **VOCABULARY** Use the terms **rock** and **mineral** in a sentence. **3.a**

4. **Critical Thinking** Gold is a soft mineral. How does this property make it useful for making jewelry? **3.a**

5. Which of these minerals is the hardest? **3.a**

A feldspar

B hornblende

C mica

D quartz

The Big Idea

6. Why is it useful to know how hard a mineral is? **3.a**

Writing ELA–W 1.1

Write to Describe

1. Observe how some small rocks are alike and different. Look at their colors, shapes, sizes, and textures.
2. Sort the rocks by two or more of these properties.
3. Write sentences to describe how you sorted the rocks.

Math NS 1.3

Put Rocks in Order by Mass

1. Choose four rocks.
2. Place one rock on one side of a balance. Place masses on the other side until the sides are even. Record the mass of the rock.
3. Repeat for the other rocks.
4. Order the rocks from the one with the least mass to the one with the greatest mass.

For more links and activities, go to **www.hspscience.com**

Edward Drinker Cope

EDWARD DRINKER COPE

- **Paleontologist**
- Told about 1,000 or more kinds of animals from long ago

Edward Drinker Cope was a famous paleontologist, a scientist who studies fossils. Dr. Cope found fossils in several states.

When Dr. Cope began his work, scientists knew about only 18 kinds of dinosaurs. Dr. Cope found bones from 56 kinds of dinosaurs and many other animals of long ago.

Dr. Cope wrote about his work. Other scientists learned from what he had done.

Think and Write

Why is it important for scientists to share information about their work?

Edward Drinker Cope was the first to find bones from the Camarasaurus.

Elizabeth Miura

Elizabeth Miura is a mineralogist. Mineralogists are scientists who study minerals. Minerals are found in rocks.

Elizabeth Miura works with other scientists. They study the water in minerals. The scientists think the information they find will help them learn about Earth's history.

ELIZABETH MIURA

- **Mineralogist, California Institute of Technology**
- Studies the water in minerals to learn about Earth's history

Think and Write

How do you think working with others can be helpful?

garnets

California Standards in This Lesson

Science Content

3.b *Students know* smaller rocks come from the breakage and weathering of larger rocks.

Investigation and Experimentation

4.f Use magnifiers or microscopes to observe and draw descriptions of small objects or small features of objects.

LESSON 2

Essential Question

What Happens As Rock Weathers?

California Fast Fact

El Capitán

El Capitán, in Yosemite National Park, is 805 meters high. It is a favorite place of many rock climbers.

Vocabulary Preview

Weathering is the change that happens when rocks are broken into smaller pieces. Wind, water, and some other things cause weathering. p. 242

Water **freezes**, or turns into a solid, when it gets cold enough. p. 244

How Rocks Change

Directed Inquiry

Ask a Question

What do you think gave these rocks their unusual shape?

▼ Paria Canyon, Vermillion Cliffs, Arizona

Get Ready

Investigation Skill Tip

When you use a hand lens to observe, you can see parts of small objects more clearly.

You Need

rock salt

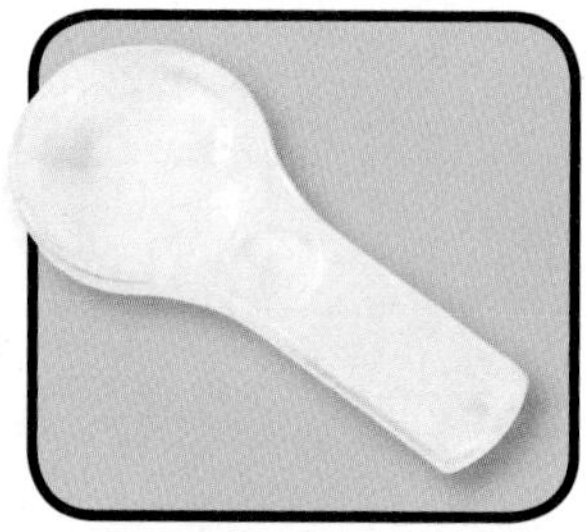

hand lens

jar, lid, sand, and water

forceps and spoon

What to Do

Step 1

Hold a grain of rock salt with forceps. Use a hand lens to **observe** its size and shape.

Step 2

Put rock salt, sand, and water in a jar. Place the lid on the jar. Shake the jar for 5 minutes.

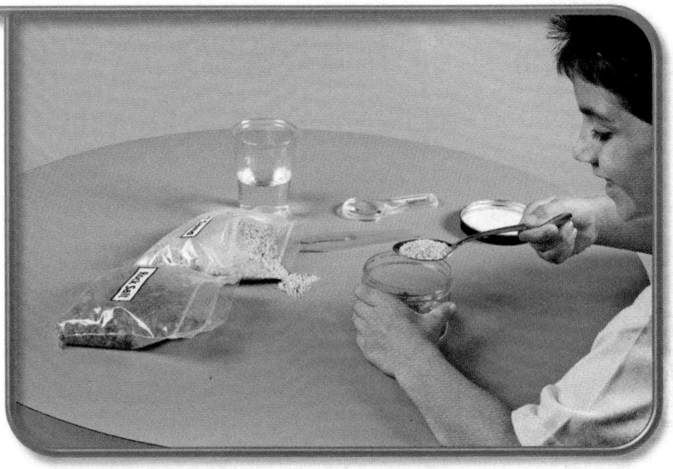

Step 3

Use forceps to remove the rock salt. Observe. How has it changed?

Draw Conclusions

Why did the rock salt change? 3.b

Independent Inquiry

Do large pieces of rock weather faster than small pieces of rock? Plan and do a test to find out. 3.b

VOCABULARY
weathering
freeze

Focus Skill CAUSE AND EFFECT

Look for causes and effects of weathering.

Weathering

Earth is made up of rock. The rock on Earth's surface is always changing.

One kind of change is caused by weathering. **Weathering** happens when wind and water break rock into smaller pieces.

The smallest bits of rock are in the top layer. Layers below have larger and larger pieces of weathered rock. ▶

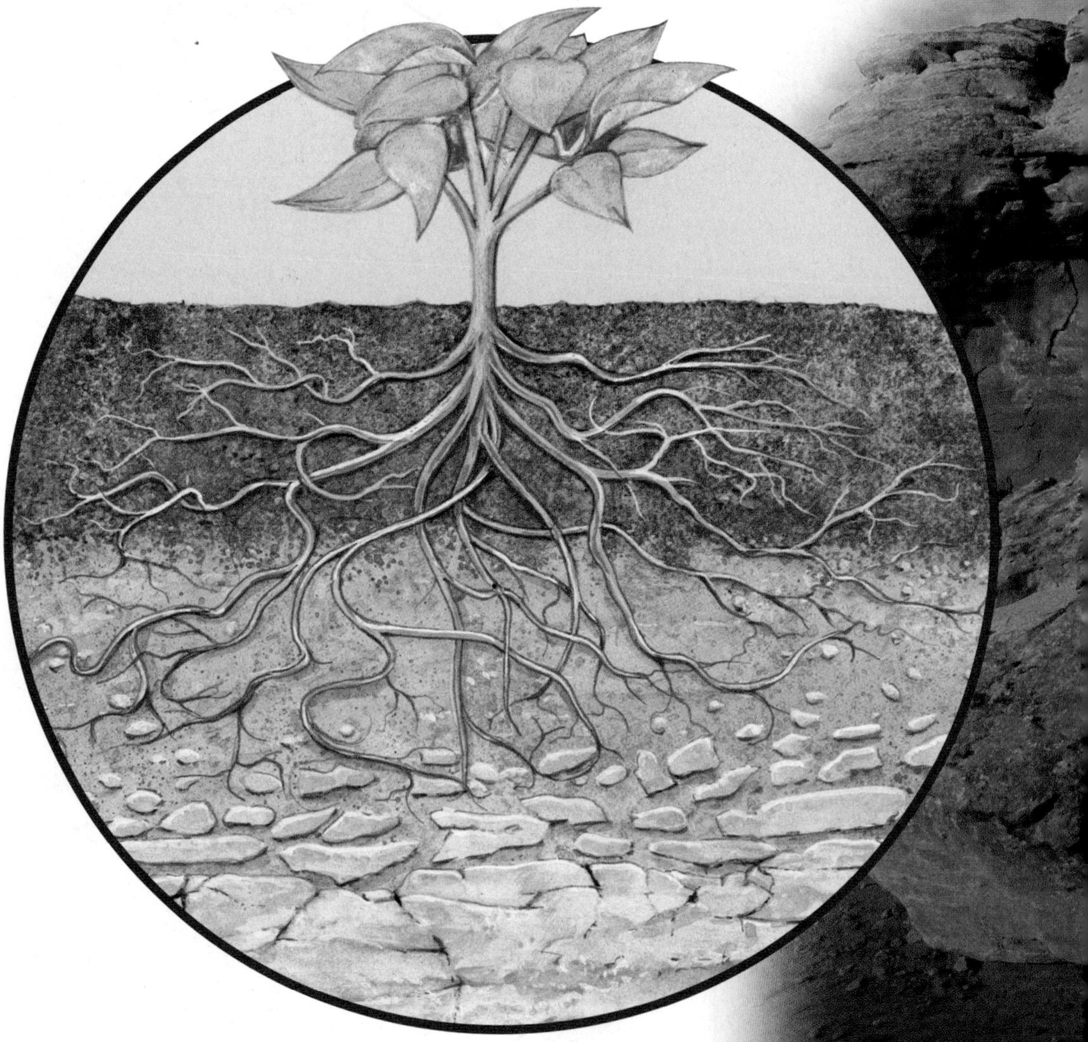

Water and wind weather all rock. But some rocks weather faster than others.

Some rocks have harder minerals. They weather very slowly. Other rocks have softer minerals. These rocks weather a little faster.

Focus Skill **CAUSE AND EFFECT** **What are two causes of weathering?**

Insta-Lab

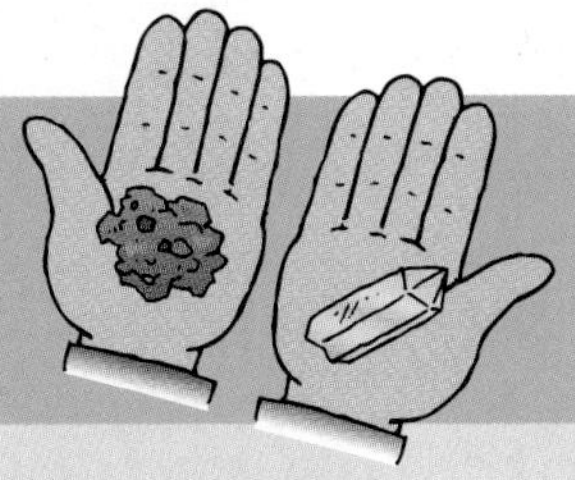

Making Rocks Change

Use a hand lens to observe two rocks. Record your observations. Rub the rocks together. Again, use a hand lens to observe the rocks. How did the rocks change? Why did they change?

natural sandstone archway

Weathering Causes Changes

Weathering can happen when water gets into the cracks of rocks. The water **freezes**, or becomes ice, when it gets cold enough. Ice takes up more space than water. So it pushes against the cracks. It makes the cracks bigger.

Then the ice thaws, or melts. More water gets into the cracks. This happens over and over. The rocks can break into pieces.

granite cracked by ice

roots of juniper tree pushing through cracks in rock

Plant roots can also cause weathering. The roots of some plants are very strong. As they grow down into the ground, they may push into cracks in rocks. They can even split a rock.

Focus Skill **CAUSE AND EFFECT** **How can ice and plant roots cause weathering?**

Weathering harmed this stonework.

Artists repaired the stonework.

Things in the Air Cause Weathering

Some things in the air cause weathering. Water causes the most weathering. Water mixes with other things in the air and rock. Then many kinds of changes happen. These changes weather rock. Often, this kind of weathering will cause the rock to change color.

Sometimes smoke is in the air. Water mixes with gases in the smoke. The mixture weathers some kinds of rock. It eats away some of the minerals in the rock.

Focus Skill **CAUSE AND EFFECT** **How does water cause weathering?**

This stonework was harmed by weathering.

Standards Wrap-Up and Lesson Review

Essential Question

What happens as rock weathers?

In this lesson, you learned that small rocks come from the weathering of larger rocks. Water, wind, and other things cause weathering.

Science Content Standard in This Lesson

3.b *Students know* smaller rocks come from the breakage and weathering of larger rocks.

1. Focus Skill **CAUSE AND EFFECT** Make a chart like this one. Show the causes of weathering. **3.b**

cause → effect

2. **SUMMARIZE** Write a lesson summary. Begin with the sentence **Weathering causes changes.** **3.b**

3. **VOCABULARY** Use the term **weathering** to tell about this picture. **3.b**

4. **Investigation** When is it helpful to use a hand lens and forceps? **4.f**

5. Which of these gets weathered by moving water or wind? **3.b**

A all rocks
B only softer rocks
C only harder rocks
D no rocks

The Big Idea

6. What causes weathering? **3.b**

Writing — ELA–W 1.1

Write to Describe

1. Find a picture in this lesson that shows weathering.
2. Write a few sentences about the picture. Do not tell which picture it is.
3. Ask a classmate to read the sentences and find the picture you described.

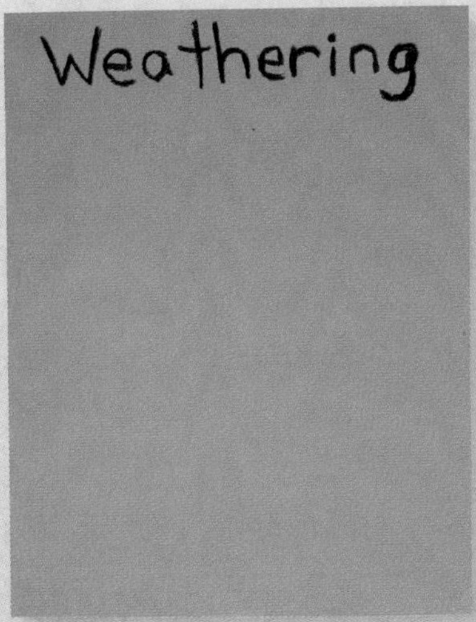

Math — MG 1.3

Measuring Water

1. Half-fill a small plastic cup with water. Mark the water line. Use a ruler to measure the height. Record.
2. Put the cup in a freezer. Wait until the water freezes.
3. Mark the ice line. Measure and record its height. Is it the same, higher, or lower?
4. How does this show why some weathering happens?

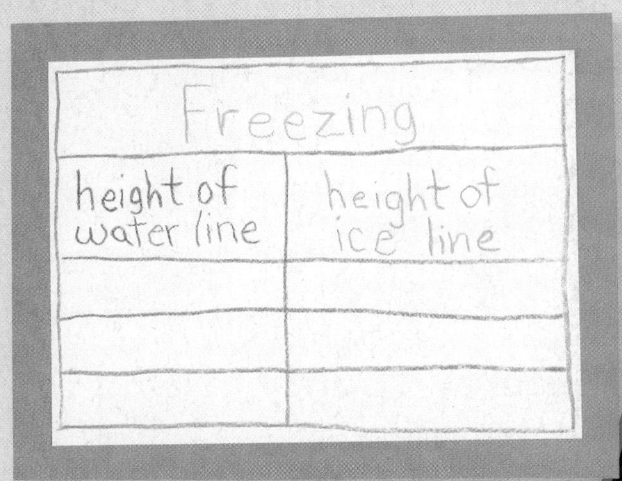

For more links and activities, go to **www.hspscience.com**

California Standards in This Lesson

Science Content

3.c *Students know* that soil is made partly from weathered rock and partly from organic materials and that soils differ in their color, texture, capacity to retain water, and ability to support the growth of many kinds of plants.

Investigation and Experimentation

4.b Measure length, weight, temperature, and liquid volume with appropriate tools and express those measurements in standard metric system units.

LESSON 3

Essential Question

How Are Kinds of Soil Different?

California Fast Fact

Monterey County

California is known for its lettuce. Much of it grows in Monterey County. The soil in Monterey County is very rich. That is one reason lettuce grows so well here.

Vocabulary Preview

Soil is made of small bits of rock mixed with material that was once living. p. 254

Humus is plant and animal material in soil. p. 254

After things die, they **rot**, or fall apart. p. 254

Investigate

Comparing Kinds of Soil

Directed Inquiry

Ask a Question

Why do you think plants can grow well in this soil?

▼ orange grove

Get Ready

Investigation Skill Tip
You can use a measuring cup to measure the amount of a liquid.

You Need

cup of sandy soil in a filter

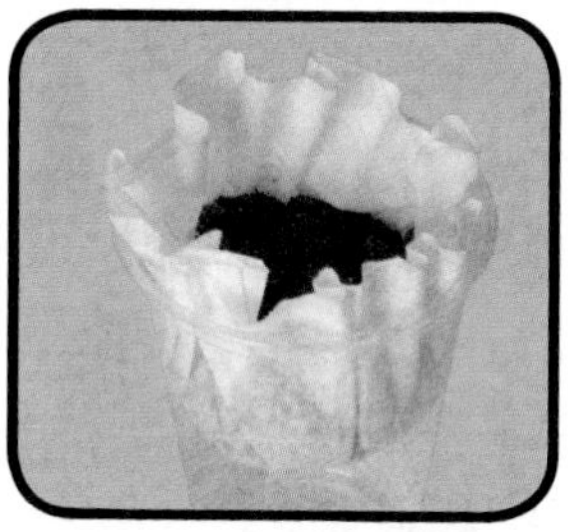

cup of potting soil in a filter

measuring cup

water

What to Do

Step 1

Pour one cup of water over the potting soil.

Step 2

Pour one cup of water over the sandy soil. **Measure** the water that comes through each filter.

Step 3

Record and compare the amounts.

Independent Inquiry

Repeat the investigation. Use a different kind of soil. **Compare** the amount of water that comes through with the amounts for the first two kinds of soil. 3.c

Draw Conclusions

What did you learn about these two kinds of soil? 3.c

3.c

VOCABULARY
soil
rot
humus

COMPARE AND CONTRAST

Look for ways kinds of soil are alike and different.

Soil

Soil is made of bits of rock mixed with material that was once living. This material may be parts of dead plants or animals.

It takes a long time for soil to form. Wind and rain can weather rock. Over time, the pieces break down into tiny grains of sand. These grains form part of the soil.

Humus is plant and animal material in soil. Parts of dead plants and animals **rot**, or fall apart. The rotted bits become part of the soil.

Animals live in soil. They dig tunnels and move about in them. When they dig and move, they mix the soil.

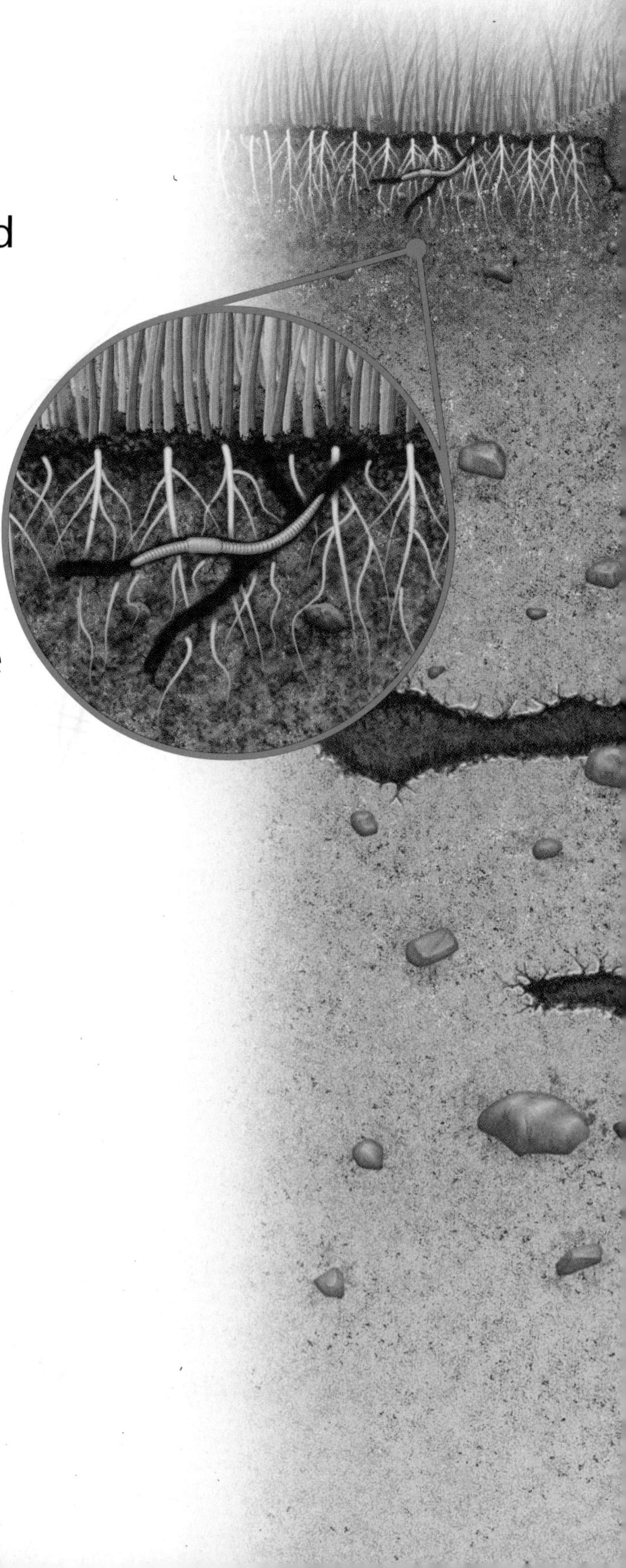

COMPARE AND CONTRAST **Compare how rock, plant material, and animal material break down to form soil.**

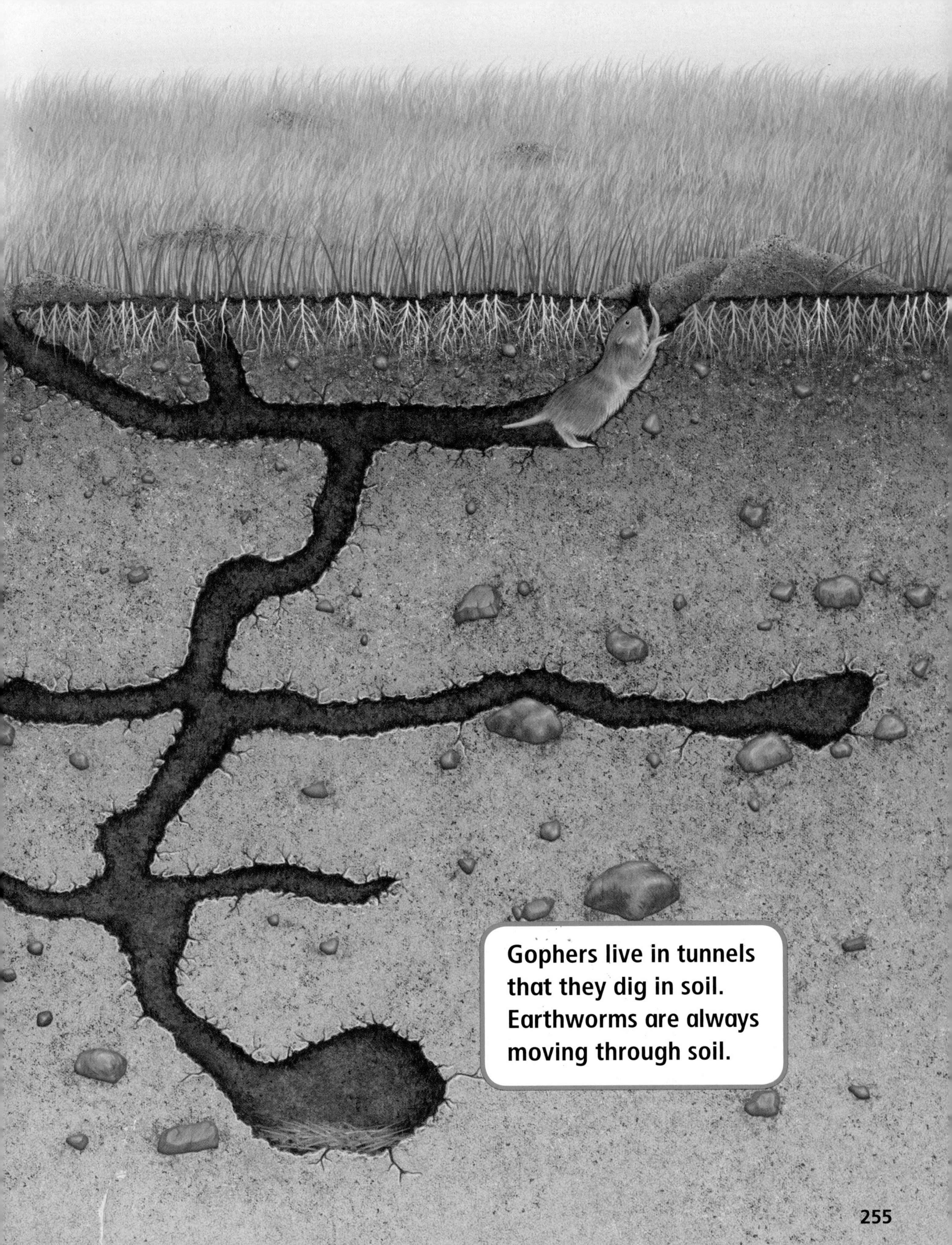

Gophers live in tunnels that they dig in soil. Earthworms are always moving through soil.

Clay

Clay is smooth when it is dry. It is sticky when it is wet.

Silt

Silt is smooth and powdery.

Humus

Humus is brown and soft. It holds water well. It is made up of once-living material.

Sand

Sand grains are rough. They are larger than grains of silt or clay.

Kinds of Soil

There are many kinds of soil. Each kind is made up of different materials. Soil may have clay, silt, sand, or humus in it. Each kind of soil has different properties.

Color is a property of soil. Soil may be dark or light. Dark soil has a lot of humus in it. Light soil is mostly sand. The red color of some soil comes from rocks that have a lot of iron in them.

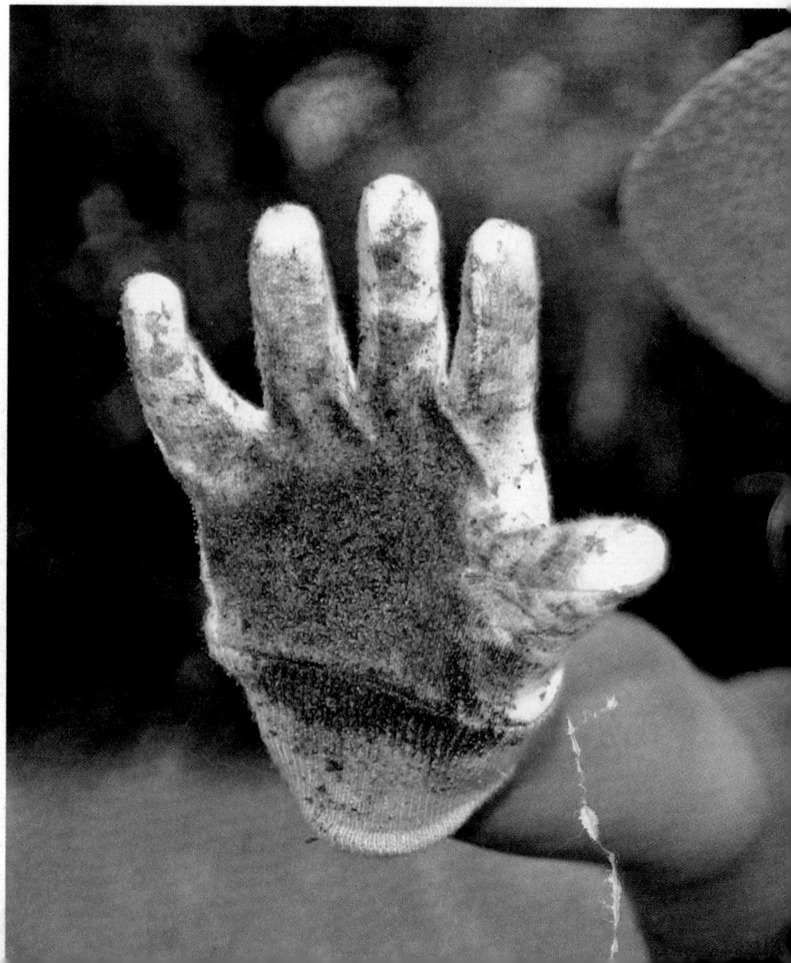

Texture is another property of soil. Sand feels grainy. Dry silt feels powdery. Wet clay feels sticky. Humus feels crumbly.

Kinds of soil are also different in how they hold in water. Clay holds in a lot of water. Sand and silt hold in less water. Humus in soil acts like a sponge. It helps the soil hold water. Plants that need more water grow well in soil that has a lot of this kind of material.

Focus Skill **COMPARE AND CONTRAST**

How are kinds of soil alike? How are they different?

Insta-Lab

A Closer Look at Soil

Use a hand lens to observe some soil. What do you see? Work with a classmate to compare observations.

Soil for Growing Things

Soil holds the roots of plants in place. This helps plants get water and nutrients.

You have learned that some kinds of soil hold water better than other kinds. It is easier for plants to get water from some kinds of soil. So some plants grow better in one kind of soil, and some grow better in another kind of soil.

corn growing in soil with a lot of clay

lettuce growing in humus

Plants need nutrients to grow and to stay healthy. Plants get nutrients from the soil. Different kinds of soil have different kinds of nutrients. They are good for different plants.

Soil that has a lot of humus has many nutrients. Most kinds of plants grow better when they have more nutrients.

cotton growing in silt

Focus Skill COMPARE AND CONTRAST **How can one kind of soil be better than another for growing plants?**

plants growing in sand

Essential Question

How are kinds of soil different?

In this lesson, you learned that soil is made of plant and animal material and bits of rock. You also learned that kinds of soil are different from one another.

Science Content Standards in This Lesson

3.c *Students know* that soil is made partly from weathered rock and partly from organic materials and that soils differ in their color, texture, capacity to retain water, and ability to support the growth of many kinds of plants.

1. Focus Skill **COMPARE AND CONTRAST** Make a chart like this one. Show how kinds of soil are the same and different from one another. **3.c**

   alike — different

2. **SUMMARIZE** Write a summary. Begin with the sentence **Soil is made of different things**. **3.c**

3. **VOCABULARY** Use the terms **soil** and **texture** to tell about the picture. **3.c**

4. **Critical Thinking** What kind of soil is best for growing plants? **3.c**

   A red soil with iron in it
   B powdery soil with silt in it
   C dark soil with a lot of humus in it
   D light soil that is mostly sand

5. How do earthworms affect soil? **3.c**

The Big Idea

6. What are some properties of soil? **3.c**

Writing ELA–W 1.1

Write to Describe

1. Observe two kinds of soil.
2. Draw a picture of each kind of soil. Show and label the things you see in the soil.
3. Write sentences to compare the different kinds of soil.

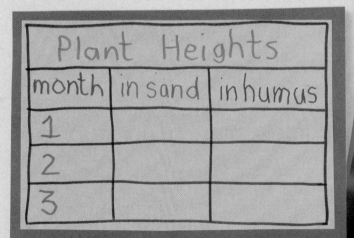

Math SDAP 1.1, 1.2

Plant Growth Bar Graph

1. Plant one bean plant in sandy soil. Plant another in soil that has humus in it. Care for both plants.
2. Once a month, measure the plants in centimeters.
3. Make a chart. Record your data.
4. Use your chart to make a bar graph.

Plant Heights

month	in sand	in humus
1		
2		
3		

For more links and activities, go to **www.hspscience.com**

Tomato says "Pass the Salt!"

According to experts, a large amount of United States farmland is too salty. They say that each year, about 101,000 square kilometers (38,000 square miles) of U.S. farmland cannot be used. The soil has too much salt.

Most plants can't grow in soil that has too much salt. Scientists have now made a new kind of tomato that grows well in salty soil. The plant can even be watered with salty water.

A New Kind of Plant

Scientists have figured out a way to change how a tomato plant grows. The change lets the tomato plant absorb salty water. The plant stores salt in its leaves, where it will not harm the plant or the fruit.

The scientists who grew the special tomatoes are also working on making other plants that can live in salty soil.

Think and Write

How might farmers be helped if plants can grow in salty soil?

Salt of the Earth

Scientists say that plants like corn, wheat, and peas could all be changed so that they can grow in salty soil.

California Standards in This Lesson

LESSON 4

Science Content

3.d *Students know* that fossils provide evidence about the plants and animals that lived long ago and that scientists learn about the past history of Earth by studying fossils.

Investigation and Experimentation

4.d Write or draw descriptions of a sequence of steps, events, and observations.

Essential Question

What Do Scientists Learn from Fossils?

California Fast Fact

Marble Mountains

Different kinds of fossils can be found in the rock of Latham Shale at Marble Mountains. Trilobites are the most common fossils found there.

Vocabulary Preview

A **dinosaur** is an animal that lived on Earth long ago. p. 268

A **fossil** is what is left of an animal or a plant that lived long ago. A fossil can be a print in a rock. It can be a bone, a tooth, or a shell that has turned to rock. p. 268

Investigate

Uncovering Fossils

Directed Inquiry

Ask a Question

Why do scientists look for and study fossils?

Get Ready

Investigation Skill Tip
You can share what you know when you record what you discover.

These scientists are digging out fossils. ▼

You Need

small objects

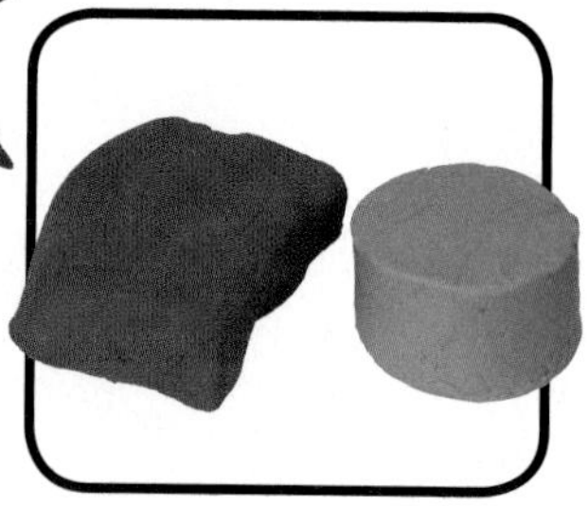

clay

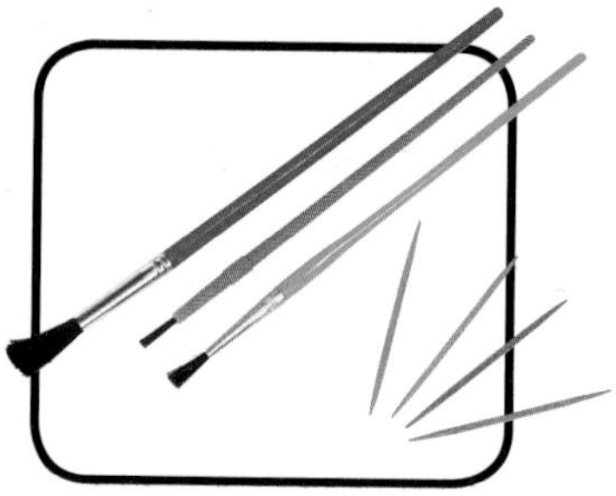

tools

What to Do

Step 1

Place a small object inside a ball of clay. Let the clay get hard.

Step 2

Trade balls of clay with a classmate. Use tools to gently remove the clay.

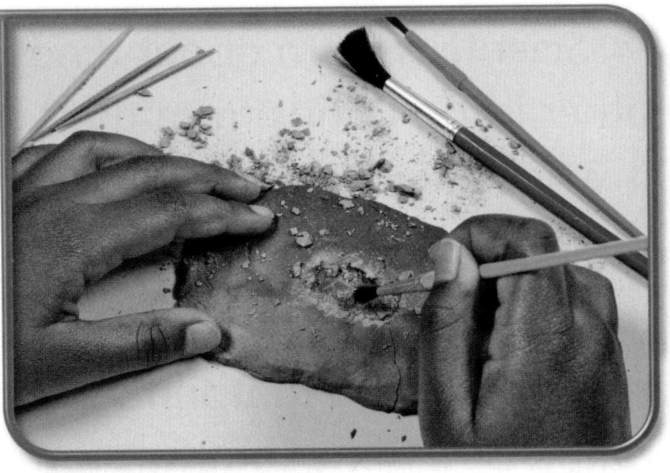

Step 3

Draw pictures and write sentences to **record** what you did and what you observed.

Independent Inquiry

Use small objects to leave prints in clay. Draw pictures and write sentences to **record** what you do and what you observe. 4.d

Draw Conclusions

Why is it helpful to record your findings? 4.d

3.d

VOCABULARY
dinosaur
fossil

Focus Skill SEQUENCE

Look for the sequence, or order, of events in the forming of fossils.

Fossils

Dinosaurs were animals that lived on Earth long ago. No dinosaurs live on Earth now.

Scientists learn about dinosaurs and other living things from their fossils. A **fossil** is what is left of an animal or a plant that lived long ago.

Fossils are found in rock. A fossil can be a print, such as a footprint. It can be a shell, a tooth, or a bone that has turned to rock.

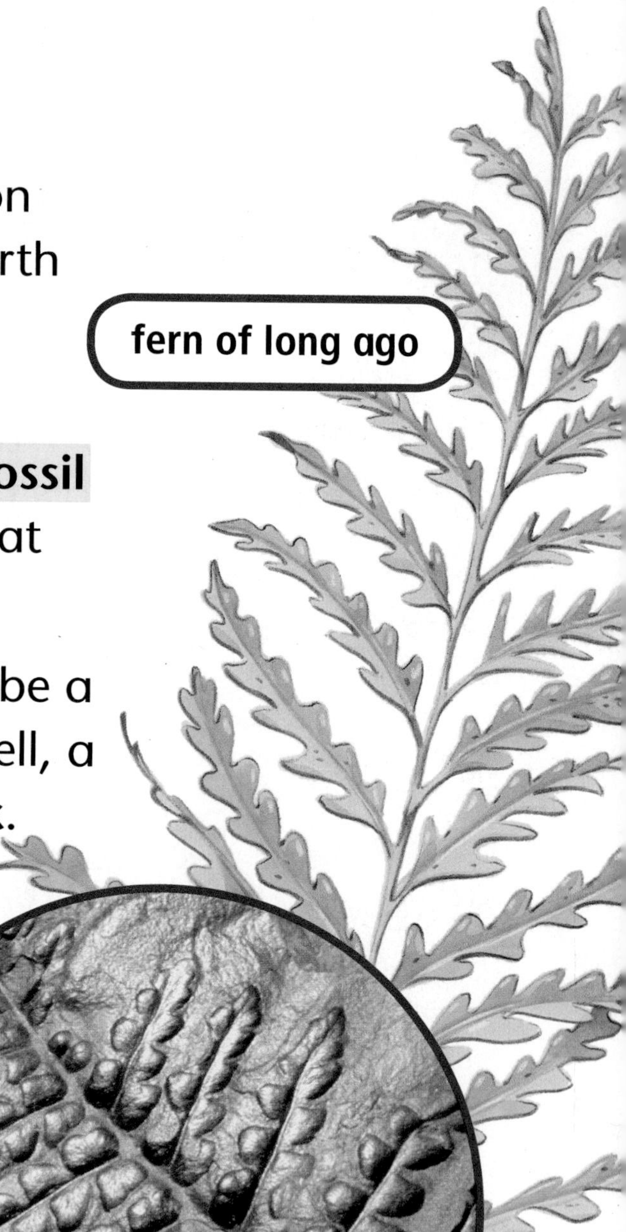

fern of long ago

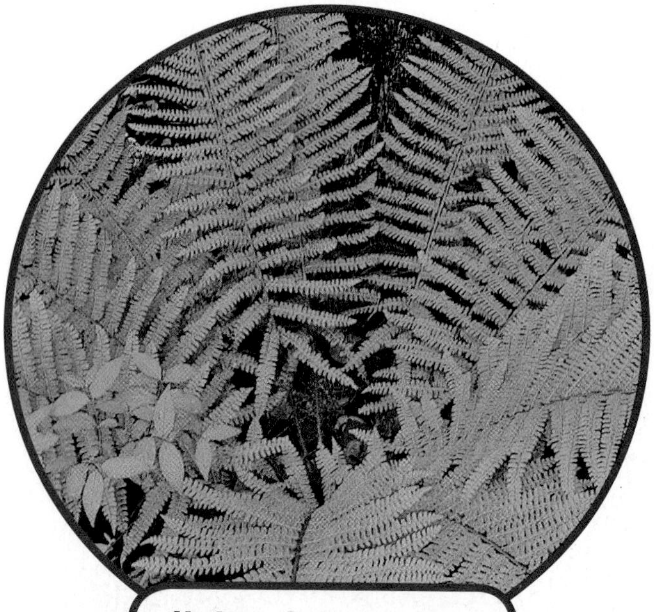

living fern today

fern fossil print in rock

Scientists observe fossils. They see how they are like and different from plants and animals of today. In this way, scientists learn about the plants and animals of long ago.

Fossils show the sizes of plants and animals. They can show how animals moved. Some fossils show what animals ate.

Focus Skill SEQUENCE What happened to some living things of long ago after they died?

▲ California mountain lion

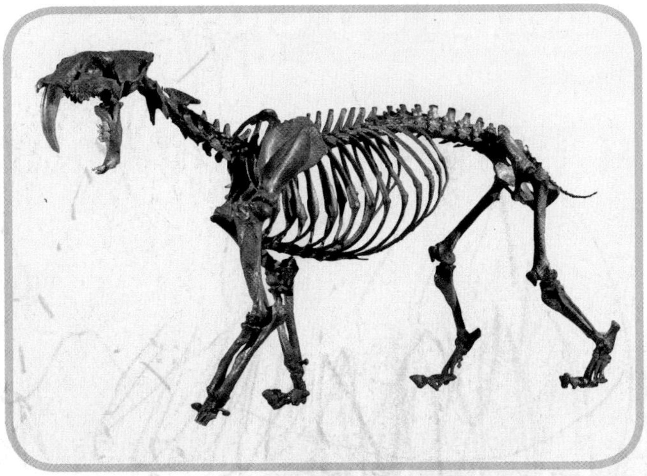

▲ fossil of saber-toothed cat

saber-toothed cat of long ago ▶

How Fossils Form

Fossils form when plants and animals are buried in mud, clay, or sand. The soft parts of the plant or animal rot away. The hard parts turn to rock. The fossils may be found many, many years later.

Science Up Close

A Trilobite Fossil Forms

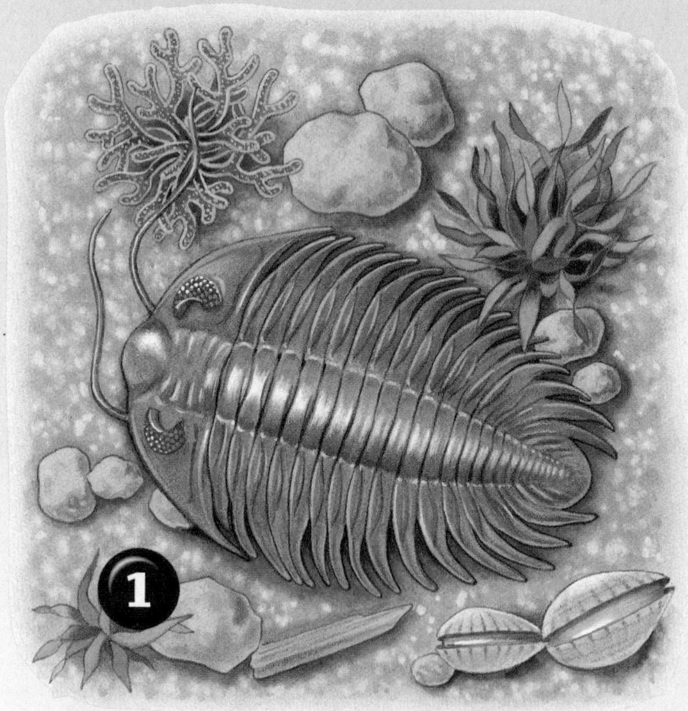

First, a trilobite died. Mud and sand covered the trilobite.

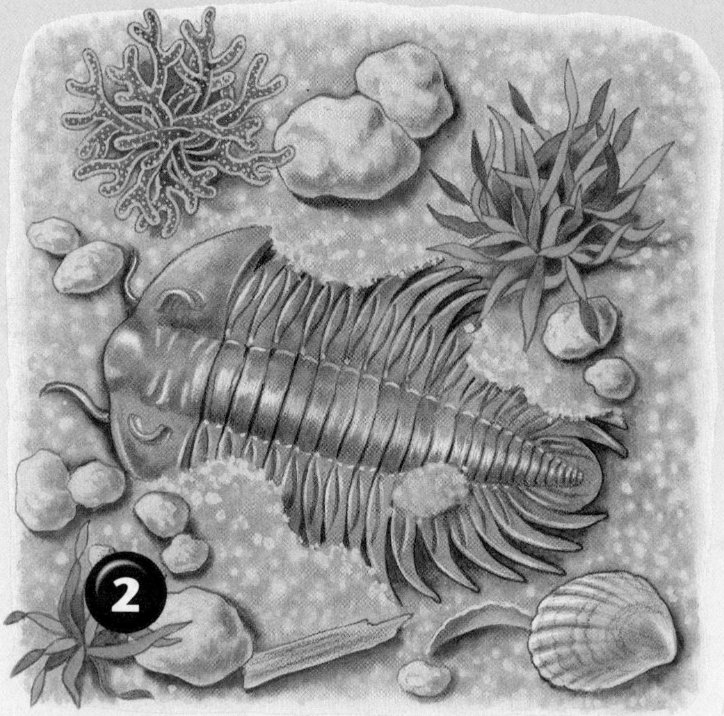

Next, the trilobite's soft parts rotted away. Its shell and other hard parts stayed.

A trilobite was an animal. It lived in the sea long ago. A shell covered its body. The pictures show how its fossil formed.

Focus Skill SEQUENCE **What happened after mud and sand covered a trilobite?**

Insta-Lab

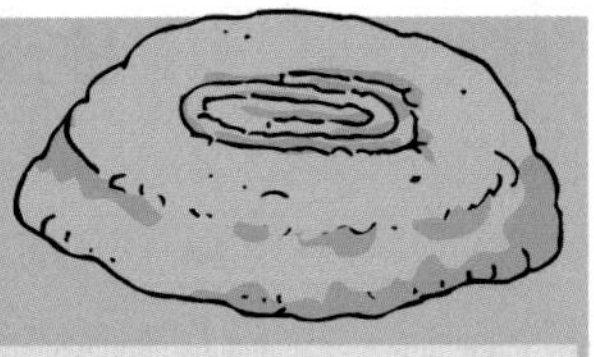

Make a Print in Clay

Flatten four pieces of clay. Press a different object into each one. Remove the objects. Trade some prints with a classmate. What object made each print fossil?

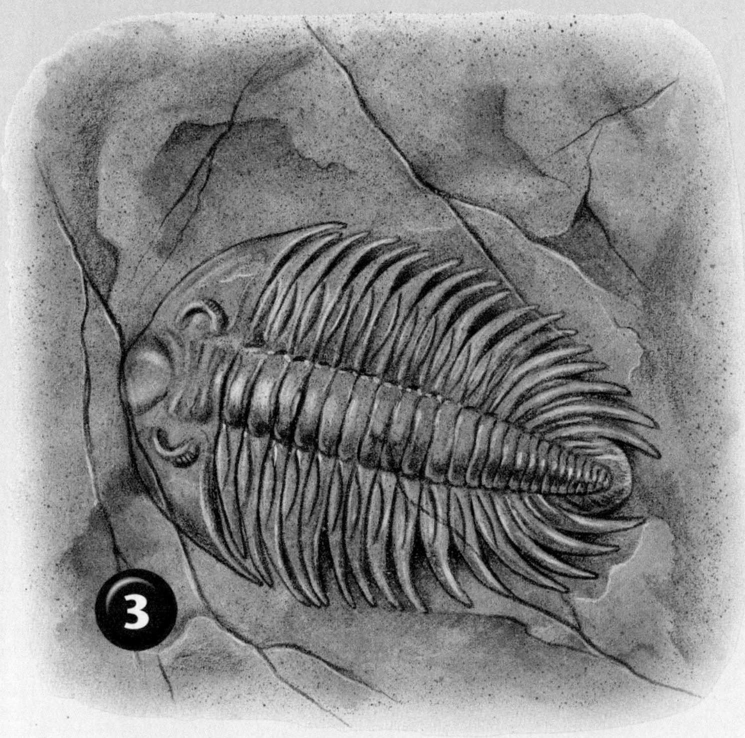

Then, the mud, the sand, and the hard parts of the trilobite slowly turned to rock.

Last, after many, many years, the rock that covered the fossil was removed by wind and water, and the fossil could be found.

For more links and animations, go to **www.hspscience.com**

What We Learn from Fossils

Scientists can learn a lot about Earth's history by studying fossils and the rocks where they were found.

pterodactyl ▶

stegosaurus

fossil of pterodactyl

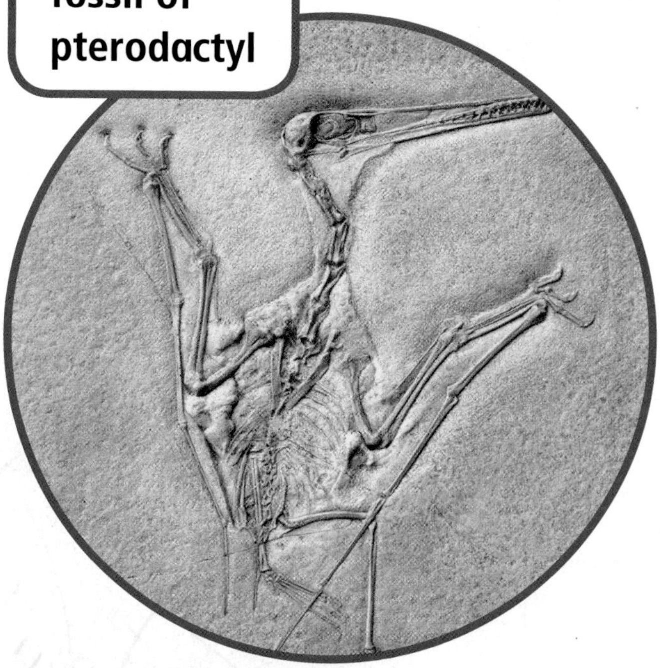

▼ fossil of stegosaurus

Eogyrinus needed to live where water was near land. The eogyrinus fossil below was found high in the mountains. This tells scientists that what is now mountains was once down near water.

Focus Skill **SEQUENCE** **What can scientists find out from fossils about Earth's history?**

eogyrinus

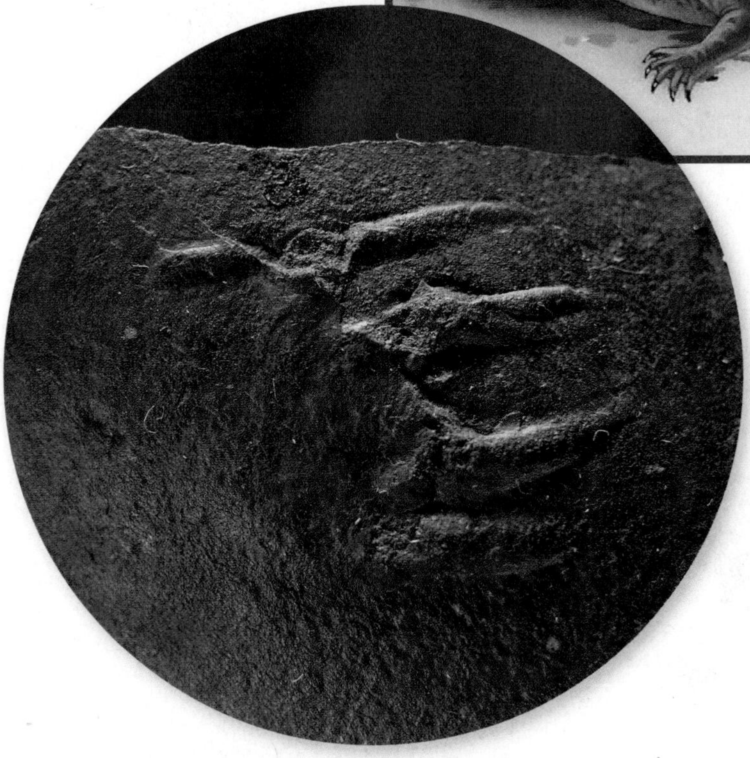

◀ **eogyrinus footprint**

Standards Wrap-Up and Lesson Review

Essential Question

What do scientists learn from fossils?

In this lesson, you learned that scientists learn about plants and animals that lived long ago by studying fossils.

Science Content Standards in This Lesson

3.d *Students know* that fossils provide evidence about the plants and animals that lived long ago and that scientists learn about the past history of Earth by studying fossils.

1. **Focus Skill SEQUENCE** Make a chart like this one. Show how some fossils are formed. **3.d**

   [ ] → [ ] → [ ]

2. **SUMMARIZE** Write a lesson summary about fossils. **3.d**

3. **VOCABULARY** Use the term **fossil** to tell about this picture. **3.d**

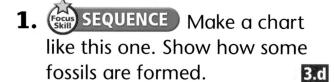

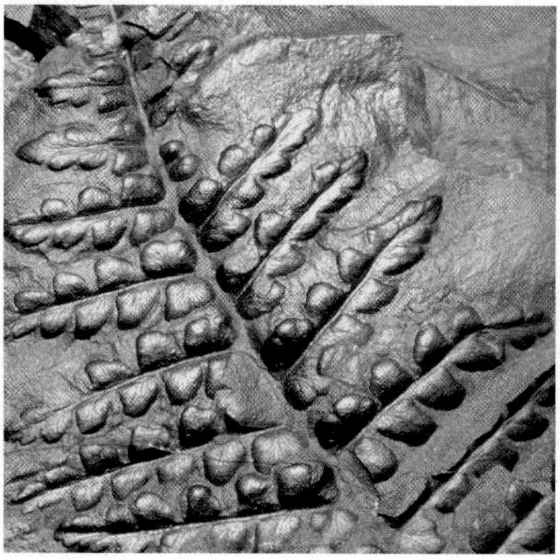

4. **Investigation** Why is it important for scientists to record what they do and what they observe? **4.d**

5. Which animal lives today? **3.d**
   A mountain lion
   B pterodactyl
   C saber-toothed cat
   D stegosaurus

The Big Idea

6. Why is it useful to study fossils? **3.d**

Writing — ELA–W 1.1

Write to Describe

1. Observe fossils. Compare them with animals and plants that live today.
2. Draw a picture of a fossil. Then draw an animal or a plant, like the fossil, that lives today.
3. Describe how they are alike and different.

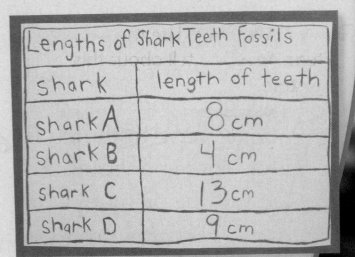

Math — MG 1.3

Shark Teeth Sizes

1. Look at the data in the chart.
2. Use a centimeter ruler to measure how long a tooth is from each shark.
3. Then list the sharks in order from the one with the smallest teeth to the one with the largest teeth.
4. Compare results.

Lengths of Shark Teeth Fossils

shark	length of teeth
shark A	8 cm
shark B	4 cm
shark C	13 cm
shark D	9 cm

For more links and activities, go to **www.hspscience.com**

THE LA BREA TAR PITS

At the La Brea Tar Pits, you can see the bones of many animals. Some are bones from animals of today. Others are fossils of bones from animals of long ago. Many are from saber-toothed cats. Others are from mammoths and birds.

Long ago, animals came here to drink water from pools on the tar. When the weather was warm, the tar became sticky. The animals walked toward the water. They sank into the tar. Some were able to pull themselves out. Many could not get out. More than one million bones have been dug from the tar. These bones tell us much about the animals of long ago.

◀ Visitors can watch as paleontologists clean and repair fossil bones from the tar pits.

Think and Write

How do the La Brea Tar Pits help us learn about animals of long ago? 3.d

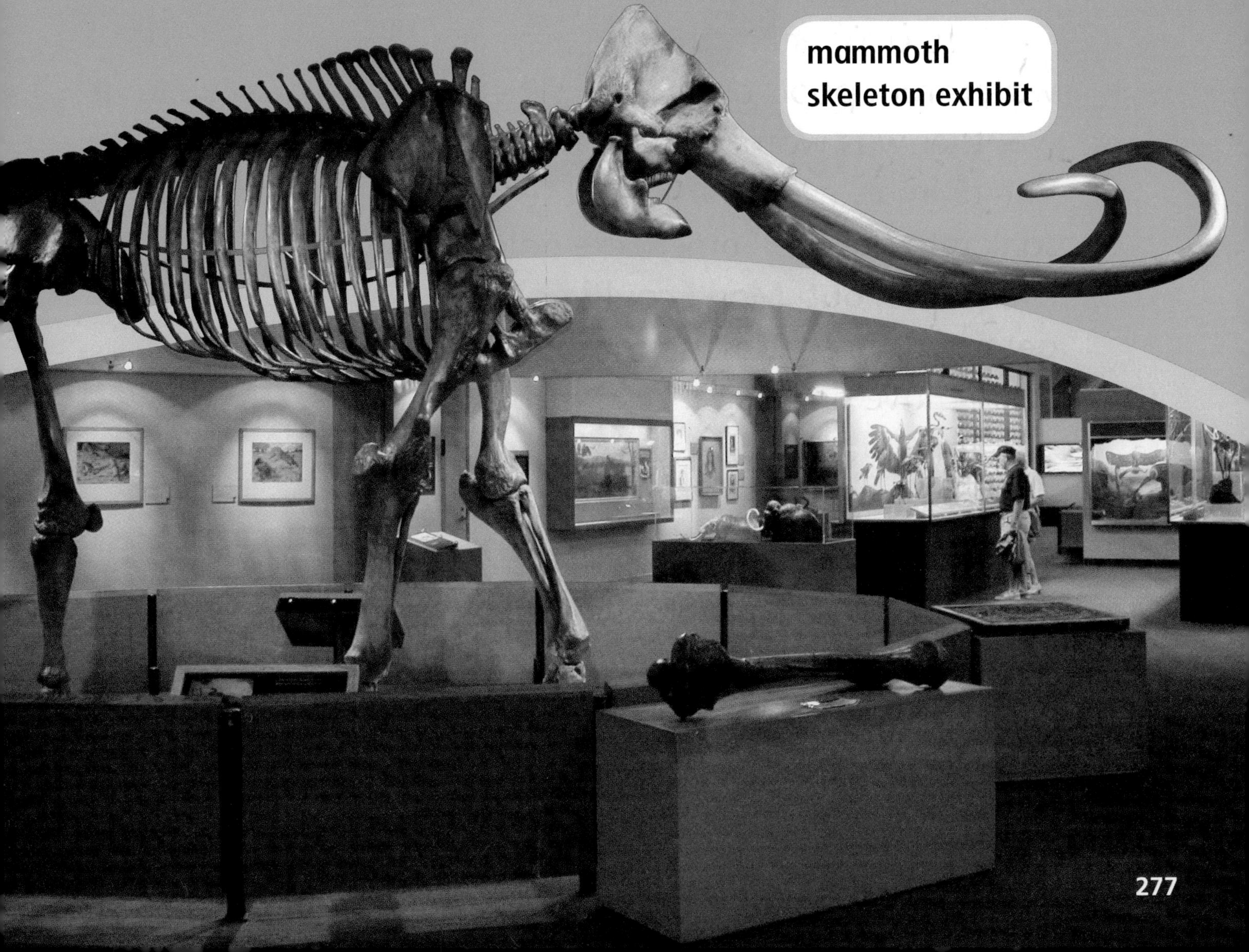

mammoth skeleton exhibit

California Standards in This Lesson

Science Content

3.e *Students know* rock, water, plants, and soil provide many resources, including food, fuel, and building materials, that humans use.

Investigation and Experimentation

4.e Construct bar graphs to record data, using appropriately labeled axes.

LESSON 5

Essential Question

What Are Natural Resources?

California Fast Fact

Lake Tahoe

Lake Tahoe contains twice the amount of water that is in all other California lakes and reservoirs together.

Vocabulary Preview

A **natural resource** is anything from nature that people can use to meet their needs. p. 282

Ways We Use Water

Directed Inquiry

Ask a Question

Why do you think farmers use sprinklers to water their crops?

Get Ready

Investigation Skill Tip

When you record data, it is easier to remember what you observe.

You Need

paper and pencil

What to Do

Step 1

List the ways you and your classmates use water in one day.

Step 2

Record the data in a chart like this one. Make a mark each time someone uses water.

Ways Our Class Uses Water in One Day	
Way	Tally
washing hands	

Step 3

Count the marks at the end of the day.

Independent Inquiry

Make a different chart. **Record** how often your class uses things that are made from plants. Then use your chart to make a bar graph that shows your data. Label the parts of your bar graph. 4.e

Draw Conclusions

For what did your class use water most often? 3.e

3.e

VOCABULARY
natural resource

Focus Skill **MAIN IDEA AND DETAILS**

Look for details about how people use natural resources.

Water

A **natural resource** is something from nature that people can use. Natural resources help people meet their needs.

Water is a natural resource. People drink water. They use it to bathe, cook, and clean. They also use it to grow plants and raise animals. People have fun doing water activities.

People use boats to travel on water. They also use boats to move things from place to place.

People also get electricity by using moving water.

Focus Skill **MAIN IDEA AND DETAILS** **How do people use water?**

copper mine

copper ore

Rocks and Soil

Rocks and soil are two important natural resources. People use rocks to build things, such as houses, walls, and roads.

People get metals, such as copper, from ores, which contain minerals. Ores are found in rocks in the ground. People dig up an ore and then get the metal out of it. Metal is used to make things such as pots, bikes, and cars. It is used for building as well.

▲ **copper roof**

▲ **rocks used for building**

People use soil to grow plants. Soil holds plants in place. It also has nutrients and water that plants need to grow.

Clay is made up of tiny bits of rock. People use clay for building. They shape the clay into bricks or blocks. The clay bricks or blocks are dried until they are hard. Then people use them to make buildings and other things.

Focus Skill MAIN IDEA AND DETAILS **How do people use rocks and soil?**

brick wall

▼ strawberries

Plants and Animals

Plants are another important natural resource. People use parts of cotton and other plants to make cloth. They use wood from trees to build houses and to make furniture and paper.

People use plants as fuel. They may burn tree branches or logs cut from trees.

People also use plants for food. They eat some plant parts. They use other plant parts to make foods such as bread. Some drinks, such as tea, are made from plants.

▲ cotton bolls on plant

Some people use animals to meet their needs for food and clothing. They eat the meat of some animals. They drink milk from cows or goats. People also use milk to make foods such as cheese. People eat eggs from chickens. They use wool from sheep to make warm clothing. They use leather to make shoes and other things.

Focus Skill **MAIN IDEA AND DETAILS** **How do people use plants and animals?**

Insta-Lab

List Natural Resources

Make a list of things in your classroom that are made from natural resources. Share your list with a classmate. What natural resources were used to make each thing?

Standards Wrap-Up and Lesson Review

Essential Question

What are natural resources?

In this lesson, you learned that people use resources that come from rocks, water, plants, and soil. People use these things for food, fuel, and building materials.

Science Content Standards in This Lesson

3.e *Students know* rock, water, plants, and soil provide many resources, including food, fuel, and building materials, that humans use.

1. **MAIN IDEA AND DETAILS** Make a chart like this one. Show the details for the main idea **We use natural resources.** 3.e

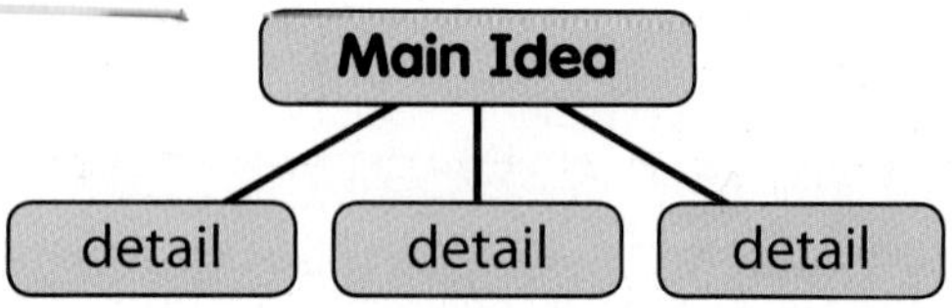

2. **DRAW CONCLUSIONS** Why might rock be a better building material than wood? 3.e

3. **VOCABULARY** Use the term **natural resource** to tell about this picture. 3.e

4. **Critical Thinking** Why is it important to protect natural resources? 3.e

5. Which natural resource is used for fuel? 3.e

   A plants
   B rocks
   C soil
   D water

The Big Idea

6. How do we use natural resources? 3.e

Writing ELA–W 1.1

Write to Describe

1. Draw and label a picture of a plant or another natural resource found in California.
2. Write a few facts about the natural resource. Tell how people use it.
3. Share your facts with classmates.

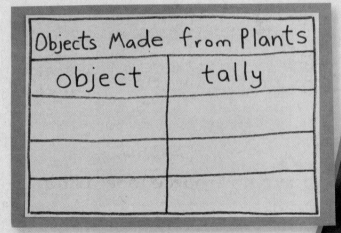

Math SDAP 1.1, 1.2

Natural Resource Bar Graph

1. List classroom objects that are made from plants.
2. Make a tally chart. Record how many times you use each of these objects.
3. Use your tally chart to make a bar graph. Label the parts of your graph.
4. Share your results.

Objects Made from Plants

object	tally

For more links and activities, go to **www.hspscience.com**

UNIT 3 EARTH SCIENCE

Wrap-Up

Visual Summary

Tell how each picture helps explain the **Big Idea**.

The Big Idea **Earth is made up of materials that are different from one another. People use these materials.**

3.a

Rocks contain different minerals. The minerals have different properties. Color, texture, size, and shininess, or luster, are some properties of minerals.

3.b, 3.c

Wind, water, and plants weather rocks. Weathering breaks down rocks to form soil. Color and texture are properties of soil.

3.d

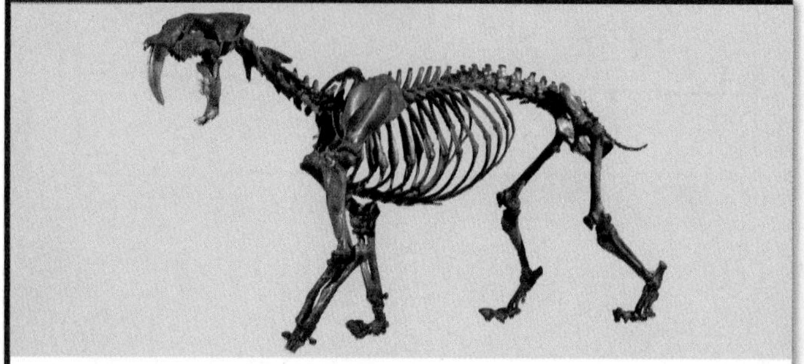

A fossil is what is left of a plant or an animal that lived long ago. Scientists study fossils.

3.e

Natural resources are things in nature that people use, such as water, soil, animals, and plants.

Show What You Know

Unit Writing Activity

Write About Fossils

Choose an animal that lived long ago. Find out where fossils of that animal can be found. What have scientists learned by studying this animal? Does it compare to an animal of today? Write sentences about what you learn. Draw pictures to go with your sentences. Share your writing and pictures with the class.

Unit Project

Rock and Mineral Collection

Go on an adventure to collect rocks and minerals. Gather as many as you can. Then go to a library or a media center and learn about your collection. Write two sentences about each rock or mineral. Bring in your collection and writing to share with the class.

UNIT 3 EARTH SCIENCE

Review

California Science Standards in ■

Vocabulary Review

Use the terms to complete the sentences. The page numbers tell you where to look if you need help.

mineral p. 229	**soil** p. 254
property p. 230	**fossil** p. 268
weathering p. 242	**natural resource** p. 282

1. The material made of small bits of rock mixed with dead plant parts is ______. 3.c
2. What is left of a plant or an animal that lived long ago is a ______. 3.d
3. The breaking down of rock by wind and water is ______. 3.b
4. Anything in nature that people can use to meet their needs is a ______. 3.e
5. A characteristic, or feature, of something is a ______. 3.a
6. A solid material, found in nature, that was never alive is a ______. 3.a

Check Understanding

7. What is the name of the dark brown material in soil that was once part of living things? **3.c**

A clay

B humus

C sand

D silt

8. How does this rock show the effects of weathering? **3.b**

Critical Thinking

9. What natural resources do you need to grow a plant? **3.e**

The Big Idea

10. What are two or three properties you can use to compare minerals? **3.a**

References

Contents

Your Senses

You have five senses that tell you about the world. Your five senses are sight, hearing, smell, taste, and touch.

Your Eyes

If you look at your eyes in a mirror, you will see an outer white part, a colored part called the iris, and a dark hole in the middle. This hole is called the pupil.

Inside of Eye

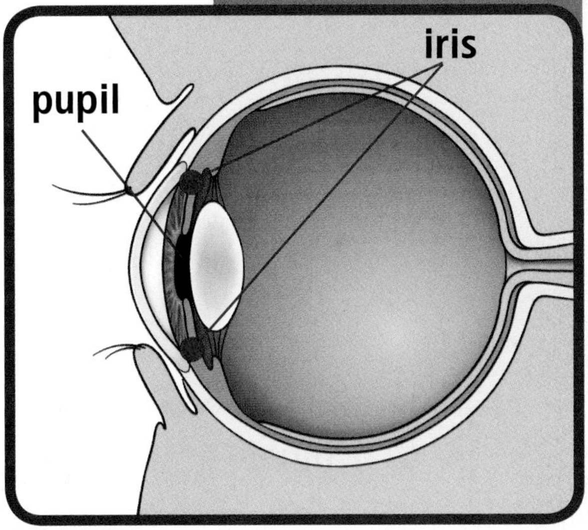

Caring for Your Eyes

- Have a doctor check your eyes to find out if they are healthy.
- Never look directly at the sun or at very bright lights.
- Wear sunglasses outdoors in bright sunlight and on snow and water.
- Don't touch or rub your eyes.
- Protect your eyes when you play sports.

Outside of Eye

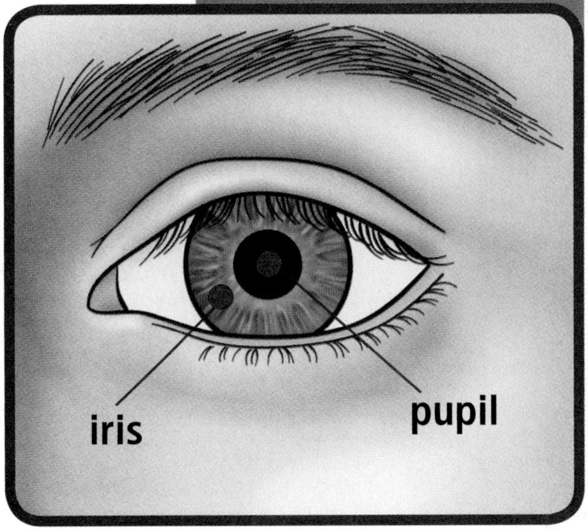

Your Ears

Your ears let you hear the things around you. You can see only a small part of the ear on the outside of your head. The parts of your ear inside your head are the parts that let you hear.

Caring for Your Ears

- Have a doctor check your ears.
- Avoid very loud noises.
- Never put anything in your ears.
- Protect your ears when you play sports.

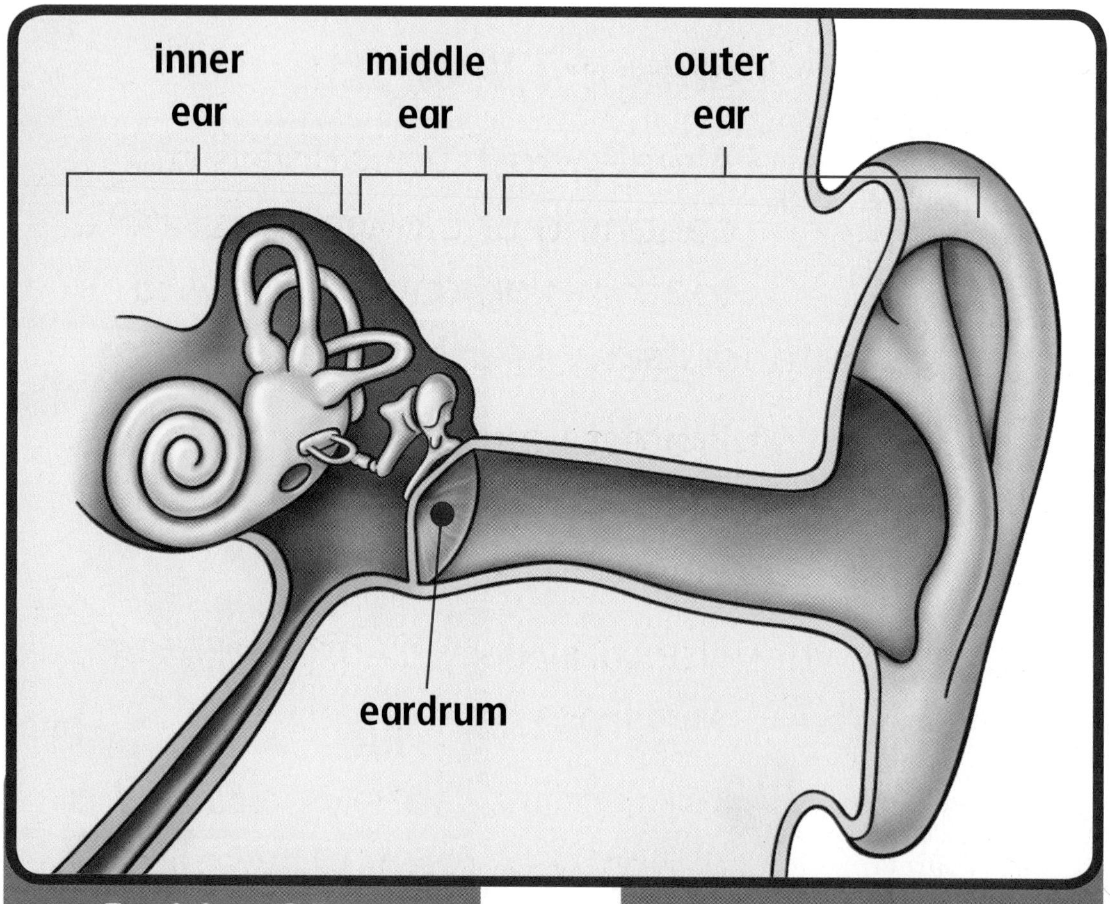

Inside of Ear

Outside of Ear

Your Senses of Smell and Taste

Your nose cleans the air you breathe and lets you smell things. Your nose and tongue help you taste things you eat and drink.

Your Skin

Your skin protects your body from germs. Your skin also gives you your sense of touch.

Caring for Your Skin

- Always wash your hands after coughing or blowing your nose, touching an animal, playing outside, or using the restroom.
- Protect your skin from sunburn. Wear a hat and clothes to cover your skin outdoors.
- Use sunscreen to protect your skin from the sun.
- Wear proper safety pads and a helmet when you play sports, ride a bike, or skate.

Your Skeletal System

Inside your body are many hard, strong bones. They form your skeletal system. The bones in your body protect parts inside your body.

Your skeletal system works with your muscular system to hold your body up and to give it shape.

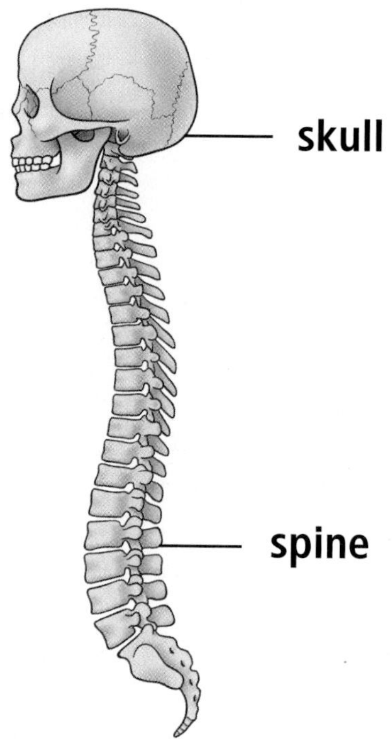

Caring for Your Skeletal System

- Always wear a helmet and other safety gear when you skate, ride a bike or a scooter, or play sports.
- Eat foods that help keep your bones strong and hard.
- Exercise to help your bones stay strong and healthy.
- Get plenty of rest to help your bones grow.

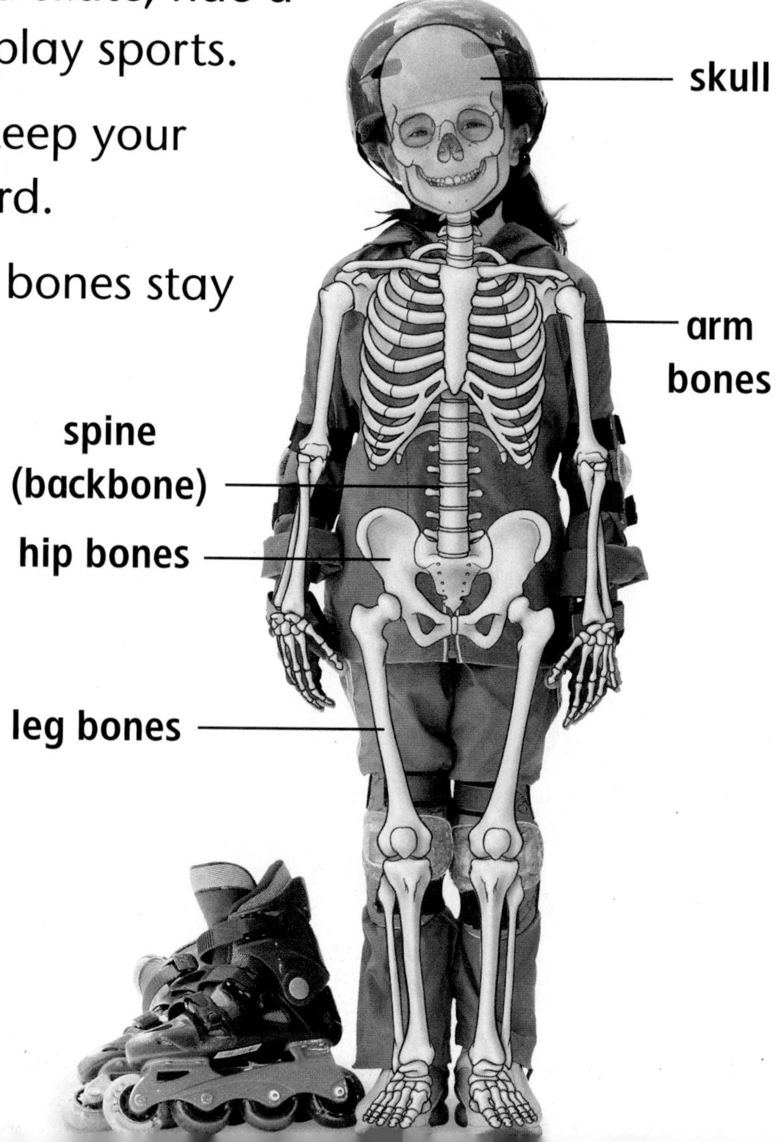

Your Muscular System

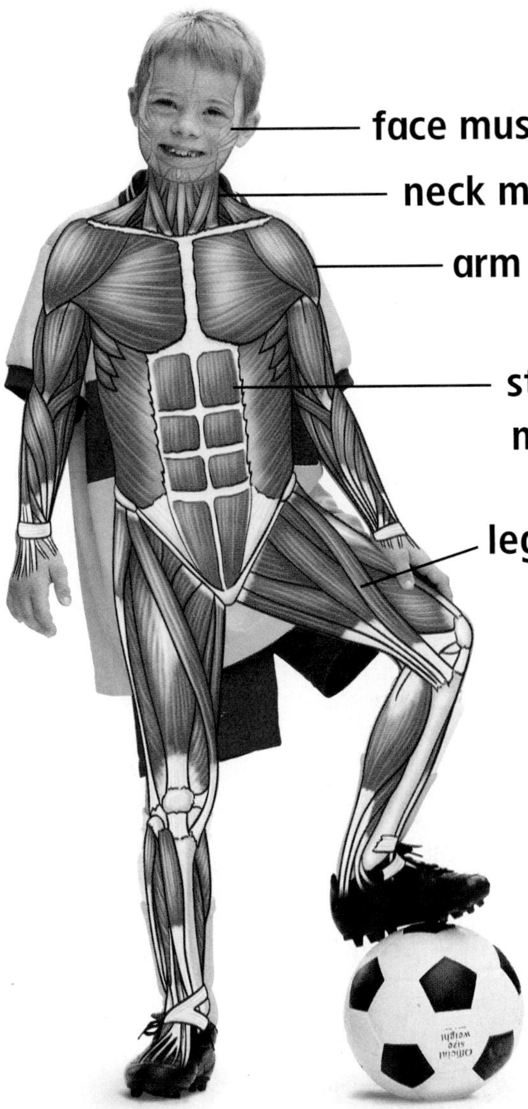

Your muscular system is made up of the muscles in your body. Muscles are body parts that help you move.

Caring for Your Muscular System

- Exercise to keep your muscles strong.
- Eat foods that will help your muscles grow.
- Drink plenty of water when you play sports or exercise.
- Rest your muscles after you exercise or play sports.

Your Nervous System

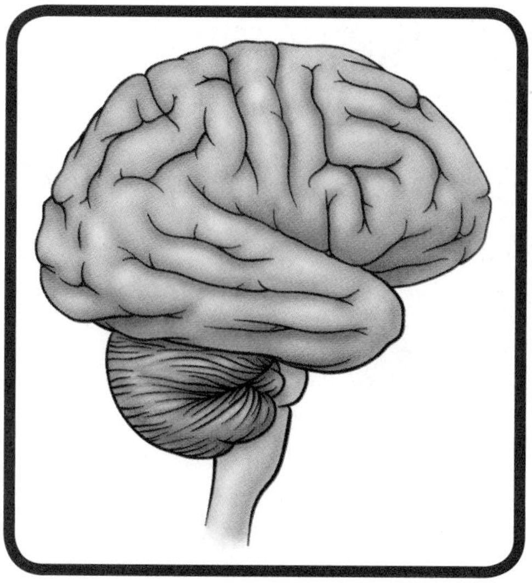

Your brain and your nerves are parts of your nervous system. Your brain keeps your body working. It tells you about the world around you. Your brain also lets you think, remember, and have feelings.

Caring for Your Nervous System

- Get plenty of sleep. Sleeping lets your brain rest.
- Always wear a helmet to protect your head and your brain when you ride a bike or play sports.

Your Digestive System

Your digestive system helps your body get energy from the foods you eat. Your body needs energy to do things.

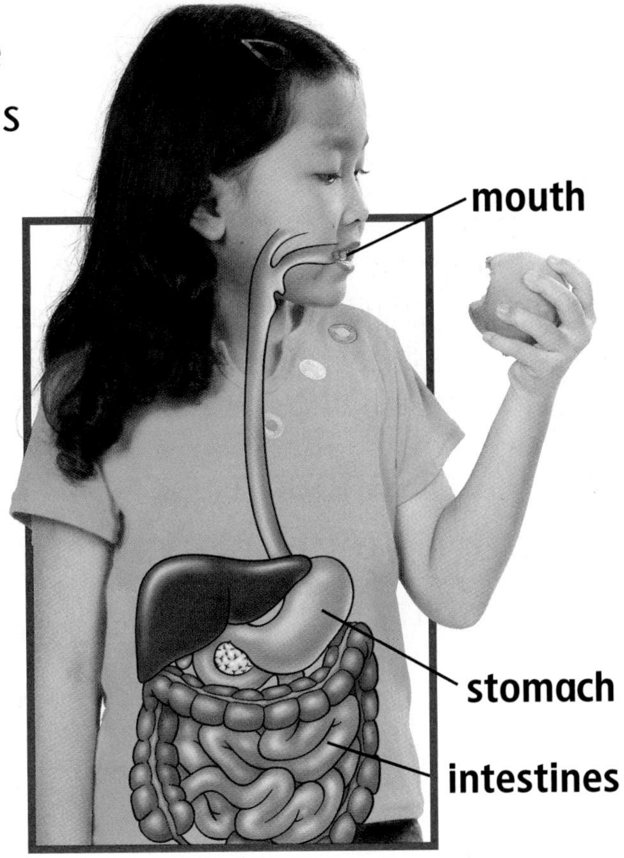

When your body digests food, it breaks the food down. Your digestive system keeps the things your body needs. It also gets rid of the things your body does not need to keep.

Caring for Your Digestive System

- Brush and floss your teeth every day.
- Wash your hands before you eat.
- Eat slowly and chew your food well before you swallow.
- Eat vegetables and fruits. They help move foods through your digestive system.

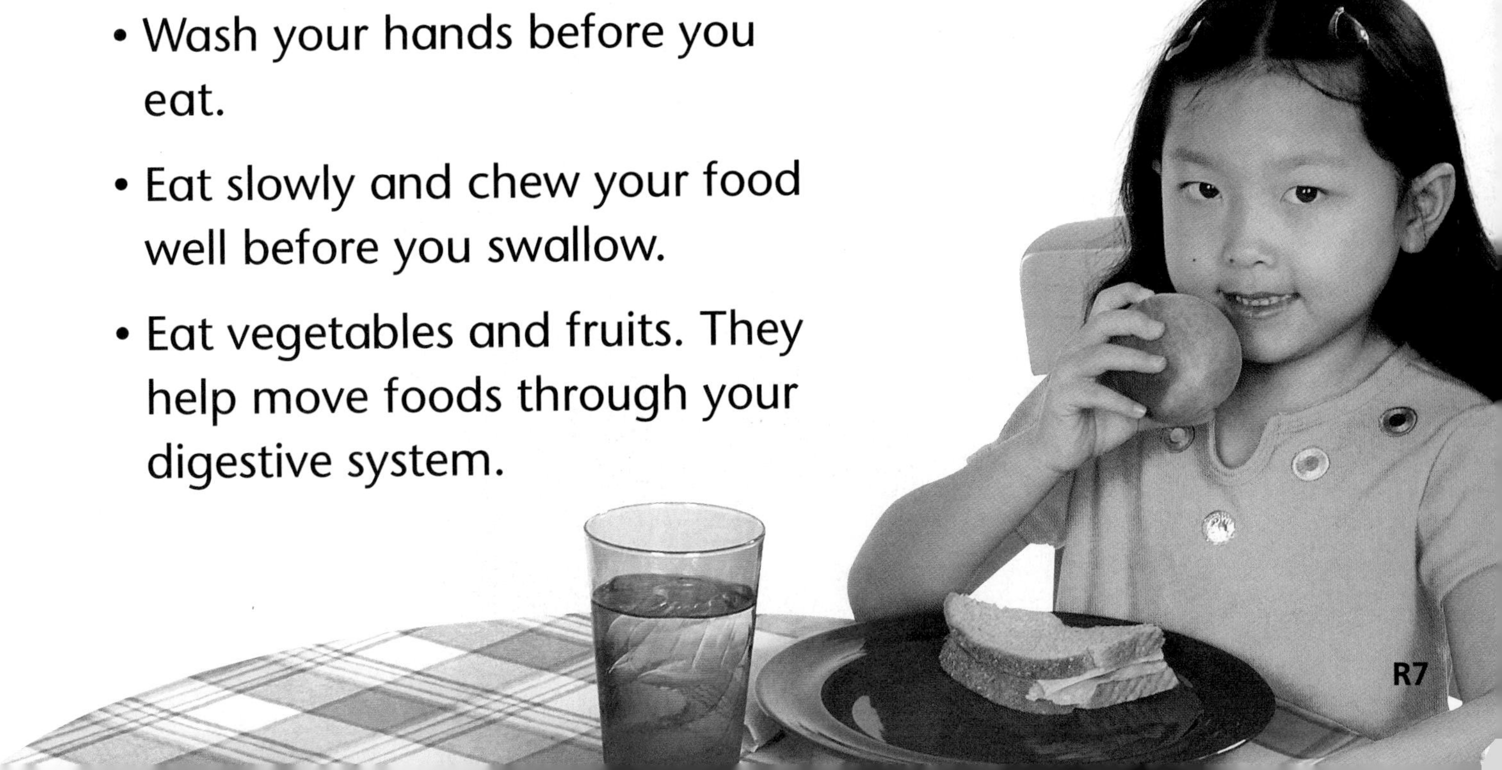

Your Respiratory System

You breathe using your respiratory system. Your mouth, nose, and lungs are all parts of your respiratory system.

Caring for Your Respiratory System

- Never put anything in your nose.
- Never smoke.
- Exercise enough to make you breathe harder. Breathing harder makes your lungs stronger.

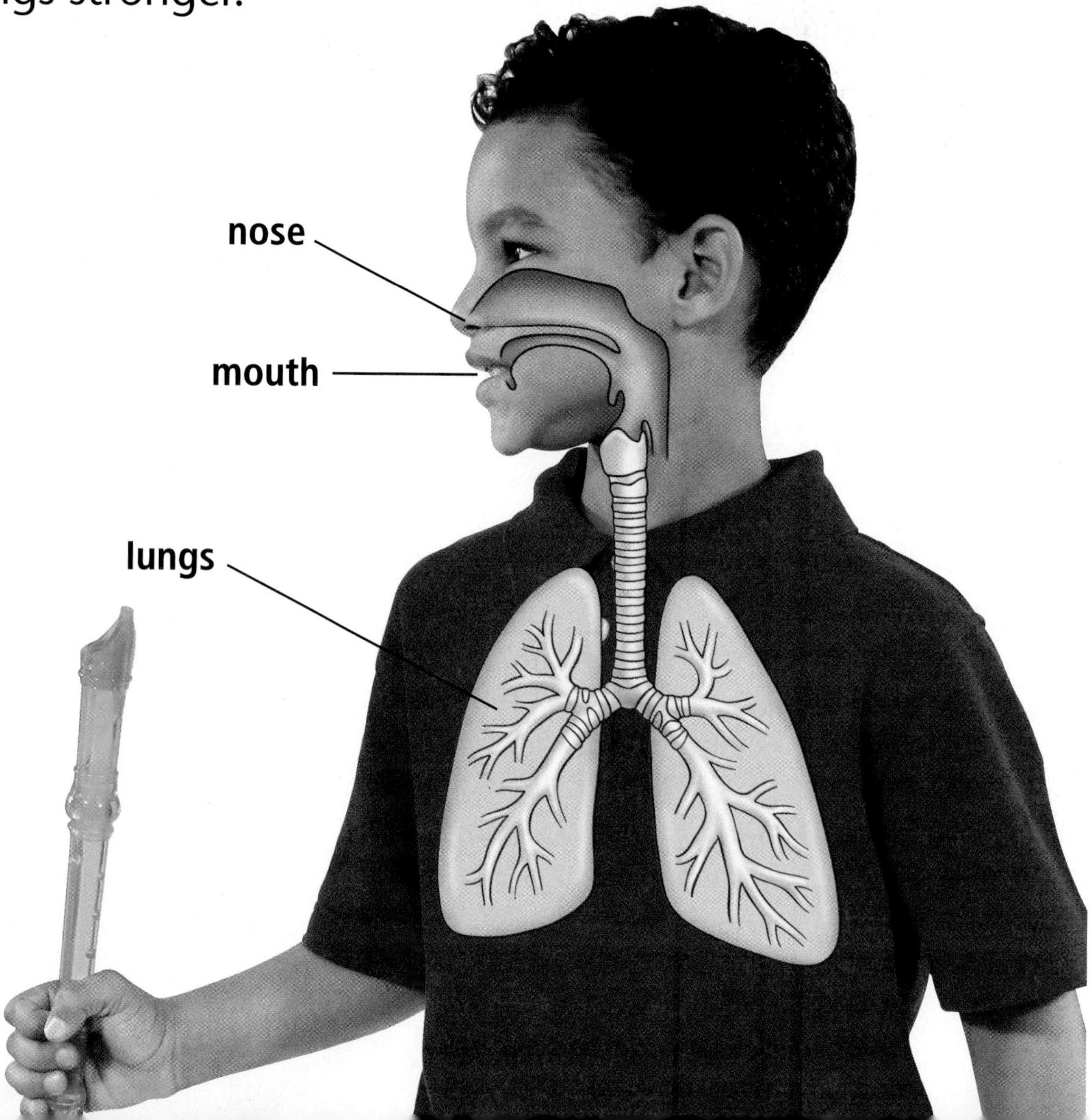

Your Circulatory System

Your circulatory system is made up of your heart and your blood vessels. Your blood carries food energy and oxygen to help your body work. Blood vessels are small tubes. They carry blood from your heart to every part of your body.

Your heart is a muscle. It is beating all the time. As your heart beats, it pumps blood through your blood vessels.

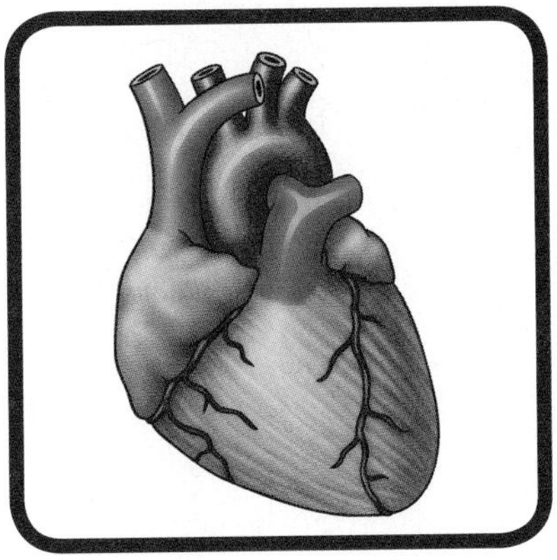

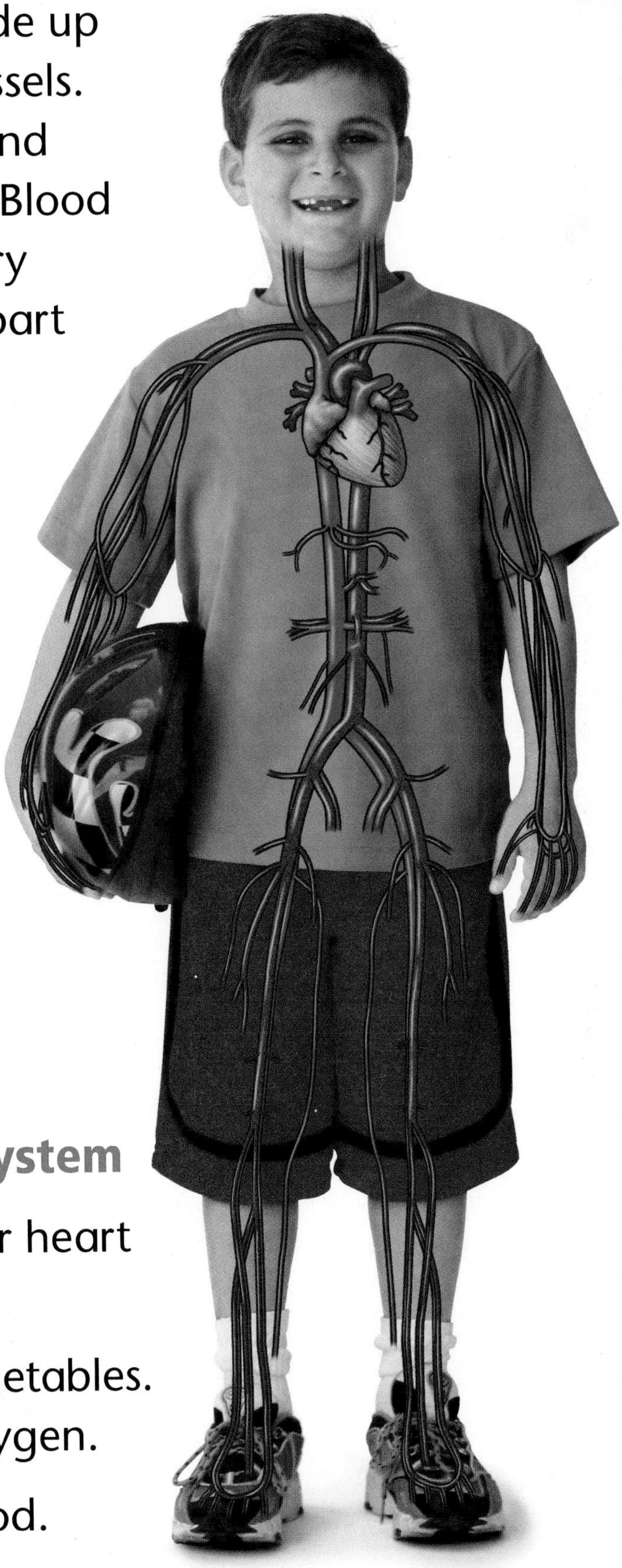

Caring for Your Circulatory System

- Exercise every day to keep your heart strong.
- Eat meats and green leafy vegetables. They help your blood carry oxygen.
- Never touch anyone else's blood.

Staying Healthy

You can do many things to help yourself stay fit and healthy.

You can also avoid doing things that can harm you.

If you know ways to stay safe and healthy and you do these things, you can help yourself have good health.

Staying away from alcohol, tobacco, and other drugs

Keeping Clean

Keeping clean helps you stay healthy. You can pick up germs from the things you touch. Washing with soap and water helps remove germs from your skin.

Wash your hands for as long as it takes to say your ABCs. Always wash your hands at these times.

- Before and after you eat
- After coughing or blowing your nose
- After using the restroom
- After touching an animal
- After playing outside

Caring for Your Teeth

Brushing your teeth and gums keeps them clean and healthy. You should brush your teeth at least twice a day. Brush in the morning. Brush before you go to bed at night. It is also good to brush your teeth after you eat if you can.

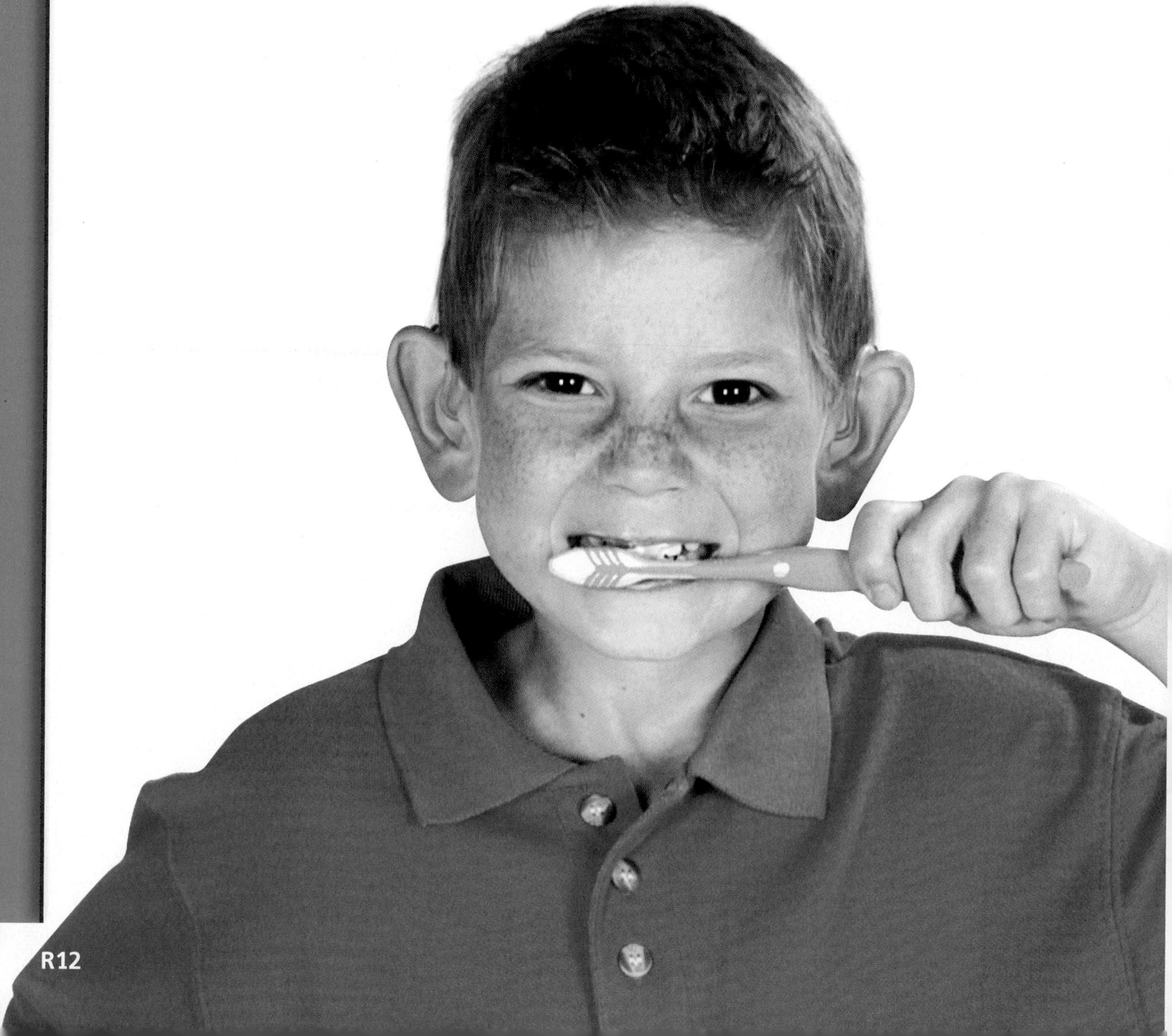

Brushing Your Teeth

Use a soft toothbrush that is the right size for you. Always use your own toothbrush. Use only a small amount of toothpaste. It should be about the size of a pea. Be sure to rinse your mouth with water after you brush your teeth.

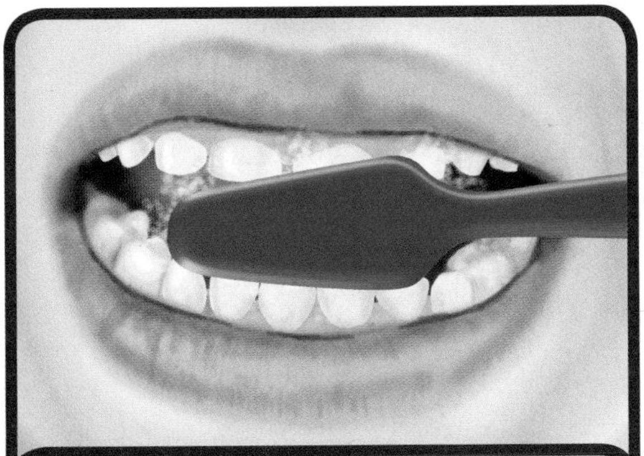

❶ **Brush the outsides of all of your teeth.**

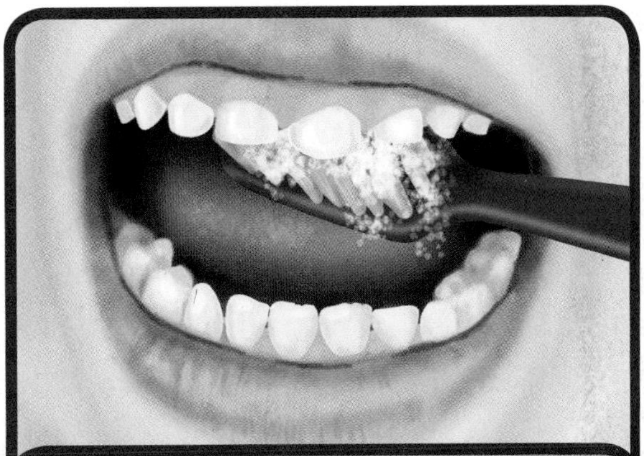

❷ **Brush the insides of all of your teeth.**

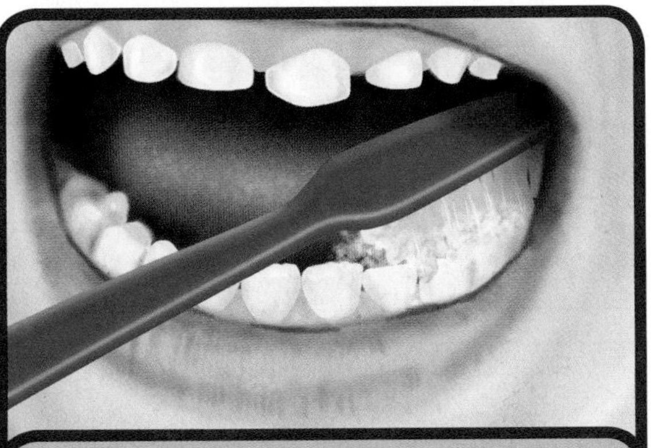

❸ **Brush the flat parts of your back teeth.**

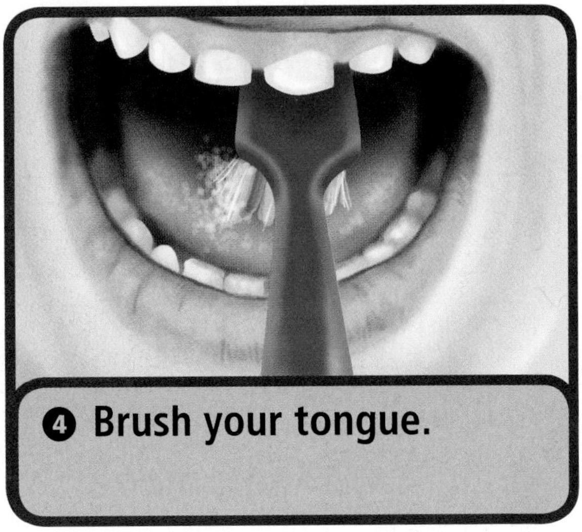

❹ **Brush your tongue.**

Identify the Main Idea and Details

Learning how to find the main idea can help you understand what you read. The main idea of a paragraph is what it is mostly about. The details tell you more about it. Read this paragraph.

> Snakes swallow their food whole. They cannot chew their food. Snakes' mouths are flexible. They can open their mouths very wide. They can move their jaws from side to side. Their skin can stretch to help open their mouths wide. Because it can open its mouth wide, a snake can swallow a larger animal.

This chart shows the main idea and details.

Detail
Snakes cannot chew.

Detail
Snakes' mouths are flexible.

Main Idea Snakes must swallow their food whole.

Detail
Snakes' skin can stretch to help open their mouths wide.

Detail
Snakes can open their mouths very wide.

Compare and Contrast

Focus Skill

Learning how to compare and contrast can help you understand what you read. Comparing is finding what is alike. Contrasting is finding what is different. Read this paragraph.

> The desert and the forest are both environments for living things. Many kinds of plants and animals live there. The desert is dry for most of the year. The forest has more rain. Plants such as cactuses live in the desert. Oak and maple trees live in the forest.

This chart shows comparing and contrasting.

Compare	Contrast
alike	**different**
Both are environments. Many kinds of plants and animals live in each environment.	Deserts are dry. Forests have more rain. Plants such as cactuses live in the desert. Oak and maple trees live in the forest.

Focus Skill Cause and Effect

Learning how to find cause and effect can help you understand what you read. A cause is why something happens. An effect is what happens. Some paragraphs have more than one cause or effect. Read this paragraph.

> People once used a poison called DDT to get rid of pests. Small birds eat bugs. Some large birds eat small birds. When small birds ate bugs sprayed with DDT, the DDT got into their bodies. When large birds ate small birds, the DDT got into their bodies, too. DDT caused birds to lay eggs that broke easily.

This chart shows cause and effect.

Cause

Small birds ate bugs sprayed with DDT.

Effects

Large birds that ate small birds got DDT into their bodies.
The DDT made the birds lay eggs that broke easily.

Focus Skill

Sequence

Learning how to find sequence can help you understand what you read. Sequence is the order in which something happens. Some paragraphs use words that help you understand order. Read this paragraph. Look at the underlined words.

> Ricky and his grandpa made a special dessert. <u>First</u>, Grandpa peeled apples and cut them into small chunks. <u>Next</u>, Ricky put the apple chunks and some raisins in a bowl. <u>Then</u>, Grandpa put the bowl into a microwave oven for about ten minutes. <u>Last</u>, when the bowl was cool enough to touch, Ricky and Grandpa ate their dessert.

This chart shows sequence.

1. <u>First</u>, Grandpa peeled apples and cut them into chunks.
2. <u>Next</u>, Ricky put apple chunks and raisins in a bowl.
3. <u>Then</u>, Grandpa put the bowl in a microwave oven for ten minutes.
4. <u>Last</u>, Ricky and Grandpa ate their dessert.

Focus Skill Draw Conclusions

When you draw conclusions, you tell what you have learned. What you learned also includes your own ideas. Read this paragraph.

The body coverings of many animals can help them hide. One kind of moth has wings with a pattern that looks like tree bark. The moth is hard to see when it is resting on a tree. A polar bear's white coat can make it hard to see in the snow. Being hard to see can help protect an animal or help it hunt other animals.

This chart shows how to draw conclusions.

What I Read

The body coverings of a moth and a polar bear can help them hide.

What I Know

I have seen an insect that looks like a leaf. The insect was very hard to see when it was on a tree branch.

Conclusion

Some animals that live near my own home have body coverings that help them hide.

Focus Skill

Summarize

When you summarize, you tell the main idea and details you remember from what you read. Read this paragraph.

> The leaves of a tree grow in the summer. They provide food for the growing tree. Leaves trap energy from the sun. They get water from the ground. They take in gases from the air. Leaves use these things to make food for the tree.

This chart shows how to summarize.

Recall Detail	Recall Detail	Recall Detail
Leaves grow in the summer.	Leaves trap sunlight.	Leaves collect water from the ground and gases from the air.

Summary Leaves use sunlight, water, and gases to make food for the tree.

Using Tables, Charts, and Graphs

Gathering Data

When you investigate in science, you need to collect data.

Suppose you want to find out what kinds of things are in soil. You can sort the things you find into groups.

Things I Found in One Cup of Soil

By studying the circles, you can see the different items found in soil. However, you might display the data in a different way. For example, you could use a tally chart.

Reading a Tally Chart

You can show your data in a tally chart.

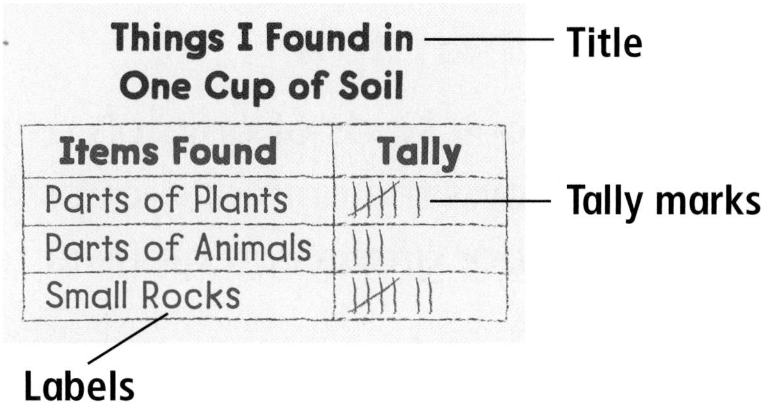
Things I Found in
One Cup of Soil
Title
Items Found
Tally
Parts of Plants
Tally marks
Parts of Animals
Small Rocks
Labels

How to Read a Tally Chart

1. **Read** the tally chart. Use the labels.
2. **Study** the data.
3. **Count** the tally marks.
4. **Draw conclusions**. Ask yourself questions like the ones on this page.

Skills Practice

1. How many parts of plants were found in the soil?
2. How many more small rocks were found in the soil than parts of animals?
3. How many parts of plants and parts of animals were found?

Using Tables, Charts, and Graphs

Reading a Bar Graph

People keep many kinds of animals as pets. This bar graph shows the animal groups most pets belong to. A bar graph can be used to compare data.

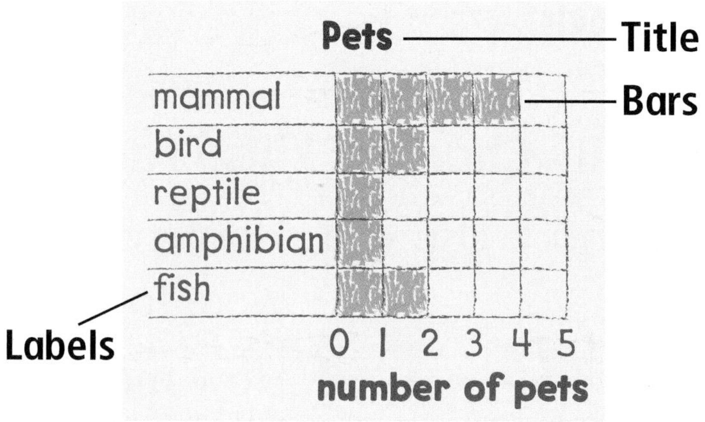

How to Read a Bar Graph

1. **Look** at the title to learn what kind of information is shown.
2. **Read** the graph. Use the labels.
3. **Study** the data. Compare the bars.
4. **Draw conclusions**. Ask yourself questions like the ones on this page.

Skills Practice

1. How many pets are mammals?
2. How many pets are birds?
3. How many more pets are mammals than fish?

Reading a Picture Graph

Some second-grade students were asked to choose their favorite season. They made a picture graph to show the results. A picture graph uses pictures to show information.

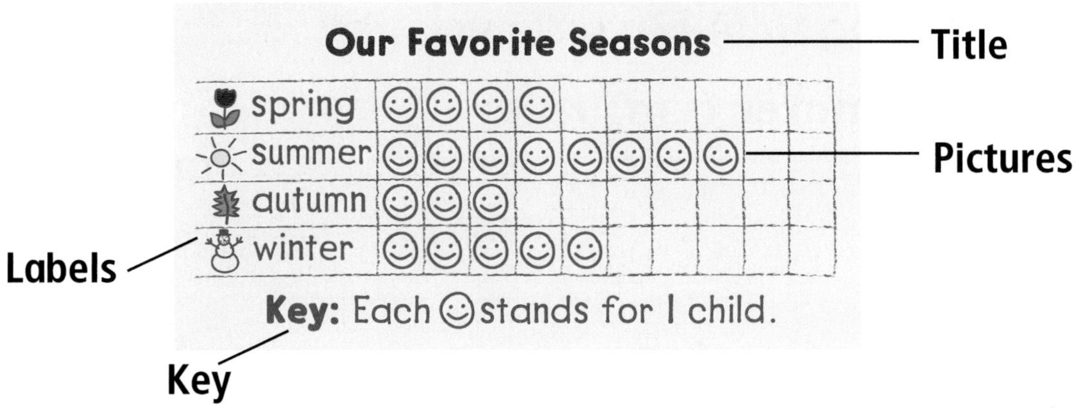

How to Read a Picture Graph

1. **Look** at the title to learn what kind of information is shown.
2. **Read** the graph. Use the labels.
3. **Study** the data. Compare the number of pictures in each row.
4. **Draw conclusions**. Ask yourself questions like the ones on this page.

Skills Practice

1. Which season did the most students choose?
2. Which season did the fewest students choose?
3. How many students in all chose summer or winter?

Measurements

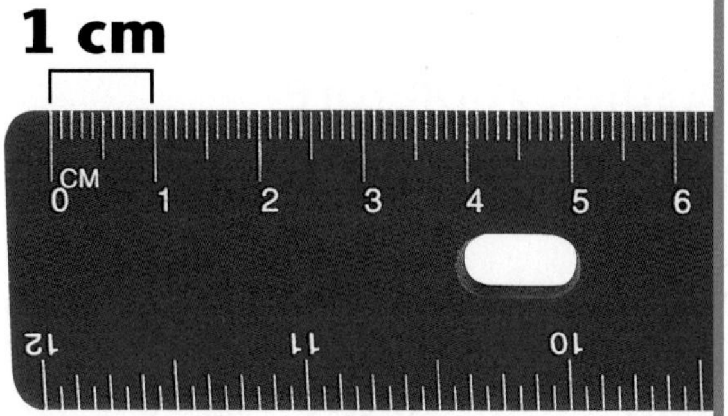

centimeter (cm) ruler

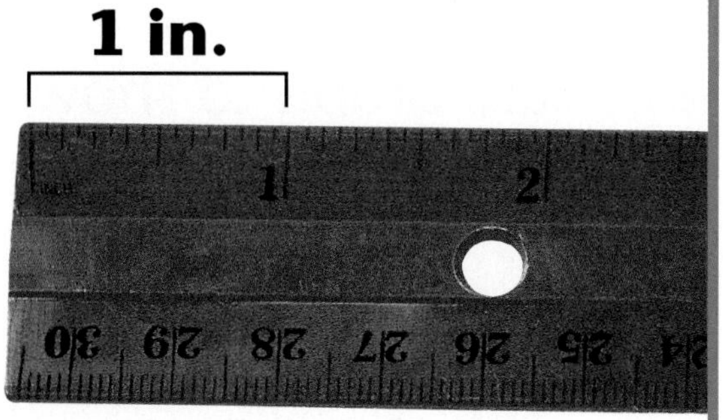

inch (in.) ruler

A **centimeter** is about the width of your index finger.

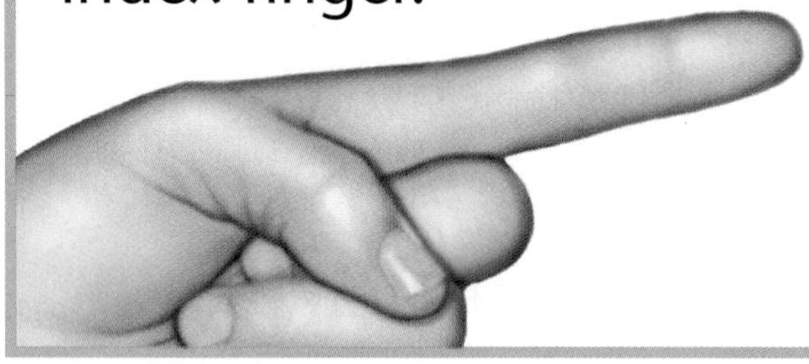

An **inch** is about the length of a paper clip.

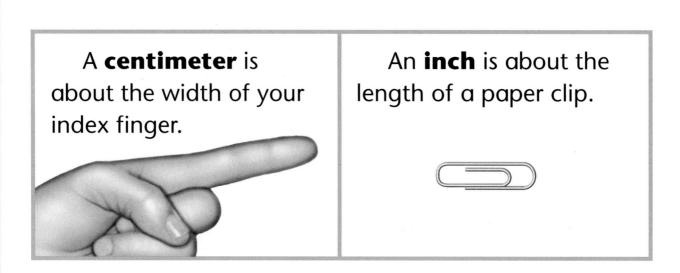

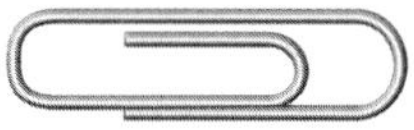

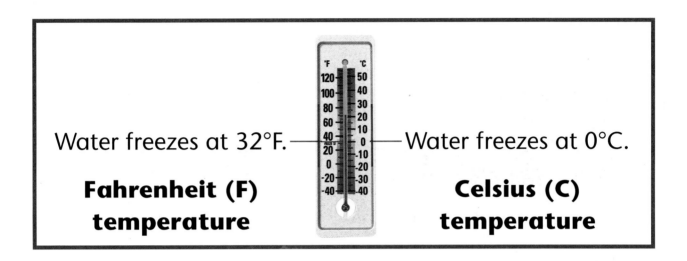

Water freezes at 32°F.

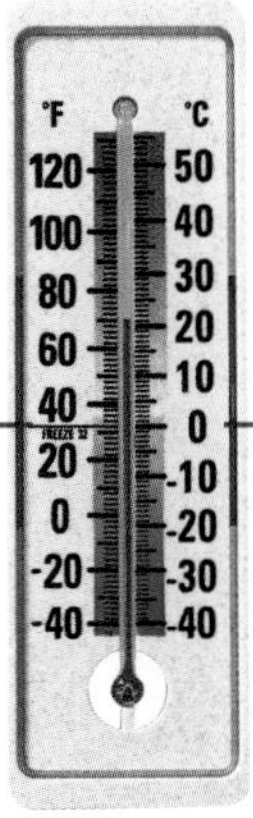

Water freezes at 0°C.

Fahrenheit (F) temperature

Celsius (C) temperature

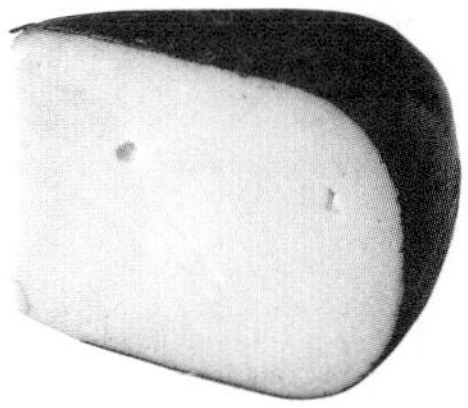

1 kilogram (kg)

1 pound (lb)

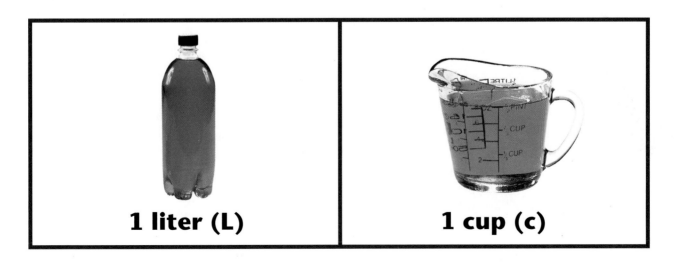

1 liter (L)

1 cup (c)

Safety in Science

Here are some safety rules to follow when you do activities.

1. **Think ahead.** Study the steps and follow them.
2. **Be neat and clean.** Wipe up spills right away.
3. **Watch your eyes.** Wear safety goggles when told to do so.
4. **Be careful with sharp things.**
5. **Do not eat or drink things.**

Visit the Multimedia Science Glossary to see illustrations of these words and to hear them pronounced.
www.hspscience.com

Every term in the glossary has a respelling. The respelling writes the term the way it sounds. This can help you say the term. The meaning of the term follows the respelling.

There may be a page number after the meaning of the term. The page number tells where the term is in your book. Many of the terms have a yellow highlight. The terms with the yellow highlight are also defined in the lessons. All of the terms have pictures to help you understand them.

The key on this page will help you understand the respellings. Each term has one or more syllables. Syllables are parts of the term. There is a • between the syllables. One syllable in each word is in capital letters. That syllable is stressed.

Pronunciation Key

Sound	As in	Phonetic Respelling	Sound	As in	Phonetic Respelling
a	**b**a**t**	(BAT)	oh	**o**ver	(OH•ver)
ah	l**o**ck	(LAHK)	oo	p**oo**l	(POOL)
air	r**are**	(RAIR)	ow	**ou**t	(OWT)
ar	**ar**gue	(AR•gyoo)	oy	f**oi**l	(FOYL)
aw	l**aw**	(LAW)	s	**c**ell	(SEL)
ay	f**a**ce	(FAYS)		**s**it	(SIT)
ch	**ch**apel	(CHAP•uhl)	sh	**sh**eep	(SHEEP)
e	t**e**st	(TEST)	th	**th**at	(THAT)
	m**e**tric	(MEH•trik)		**th**in	(THIN)
ee	**ea**t	(EET)	u	p**u**ll	(PUL)
	f**ee**t	(FEET)	uh	med**a**l	(MED•uhl)
	sk**i**	(SKEE)		tal**e**nt	(TAL•uhnt)
er	pap**er**	(PAY•per)		penc**i**l	(PEN•suhl)
	f**er**n	(FERN)		**o**nion	(UHN•yuhn)
eye	**i**dea	(eye•DEE•uh)		playf**u**l	(PLAY•fuhl)
i	b**i**t	(BIT)		d**u**ll	(DUHL)
ing	go**ing**	(GOH•ing)	y	**y**es	(YES)
k	**c**ard	(KARD)		r**i**pe	(RYP)
	kite	(KYT)	z	ba**g**s	(BAGZ)
ngk	ba**nk**	(BANGK)	zh	trea**s**ure	(TREZH•er)

Multimedia Science Glossary **www.hspscience.com**

A

adult [uh•DUHLT]

A fully grown person or animal. (152)

appearance [uh•PEER•uhns]

The way something looks. (169)

attract [uh•TRAKT]

To pull. The north and south poles of two magnets attract each other. (120)

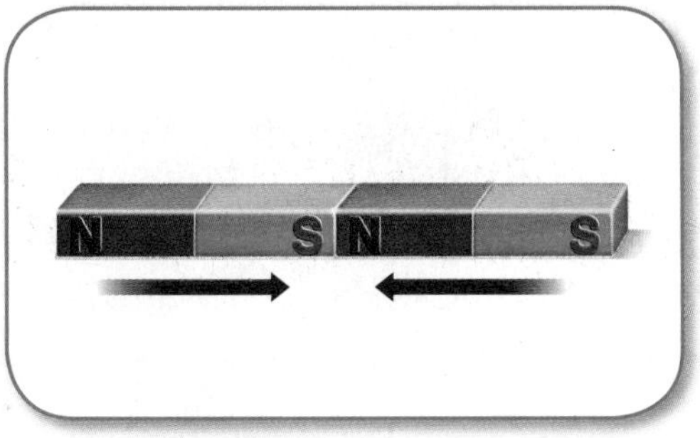

axis [AK•sis]

In a bar graph, one of the two directions along which information is given.

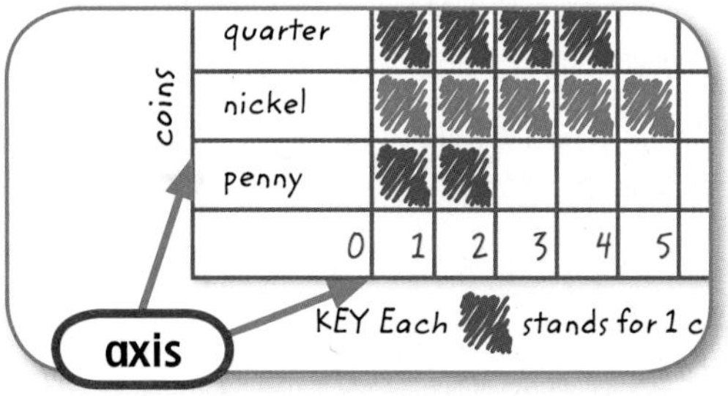

B

balance [BAL•uhns]

A science tool used to measure the mass of an object. (20)

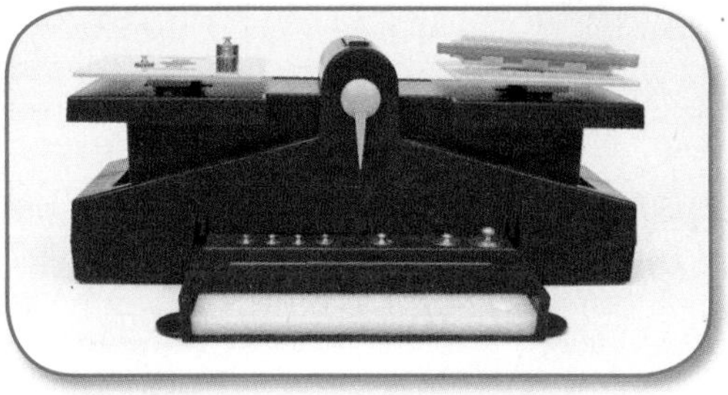

bar graph [BAR GRAF]

A diagram that uses bars to compare numbers or amounts of things. The bars show how many or how much. (32)

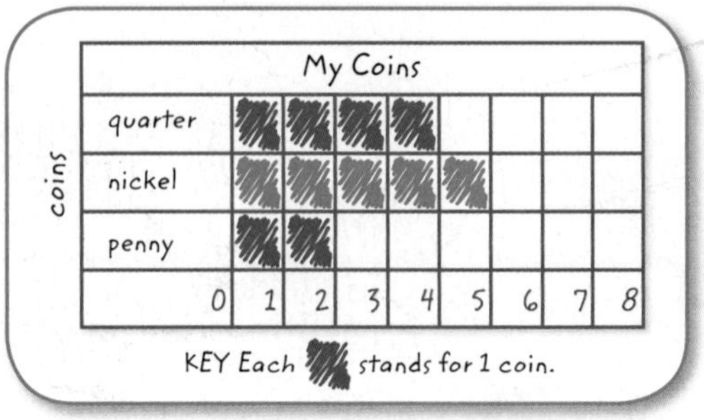

behavior [bee•HAYV•yer]

The way a living thing acts.

C

centimeter

[SEN•tuh•mee•ter]

A metric unit used to measure how long something is. (60)

characteristic

[kar•ik•tuh•RIS•tik]

A feature, or trait, of an object, such as its color, size, or shape. (196)

classify [KLAS•uh•fy]

To sort into groups by traits. (6)

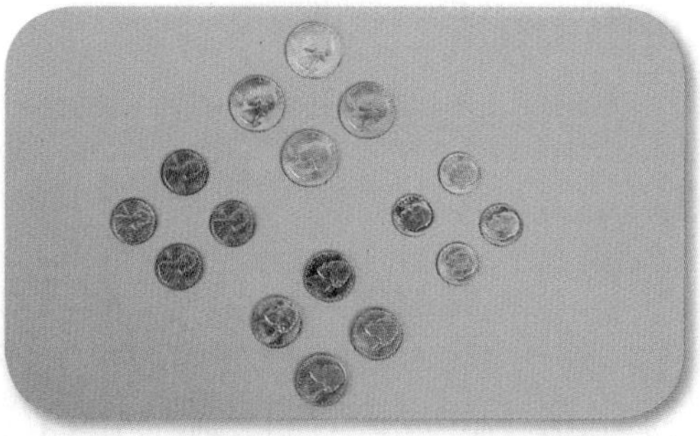

communicate

[kuh•MYOO•nuh•kayt]

To share what you know by telling or showing. (9)

compare [kuhm•PAIR]

To tell how things are alike and how they are different. (6)

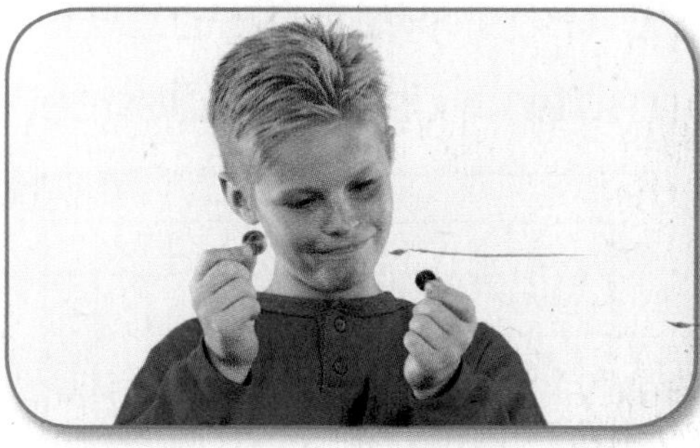

crack [KRAK]

A break or narrow opening in something. (244)

crust [KRUHST]

Earth's outer layer, which includes the ocean floor as well as the land.

D

data [DAY•tuh OR DA•tuh]

Information used in science. (28)

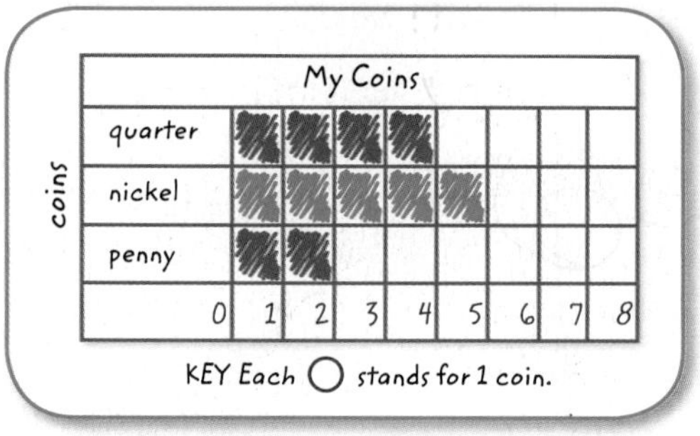

decay [dih•KAY]

To break down. Dead plant and animal matter decays over time.

dinosaur [DY•nuh•sawr]

A kind of animal that lived on Earth long ago. (268)

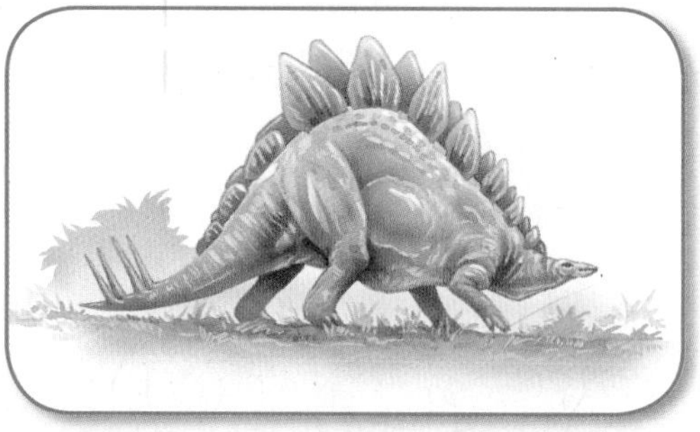

distance [DIS•tuhns]

The measure of the length between two things. (60)

draw conclusions
[DRAW kuhn•KLU•zhuhnz]
To use the information you have gathered to decide what something means. (8)

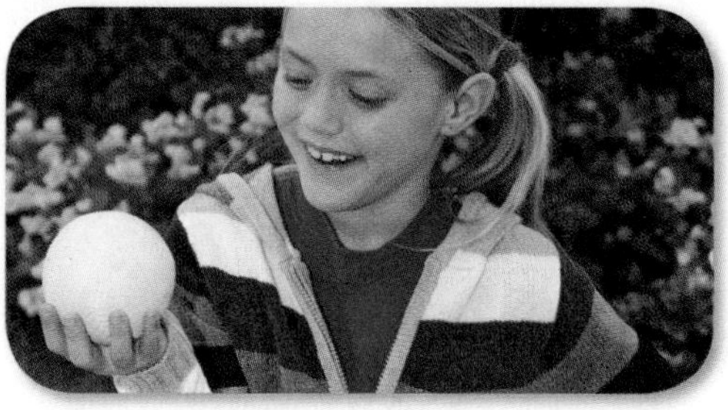

dropper [DRAH•per]
A science tool used to place a small amount of liquid. (19)

E

egg [EG]
A round or oval object in which some kinds of animals begin life. (154)

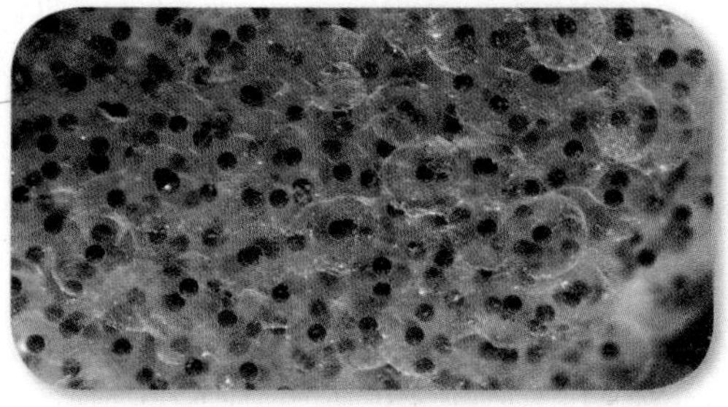

environment
[en•VY•ruhn•muhnt]
Everything around a living thing. (172)

F

float [FLOHT]
To stay on top of a liquid or to move gently through the air. (110)

flower [FLOW•er]
A part of some plants that helps a plant make seeds that can become new plants. (184)

force [FAWRS]

A push or a pull that can cause an object to move. A force can also change the way an object is moving. (80)

forceps [FAWR•seps]

A science tool that is used to hold or separate small objects. (17)

fossil [FAHS•uhl]

What is left of an animal or a plant that lived long ago. (268)

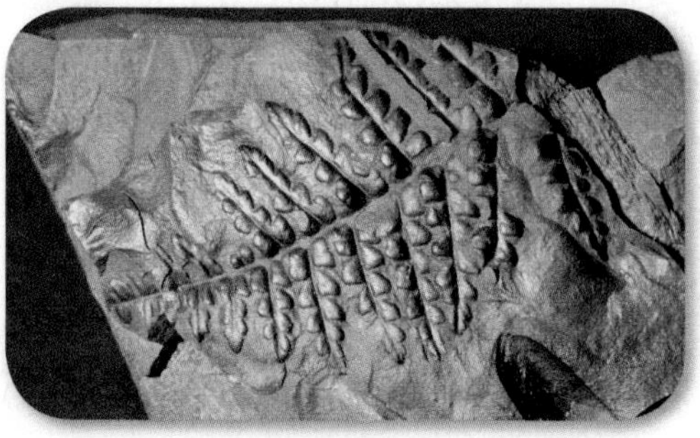

freeze [FREEZ]

To change from a liquid, such as water, to a solid, such as ice. (244)

friction [FRIK•shuhn]

A force that slows down or stops a moving object when it rubs against something. (84)

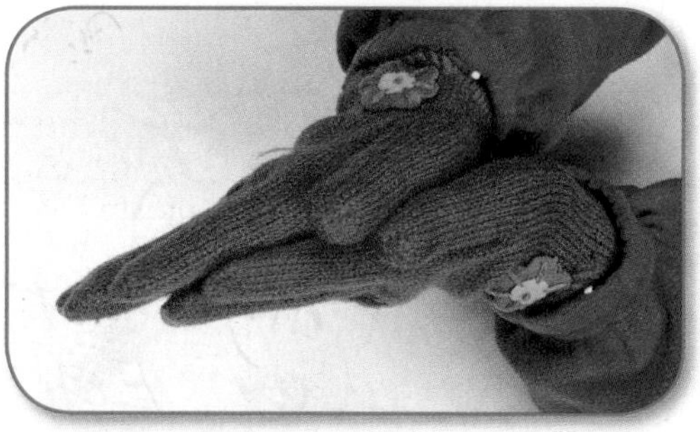

fruit [FROOT]

A part of some plants that holds and protects seeds. (184)

G

germinate [JER•muh•nayt]
What a seed does when it gets what it needs to grow. (182)

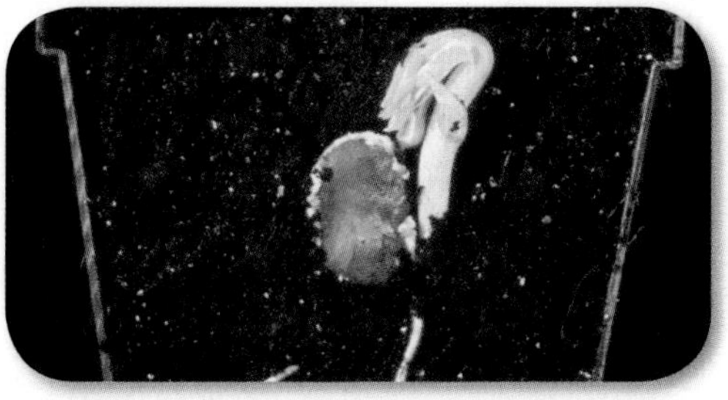

gravity [GRAV•ih•tee]
A force that pulls things toward one another. Earth's gravity pulls other things toward the center of Earth. (108)

H

hand lens [HAND LENZ]
A science tool that is used to make small objects appear larger. (16)

human-made [HYOO•muhn•mayd]
Made by people, not found in nature.

humus [HYOO•muhs]
Plant and animal matter in soil. (254)

hypothesize [hy•PAHTH•uh•syz]
To think of a scientific statement that you can test. (8)

I

infer [in•FER]

To use what you observe to explain why something happened. (8)

influence [IN•floo•uhns]

To affect the way something changes or acts.

inherit [in•HAIR•it]

To get a characteristic, or trait, from parents.

interpret [in•TER•pruht]

To explain the meaning of something, such as a graph.

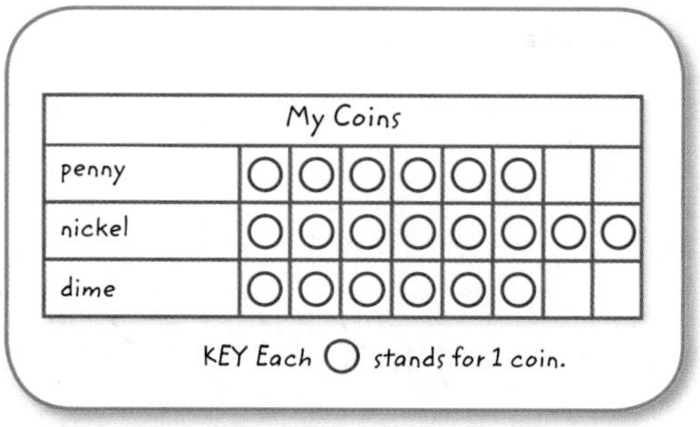

investigate [in•VES•tuh•gayt]

To plan and do a test to find out about something. (40)

investigation skills [in•ves•tuh•GAY•shuhn SKILZ]

A set of skills that people can use to find out about things. (6)

K

key [KEE]

The part of a picture graph or pictograph that tells how many objects each picture stands for. (30)

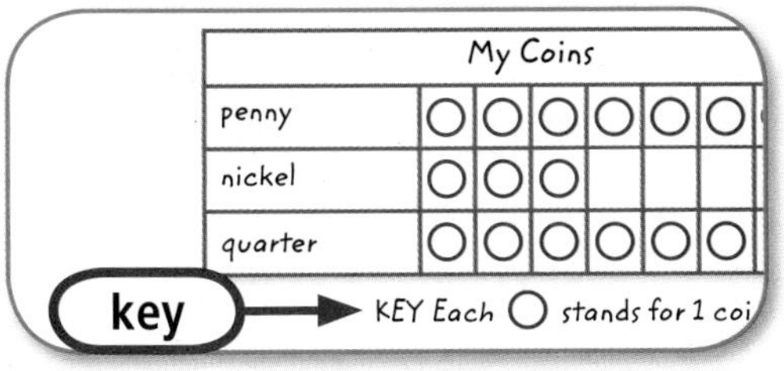

L

label [LAY•buhl]

A word that tells what kind of information is in a chart or a graph. (29)

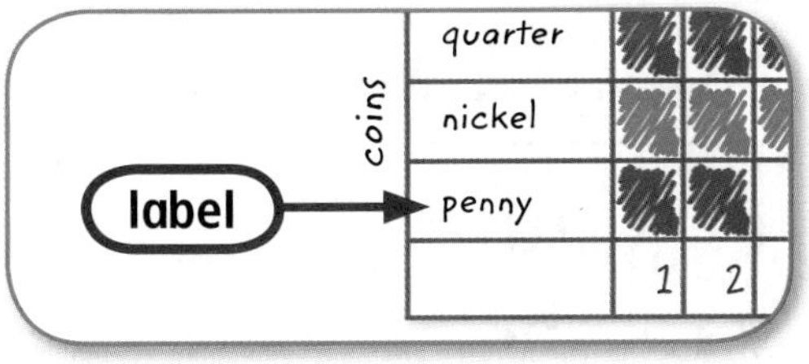

larva [LAR•vuh]

The newly hatched form of some insects. A caterpillar is a larva. (156)

length [LAYNKTH]

The distance from one end of an object to the other end. (18)

life cycle [LYF SY•kuhl]

All the stages, or times, of the life of an animal or a plant. (152)

luster [LUS•ter]

The shininess of an object. (230)

M

machine [muh•SHEEN]

A device that helps people produce more force than they can without it. (96)

magnet [MAG•nit]

An object that can pull things made of iron or steel and can push or pull other magnets. (118)

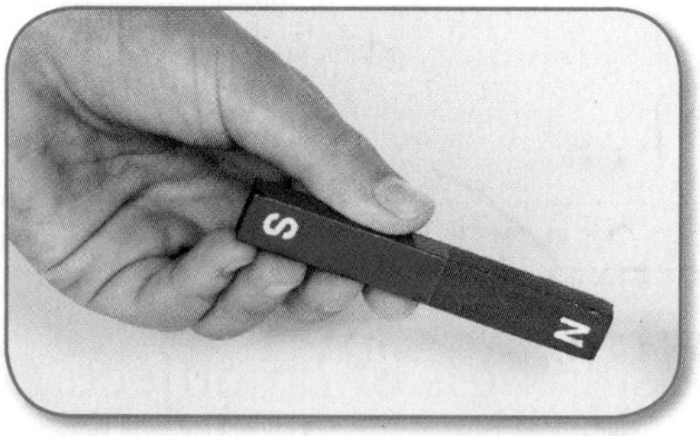

magnetic [mag•NET•ik]

Acting like a magnet.

magnetism [MAG•nuh•tiz•uhm]

The kind of force magnets have.

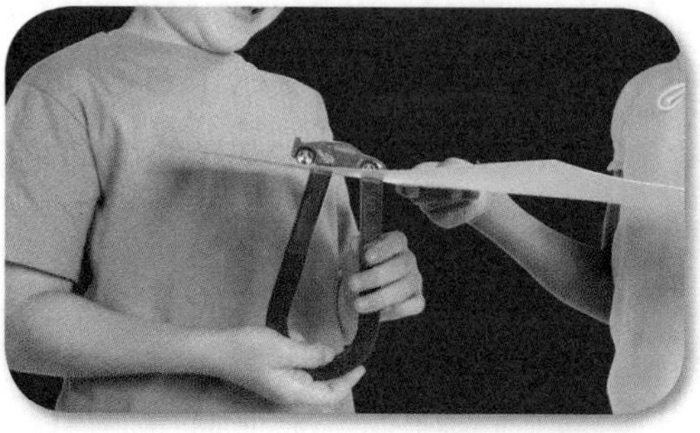

magnify [MAG•nuh•fy]

To make something look bigger than it is. (16)

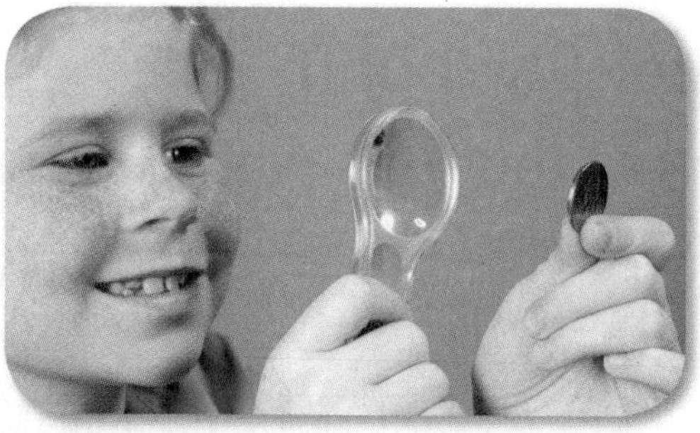

magnifying box [MAG•nuh•fy•ing BAHX]

A science tool that makes small objects placed in it look bigger. (17)

make a model [MAYK uh MAH•duhl]

To make an object or a drawing to show what something is like or how it works. (7)

measure [MEZH•er]

To find the size or amount of something. (7)

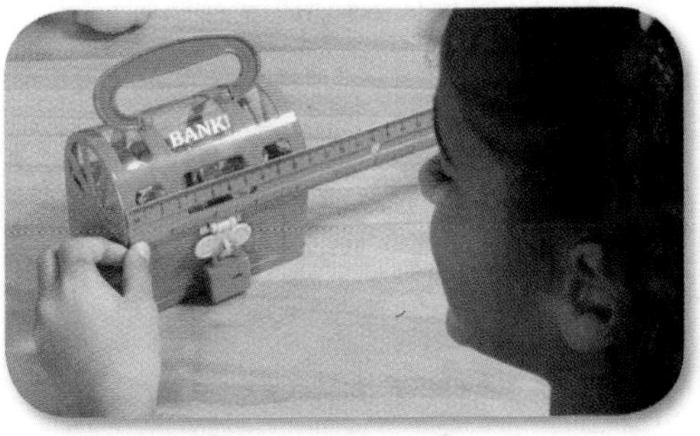

measuring cup [MEZH•er•ing KUHP]

A science tool that is used to measure a liquid. (19)

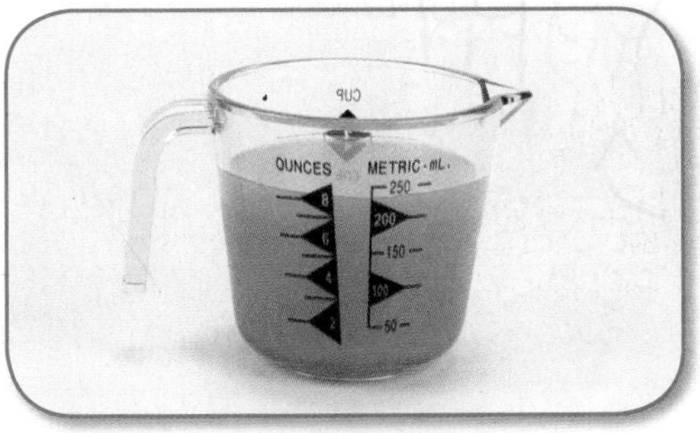

metamorphosis [met•uh•MAWR•fuh•sis]

A set of changes that some animals go through.

meter [MEE•ter]

A metric unit that is used to measure how long something is. One meter equals about 39 inches. (60)

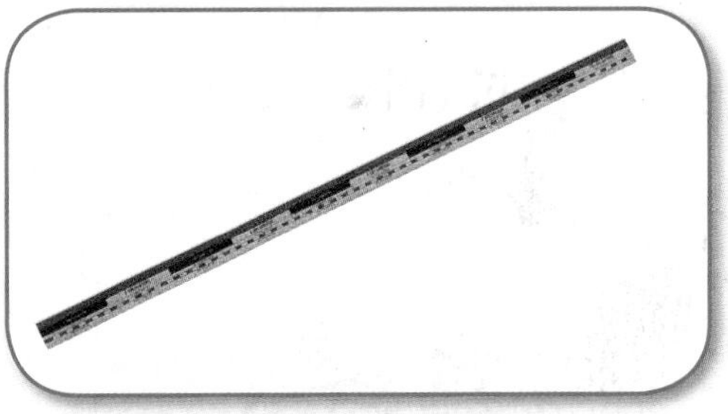

metric system [MEH•trik SIS•tuhm]

A set of units that are used for measuring. Meters and centimeters are metric units.

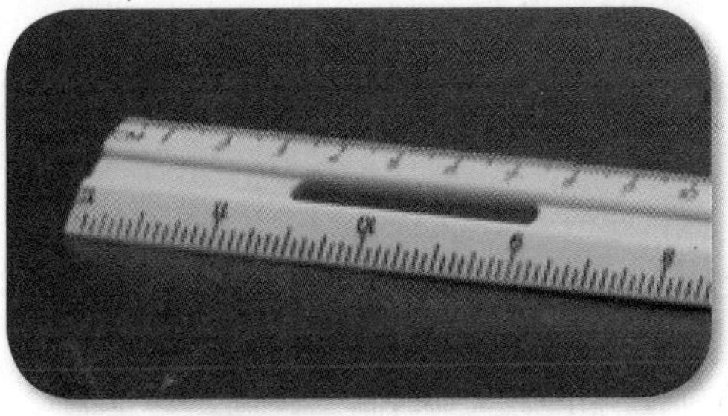

mineral [MIN•er•uhl]

A solid material, found in nature, that has never been alive. (229)

molt [MOHLT]

To shed, or get rid of, skin, feathers, or hair at certain times. (156)

motion [MOH•shuhn]

A change of position. When something moves, it is in motion. (68)

N

natural resource [NACH•er•uhl REE•sawrs]

Anything in nature that people can use to meet their needs. (282)

north pole [NAWRTH POHL]

One of two places on a magnet where the pull is the strongest. (120)

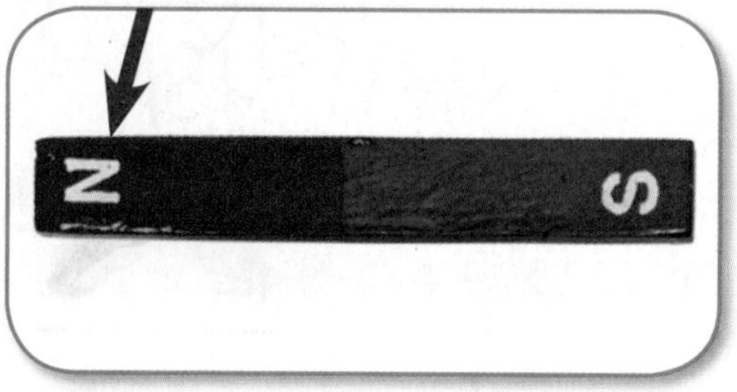

nutrients [NOO•tree•uhnts]

Things that plants and animals need to take in to help them live and grow. (215)

nymph [NIMF]
The young of certain insects, such as the grasshopper. (158)

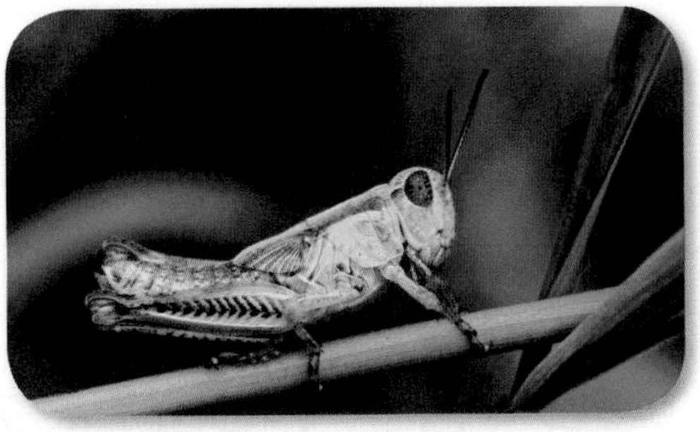

O

observe [ahb•ZERV]
To use the senses to find out about something. (6)

offspring [AWF•spring]
The young of any living thing.

organic [awr•GA•nik]
Having to do with living things.

organism [AWR•guh•niz•uhm]
Any living thing.

organize [AWR•guh•nyz]
To arrange in a certain way.

My Coins	
Coin	Tally
penny	~~IIII~~ II
nickel	III
quarter	~~IIII~~ I

P

picture graph [PIK•cher GRAF]

A diagram that uses pictures to compare numbers of things. Each picture stands for one thing. (30)

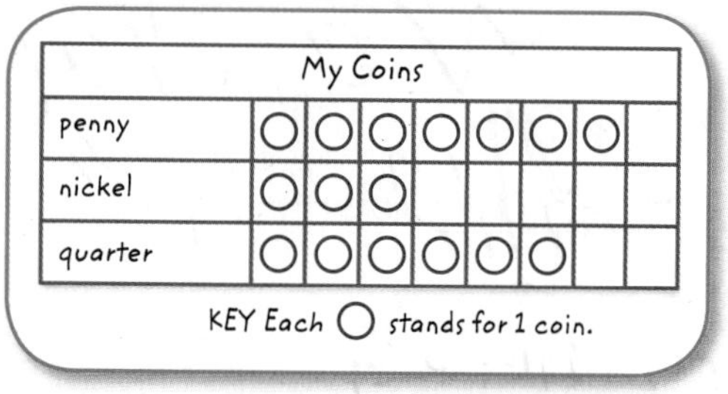

pitch [PICH]

The highness or lowness of a sound. (134)

plant [PLANT]

A kind of living thing that makes its own food. (182)

position [puh•ZISH•uhn]

The place where something is. (56)

predict [pree•DIKT]

To use what you know to make a good guess about what will happen. (9)

property [PRAH•per•tee]

A characteristic, or trait, of an object, such as its color, size, or shape. (230)

pull [PUL]

To move something toward oneself. (80)

pupa [PYOO•puh]

The stage of a butterfly's life cycle in which the caterpillar changes into an adult butterfly. (157)

push [PUSH]

To move something away from oneself. (80)

R

record [rih•KAWRD]

To keep information by writing, drawing, or using numbers. (9)

repel [rih•PEL]

To push away. The two north or two south poles of two magnets repel each other. (120)

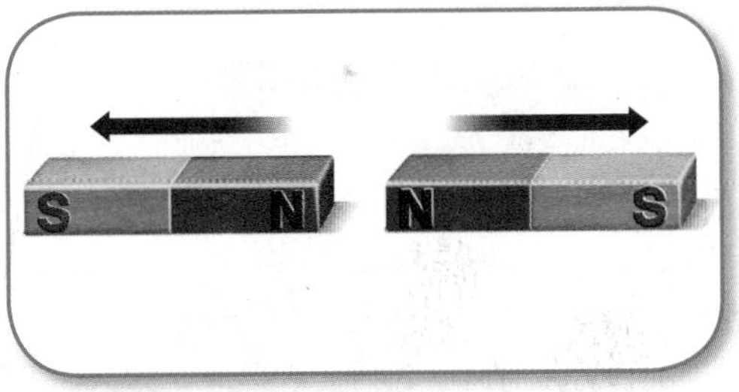

reproduce [ree•pruh•DOOS]

To produce offspring, or new living things like the parent living things.

resemble [rih•ZEM•buhl]
To look like or be similar to something else.

rock [RAHK]
A solid material, found in nature, that is made up of one or more minerals. (228)

roots [ROOTS]
The parts of a plant that hold it in the soil and take in water and nutrients. (183)

rot [RAHT]
To decay, or break down. Dead plant and animal parts rot in soil. (254)

ruler [ROO•ler]
A science tool that is used to measure the length, width, or height of an object. (18)

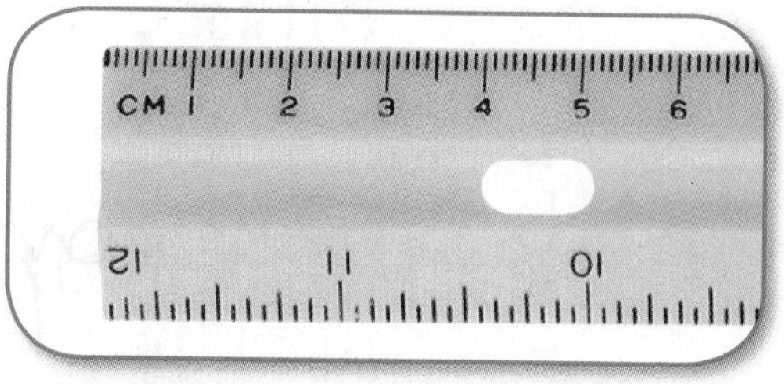

S

scale [SKAYL]
A science tool that is used to measure weight, or the pull of Earth's gravity on an object. (20)

science tools
[SY•uhns TOOLZ]
Tools people use to find out about things. (16)

seed [SEED]
A plant part from which some new plants grow. (182)

sequence [SEE•kwens]
To arrange things to show the order in which they happen. (7)

similar [SIH•muh•ler]
Like something else in some ways but not exactly like it.

simple microscope
[SIM•puhl MY•kruh•skohp]
A science tool that is used to make very small things look bigger. (17)

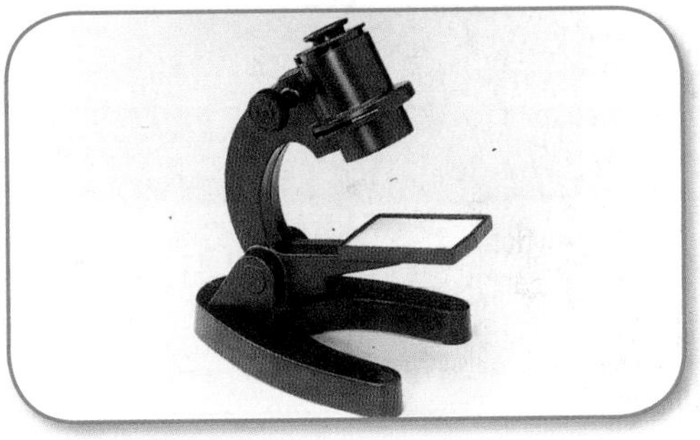

soil [SOYL]
The top layer of Earth, made up of small bits of rock. Soil that is good for growing plants also contains matter that was once living. (254)

sound [SOWND]

What you hear when an object vibrates. (130)

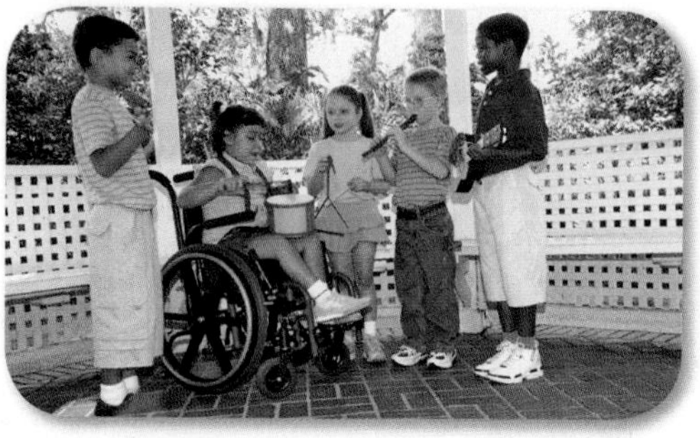

south pole [SOWTH POHL]

One of two places on a magnet where the pull is the strongest. (120)

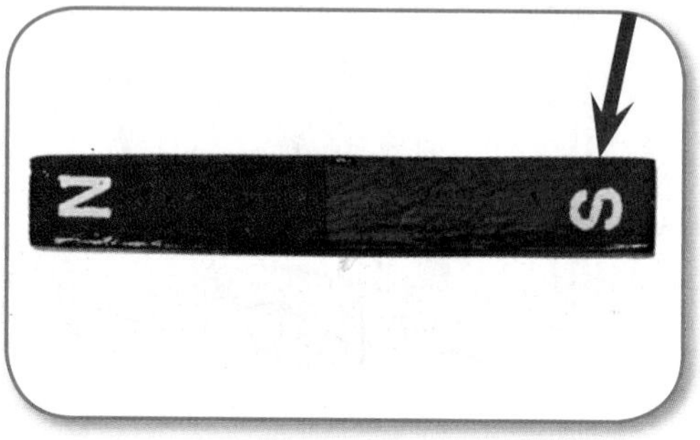

speed [SPEED]

The measure of how fast an object moves, or how far it moves in a certain amount of time. (70)

stem [STEM]

The plant part that holds up leaves. The stem carries food and water to the other parts of a plant. (183)

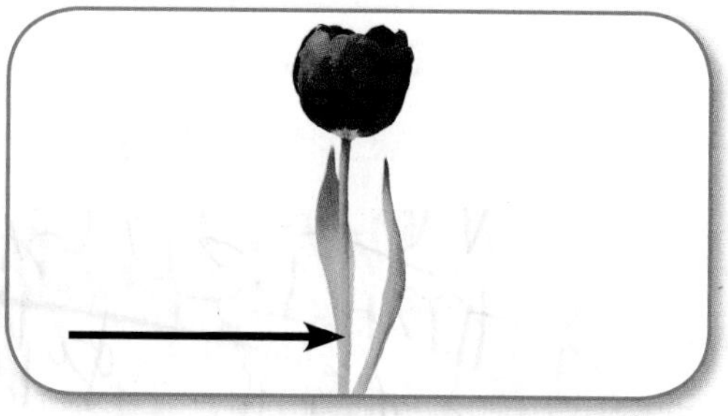

T

tadpole [TAD•pohl]

A young frog that hatches from an egg and lives in water. (154)

tally chart [TA•lee CHART]

A chart that is used to record numbers. Each tally stands for one. (28)

My Coins	
Coin	Tally
penny	~~IIII~~ II
nickel	III
dime	~~IIII~~ I

tape measure
[TAYP MEZH•er]
A science tool that is used to measure how long, tall, or wide an object is. It is also used to measure around an object. (18)

tell [TEL]
To share what you know. (9)

temperature
[TEM•per•uh•cher]
The measure of how hot, warm, or cold something is. (21)

texture [TEKS•cher]
The way something feels when you touch it. (230)

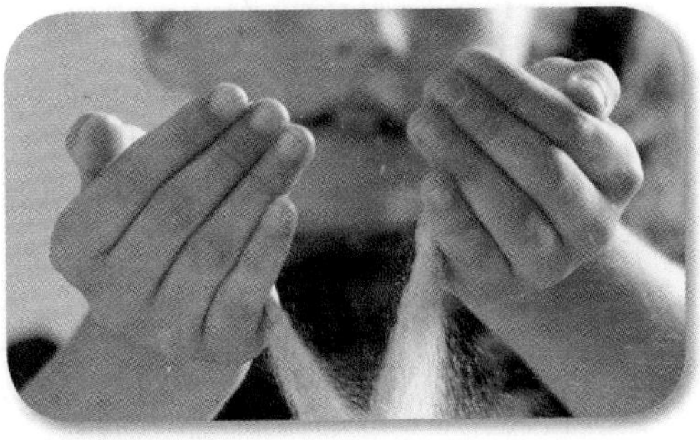

thaw [THAW]
To change from a frozen to an unfrozen state. (244)

thermometer
[ther•MAHM•uh•ter]
A science tool that is used to measure temperature, or how hot, warm, or cold something is. (21)

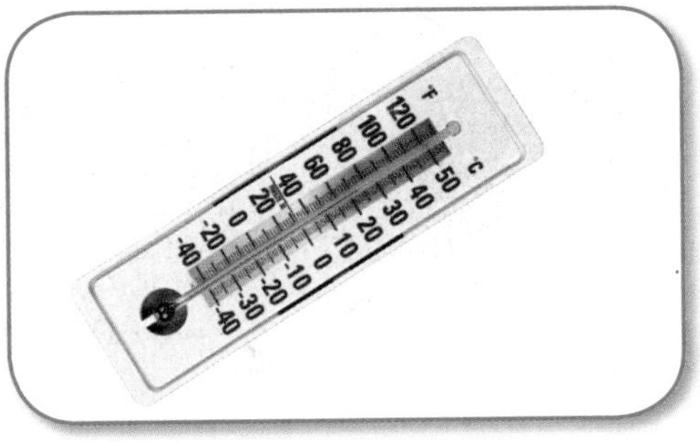

title [TY•tuhl]

The name of something. The title of a chart or a graph tells the kind of information it shows. (29)

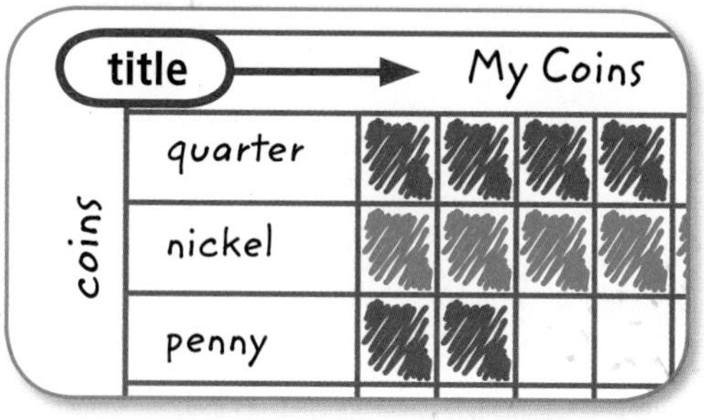

tool [TOOL]

An object that helps people do something more easily than they could do it without the tool. (94)

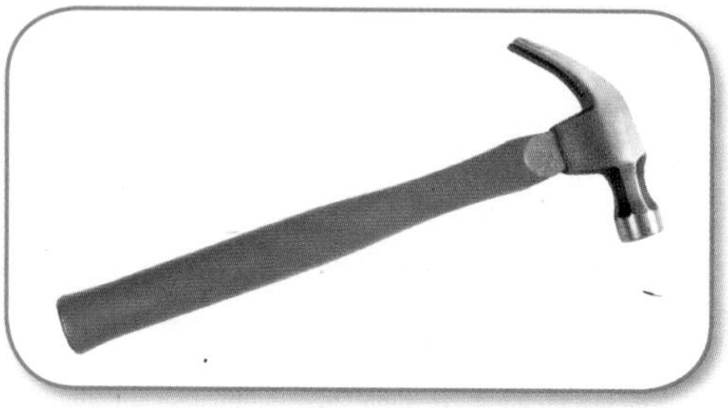

V

vibration [vy•BRAY•shuhn]

A movement back and forth. Vibrations can cause sound. (131)

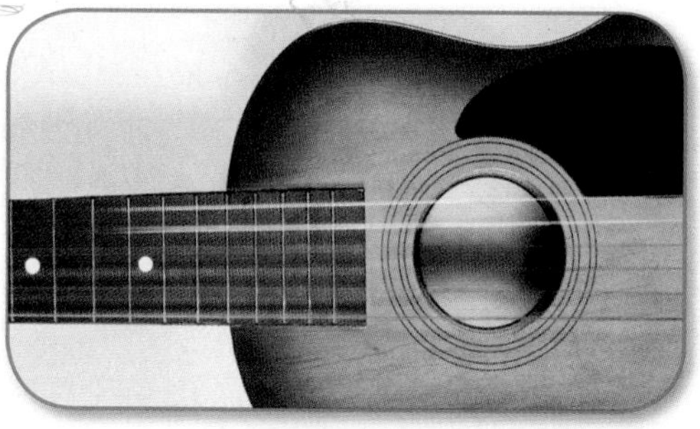

volume [VAHL•yoom]

The amount of space something takes up.

volume [VAHL•yoom]

The loudness of a sound. (132)

W

water [WAWT•er]

Liquid that falls as rain and forms oceans, rivers, and lakes. (244)

weathering [WETH•er•ing]
The breaking down of rocks into smaller pieces by water, ice, wind, and plants. (242)

wedge [WEJ]
An object that is thick at one end and thin at the other. A wedge can split some things apart.

weight [WAYT]
The measure of the pull of Earth's gravity on an object. (109)

Index

A

B

C

N

O

P

R

S

W

Y

Photo Credits

KEY: (t) top, (b) bottom, (l) left, (r) right, (c) center, (bg) background, (fg) foreground

Front Cover: Dave Fleetham/Pacific Stock;

Front Endsheets:
Page 1: Flip Nicklin/Minden Pictures; (bg) Don Paulson Photography/SuperStock; Page 2: (t) Marc Chamberlain/Seapics; (b) Tom Walmsley/Nature Photo Library; (bg) Don Paulson Photography/SuperStock; Page 3: (t) Flip Nicklin/Minden Pictures; (b) Augusto Stanzani/ARDEA LONDON; (bg) Don Paulson Photography/SuperStock;

Title Page: Dave Fleetham/Pacific Stock;

Copyright Page: Flip Nicklin/Minden Pictures;

Back Endsheets:
Page 1: (t) Flip Nicklin/Minden Pictures; (b) Copyright © Brandon Cole; (bg) Don Paulson Photography/SuperStock; Page 2: (t) Francois Gohier/ARDEA LONDON; (cl) Flip Nicklin/Minden Pictures; (b) Augusto Stanzani/ARDEA LONDON; (bg) Don Paulson Photography/SuperStock; Page 3: (t) Francois Gohier/ARDEA LONDON; Flip Nicklin/Minden; (bg) Don Paulson Photography/SuperStock;

Back Cover: Flip Nicklin/Minden Pictures;

Introduction:
1 (t) Bruce Burkhardt/Corbis, (inset) Courtesy of roundmetal/Coinpage.com; 2 (r) Robert Holmes Photography; 20 (bl) David Young-Wolff/PhotoEdit; 24 (r) Lawrence Migdale/Photo Researchers; 25 (tcl) www.coinpage.com; 26 (bl) Kathleen Finlay/Masterfile; 36 (r) Gilbert Iundt/Tempsport/Corbis; 37 (tl) The British Museum/Topham-HIP/The Image Works; 47 (b) Siede Preis/PhotoDisc/Getty Images;

UNIT 1:
51 (t) John Lamb/Getty Images; 52 (r) Medioimages/PunchStock; 53 (tr) Roy Ooms/Masterfile; 54 (bl) Masterfile 58 (b & tr) Mark E. Gibson/Corbis; 59 (b) Roy Ooms/Masterfile, (tr) Ron Stroud/Masterfile; 64 (r) Bob Torrez/Getty Images; 65 (tr) Mike Timo/Stone/Getty Images, (cr) Peter Walton/Index Stock Imagery; 66 (bl) Jeff Greenberg/Photo Edit; 70 (b) Roy Ooms/Masterfile, (cr) Bob Krist/Corbis; 71 (cr) Joseph Sohm; ChromoSohm Inc./Corbis; 72 (tr & b) Gemma Giannini/Grant Heilman Photography; 74 (bl) Roy Ooms/Masterfile; 76 (r) Emily Hart-Roberts/Imagestate; 81 (tr) Mary Kate Denny/PhotoEdit, (cl) David Woods/Corbis; 82 (tr) Getty Images, (bl) Corbis; 83 (t) Lisa Pines/Getty Images; 88 (br) Ian Leonard/Alamy; 89 (t) Visions of America, LLC/Alamy, (br) Andrew Lepley/Redferns Music Picture Library/Alamy; 90 (r) Greg Stott/Masterfile; 94 (bl) Comstock/PictureQuest, (br) Tony Freeman/Photo Edit; 95 (t) Purestock/SuperStock, (b) Mark Gilbert/Getty Images; 96 (br) Bill Tucker/Imagestate; 97 (cl) Michael Newman/Photo Edit, (tr) ASAP Ltd./Index Stock Imagery; 98 (cl) Jeff Greenberg/PhotoEdit; 99 (b) GM Media Archive; 102-103 (all) Courtesy of American Honda Motor Co.; 104 (r) John Kelly/Getty Images; 105 (tr) Mel Yates/Taxi/Getty Images, (br) Jay S Simon/Stone/Getty Images; 106 (bl) Mel Yates/Taxi/Getty Images; 108 (bl) Geoff Manasse/Photodisk/Getty Images; 112 (bl) Tony Freeman/PhotoEdit; 114 (r) BruceGray.com; 118 (b) Richard Megna/Fundamental Photographs; 119 (tr) Richard Megna/Fundamental Photographs; 126 (r) J. Emilio Flores/Corbis; 132 (tr) David Young-Wolff/Photo Edit, (b) Scott Barrow, Inc./SuperStock; 133 (cl) Pat LaCroix/The Image Bank/Getty Images; 134 (bl) Eduardo Garcia/Getty Images; 135 (b) Tom Carter/Photo Edit, (tr) C Squared Studios/PhotoDisc/Getty Images; 136 (bl) Spencer Grant/Photo Edit, (br) Photodisc Blue/Getty Images; 137 (br) Spencer Grant/Photo Edit; 138 (bl) Tony Freeman/Photo Edit; 140 (tl) The Granger Collection, New York, (bl) Steve Prezant/Corbis; 141 (tr) NASA/JPL, (br) Ken Brown/NASA/JPL, (bg) NASA/JPL/Cornell; 142 (cl) Roy Ooms/Masterfile, (cr) Comstock/PictureQuest; 143 (b) Rosanne Olson/PhotoDisc/Getty Images;

UNIT 2:
147 (tc) Alejandro Balaquer/Getty Images; 148 (r) Tom Walker/Getty Images; 149 (cr) John M. Burnley/Photo Researchers, (br) E.R. Degginger/Color-Pic; 152 (bl) Larry Ulrich/Getty Images, (cr) Chris Warbey/Stone/Getty Images; 153 (cl) Steven Begleiter/Index Stock Imagery, (br) Photodisc/Getty Images; 154 (bg) Ed Reschke/Peter Arnold, Inc.; 154 (cl) Breck P. Kent/Animals Animals, (cr) John M. Burnley/Photo Researchers; 155 (cl) John M. Burnley/Photo Researchers, (c) Runk/Schoenberger/Grant Heilman Photography, (br) Joe McDonald/Animals Animals; 156 (cl, bcr & bg) E.R. Degginger/Color-Pic; 157 (all) E.R. Degginger/Color-Pic; 158 (cl & bcr) Dwight Kuhn/Dwight Kuhn Photography; 159 (b) Dwight Kuhn/Dwight Kuhn Photography; 160 (bl) John M. Burnley/Photo Researchers; 162 (tl) Cartesia/Photodisc/Getty Images,(br) John W Banagan/Getty Images; 163 (tl) San Diego Zoo/Associated Press, (bg) Chad Ehlers/Alamy, (c) John Giustina/Getty Images; 164 (r) William Dow/Corbis; 165 (cr) Jane Grushow/Grant Heilman Photography; 166 (tl & cl) PhotoDisc, (bl) Photodisc/Getty Images; 168 (b) Jeff Rotman/naturepl.com; 169 (br) Yva Momatiuk/John Eastcott/Minden Pictures, (cl) David Tipling/naturepl.com; 170 (b) Getty Images; 171 (c) Norvia Behling/Fox Hill Photography, (tcl & tcr) Jorg & Petra Wegner/Animals Animals; 172 (cr) Yva Momatiuk & John Eastcott/Minden Pictures, (b) Sumio Harada/Minden Pictures; 173 (t) Steve Kaufman/Corbis, (cr) Kennan Ward/Corbis; 174 (tl) Mitch Epstein/Getty Images; 175 (b) Yva Momatiuk & John Eastcott/Minden Pictures; 176 (bl) Getty Images; 178 (r) Color-Pic/Animals Animals; 179 (tr) Jerome Wexler/Photo Researchers, (cr) Adam Hart-Davis/Science Photo Library/Photo Researchers; 180 (bl) Corel; 182 (bcl) D. Cavagnaro/Visuals Unlimited, (bcr) Adam Hart-Davis/Science Photo Library/Photo Researchers; 183 (bcl) Science Photo Library/Photo Researchers, (bcr) Adam Hart-Davis/Science Photo Library/Photo Researchers, (tr) Holt Studios International Ltd./Alamy; 184 (cr) Digital Vision/Getty Images, (tr) Markus Dlouhy/Peter Arnold, Inc., (tl) Cwener Photography/Index Stock Imagery; 185 (b) H. Reinhard/zefa/Corbis; 186 (bcl) Barry Runk/Stan/Grant Heilman Photography, (bcr) Dwight Kuhn/Dwight Kuhn Photography, (bg) A. Riedmiller/Peter Arnold, Inc.; 187 (c) Werner H. Muller/Peter Arnold, Inc.; 188 (br) Holt Studios International Ltd./Alamy; 190 (tl) USDA-Agricultural Research Service, (bg) Steve Austin; Papilio/Corbis; 191 (tr) Stock Montage/Getty Images, (cr) Isabella Rozenbaum & Frederic Cirou/PhotoAlto/Getty Images, (bg) AGStockUSA, Inc./Alamy; 192 (r) Chris Fredriksson/Alamy; 194 (l) Evan Sklar/Picture Arts; 196 (bl) Christi Carter/Grant Heilman Photography, (br) Richard Shiell/Animals Animals; 197 (b) Peter Marbach/Grant Heilman Photography; 198 (bl) The Garden Picture Library/Alamy; 199 (bg) Craig Lovell/Alamy, (tr) The Garden Picture Library/Alamy; 200 (cr) Nigel Cattlin/Alamy, (bg) Dynamic Graphics Group/Creatas/Alamy; 201 (tr & tl) Nigel Cattlin/Alamy; 202 (bl) Richard Shiell/Animals Animals; 204 (bl) California Agricultural Technology Institute, (br) Ted Rieger, (bg) Daryl Benson/Masterfile; 205 (cr) FoodCollection/Stockfood America; 206 (r) Dennis Hallinan/Alamy; 207 (tr) Photodisc/Getty Images; 208 (bl) Barry Runk/Grant Heilman Photography; 210 (cr) Damian Pointon/Alamy, (br) B. Runk/S. Schoenberger/Grant Heilman Photography; 211 (cr) Mark Boulton/Alamy, (b) Jerome Wexler/Visuals Unlimited; 212 (cr) Dan Suzio/Photo Researchers, (tr) Adam Jones/Visuals Unlimited, (b) B. Runk/S. Schoenberger; 213 (bl & br) Nigel Cattlin/Photo Researchers; 214 (bg) Photolibrary.com pty. ltd/Index Stock Imagery; 215 (bcr) Richard Megna/Fundamental Photographs, (bcl) Elizabeth Whiting & Associates/Alamy; 216 (bl) Elizabeth Whiting & Associates/Alamy; 218 (cl) Jeff Rotman/naturepl.com, (cr) Dwight Kuhn/Dwight Kuhn Photography, (bl) Nigel Cattlin/Photo Researchers, (br) Holt Studios International Ltd./Alamy; 219 Masterfile;

UNIT 3:
223 (tc) Anne Rippy/Getty Images; 224 (r) David Muench/Corbis; 225 (tr) Visuals Unlimited, (cr) Mark A. Schneider/Visuals Unlimited, (br) Michael Pole/Corbis; 226 (cl) Pat Behnke/Alamy, (bcl) SuperStock, Inc./SuperStock; 22008 (r) Wes Walker/Getty Images; 230 (bcl, br & bl) GC Minerals/Alamy, (cr) PhotoDisc/Getty Images; 231 (cl & c) E.R. Degginger/Color-Pic, (tr) Phil Degginger/Color-Pic, (tcr) Paul Silverman/Fundamental Photographs, (tl) Roberto de Gugliemo/Photo Researchers, (r) Biophoto Associates/Photo Researchers; 232 (br) GC Minerals/Alamy, (cr) Mark A. Schneider/Visuals Unlimited, (bl) Doug Martin/Photo Researchers; 233 (cl) Charles D. Winters/Photo Researchers, (bl) Albert J. Copley/Visuals Unlimited; 236 (tl) Mary Evans Picture Library, (br) Francois Gohier/Photo Researchers, (bg) Royal Gorge Regina Museum & History Center; 237 (tr & c) Elizabeth Miura Boyd, (bg) Gary Retherford/Photo Researchers; 238 (c) Kari Weiss Sharp/Grant Heilman Photography; 239 (tr) John Shaw/Panoramic Images, (cr) E.R. Degginger/Color-Pic; 240 (bl) Gavin Hellier/The Image Bank/Getty Images; 243 (b) Design Pics Inc./Alamy; 244 (b) E.R. Degginger/Color-Pic; 245 (t) Stanley Schoenberger/Grant Heilman Photography; 246 (tl & tr) Pizzoli Alberto/Corbis SYGMA; 247 (b) Andrew McClenaghan/Science Photo Library/Photo Researchers; 248 (bl) Pizzoli Alberto/Corbis SYGMA; 250 (r) Peter Arnold/Alamy; 251 (tr) Craig Lovell/Corbis, (br) Peter Anderson/Getty Images; 252 (bl) Mary Rhodes/Animals Animals; 258 (b) Edward Bock/Corbis, (tr & br) Ed Degginger/Color-Pic; 259 (tr & br) Ed Degginger/Color-Pic; 262 (r) Corbis; 263 (tc) Randy M. Ury/Corbis, (cr) Digital Stock; 265 (cr) Martin Land/Science Photo Library; 266 (bl) Richard T. Nowitz/Photo Researchers; 268 (bl) Dex Image/Getty Images, (br) Martin Land/Science Photo Library; 269 (tr) Robert E. Barber/Alamy, (cr) Tom McHugh/Photo Researchers; 271 (cr) Phil Degginger/Color-Pic, Inc.; 272 (cr) Alamy Images, (bc) Francois Gohier/Western Paleontological Labs/Photo Researchers; 273 (br) John Warburton-Lee/Alamy; 274 (bl) Martin Land/Science Photo Library; 276 (bc) W. Cody/Corbis; 277 (tr) Soqui Ted/Corbis SYGMA, (b) Greg Vaughn/Alamy; 278 (r) Lee Foster/Getty Images; 279 (tr) Michael Melford/National Geographic Image Collection; 280 (bl) H. Reinhard/Zefa/Masterfile; 282 (b) Mark Gibson/Index Stock Imagery, (cr) Peter Griffith/Masterfile; 283 (t) Larry Mulvehill/The Image Works; 284 (t & br) Photodisc/Getty Images, (tcr) Charles D. Winters/Photo Researchers, (cr) Larry Lefever/Grant Heilman Photography; 285 (b) Craig Lovell/Corbis, (cr) Peter Griffin/Alamy; 286 (br) Beateworks Inc./Alamy, (bl) Grant Heilman/Grant Heilman Photography; 287 (bl) Richard T. Nowitz/Corbis, (tl) Photodisc/Getty Images, (cl) J. David Andrews/Masterfile, (bcl) David Toase/PhotoDisc/Getty Images; 288 (bl) Beateworks Inc./Alamy; 290 (cl) Doug Martin/Photo Researchers, (cr) Craig Lovell/Corbis, (bl) Tom McHugh/Photo Researchers, (br) Michael Melford/National Geographic Image Collection;

GLOSSARY:
R28 (tl) Michael & Patricia Fogden/Corbis; R30 (tr) Image Source/Getty Images; R31 (bl) Breck P. Kent/Animals Animals/Earth Scenes; R31 (tr) Jane Grushow/Grant Heilman Photography; R31 (cr) Jay S Simon/Stone/Getty Images; R31 (br) Wardene Weisser/Bruce Coleman; R32 (tr) E.R. Degginger/Color-Pic; R32 (bl) Martin Land/Science Photo Library; R32 (br) Royalty-Free/Corbis; R33 (tl) Adam Hart-Davis/Science Photo Library/Photo Researchers; R33 (cl) Mel Yates/Taxi/Getty Images; R34 (bl) Joseph Van Os/The Image Bank/Getty Images; R34 (cl) Yva Momatiuk/John Eastcott/Minden Pictures; R35 (bl) E.R. Degginger/Color-Pic; R35 (cr) John M. Burnley/Photo Researchers; R38 (bl) Fritz Polking/Peter Arnold, Inc.; R38 (tl) Mark A. Schneider/Visuals Unlimited; R38 (tr) Michael Melford/National Geographic Image Collection; R38 (bl) Mike Timo/Stone/Getty Images; R38 (br) Photodisc Green (Royalty-free)/Getty Images; R39 (tl) Ed Reschke/Peter Arnold, Inc./Alamy Images; R39 (bl) Jean-Marc Truchet/Photographer's Choice/Getty Images; R39 (tr) Michael H. Black/Bruce Coleman, Inc.; R39 (cr) Stone/Keren Su/Getty Images; R40 (tr) Roy Ooms/Masterfile; R41 (cl) E.R. Degginger/Color-Pic; R42 (br) Angelo Cava III/Getty Images; R42 (tr) Peter Anderson/Getty Images; R42 (tl) Usher/Premium Stock/PictureQuest; R42 (cl) Visuals Unlimited; R43 (br) Craig Lovell/Corbis; R43 (cl) Jerome Wexler/Photo Researchers; R43 (tr) Ron Austing; Frank Lane Picture Agency/Corbis; R44 (bl) Peter Walton/Index Stock Imagery; R44 (tr) Royalty-Free/Corbis; R44 (cr) Runk/Schoenberger/ Grant Heilman Photography; R45 (cr) David Hosking/Alamy; R45 (bl) Getty Images; R45 (tr) Michael Pole/Corbis; R47 (cl) Corbis; R47 (tl) John Shaw/Panoramic Images;

All other photos © Harcourt School Publishers. Harcourt Photos provided by the Harcourt Index, Harcourt IPR, and Harcourt photographers; Weronica Ankarorn, Eric Camden, Doug Dukane, Ken Kinzie, April Riehm, and Steve Williams.

CHARACTERISTICS The bones inside a bottlenose dolphin's flipper look a lot like the bones in your hand.

MOVEMENT Bottlenose dolphins can jump as high as 3 meters.

DIET Bottlenose dolphins eat squid and many kinds of fish.
MOVEMENT Bottlenose dolphins swim by moving their tails up and down.
CHARACTERISTICS Bottlenose dolphins can live up to 30 years.